"Here's an invaluable guide from a trusted expert who loves Jesus and the Jewish people. Michael Brown provides authoritative answers—in an accessible form—about the questions you've probably had for years but didn't know who to ask."

—**Lee Strobel**, author, *The Case for Christ* and
The Case for the Real Jesus

"Every age has produced Christian scholars who are Jews. Michael Brown is the best scholar among Messianic Jews today. He has written a much-needed book to help his fellow Christians understand the Jews. He has a balanced view as to what Jews, Jewishness and Jewish customs mean that will help Christians appreciate the earthly family of Jesus.

"There are certain teachings attributed to Messianic teachers that need to be corrected. For example, some have taught that the name *Jesus* (*Iēsous* in Greek) is really a pagan corruption of the name *Zeus*. Michael deals with Jewish history and traditions by answering questions such as 'What are the main differences between Judaism and Christianity?' and 'Should all Jews move back to Israel?'

"Michael Brown believes that every living Jew, whether or not a believer in Jesus, is evidence that the God of the Bible *is* and that He keeps His promises!"

—**Moishe Rosen**, founder, Jews for Jesus

"This is an amazing book, even for people like me who have walked with our Jewish brothers of faith for many years. Michael Brown's own Jewish background, coupled with his years of fruitful ministry in the Church, make him singularly capable for the task. The book is astonishing for its background in Jewish thought, its presentation of modern-day Judaism, its challenges to the Church and its insights into the issues that confront believers today. This is especially helpful to the Church as she continues to awaken to her Jewish roots. We learn better how to be sensitive to Jewish people who have already come to faith in Messiah Yeshua, as well as to those who have yet to receive the revelation of Jesus. I pray the book will have a long and useful life. God bless Michael Brown!"

—**Don Finto**, director, The Caleb Company;
pastor emeritus, Belmont Church, Nashville;
author, *Your People Shall Be My People*

What Do Jewish People Think about Jesus?

And Other Questions Christians Ask
about Jewish Beliefs, Practices & History

MICHAEL L. BROWN

Chosen
Grand Rapids, Michigan

Published by Chosen Books
A division of Baker Publishing Group
P.O. Box 6287, Grand Rapids, MI 49516-6287
www.chosenbooks.com

Printed in the United States of America

Library of Congress Cataloging-in-Publication Data

Brown, Michael L., 1955–
    What do Jewish people think about Jesus? : and other questions Christians ask about Jewish beliefs, practices, and history / Michael L. Brown.
        p. cm.
    Includes bibliographical references and index.
    ISBN 10: 0-8007-9426-5 (pbk.)
    ISBN 978-0-8007-9426-2 (pbk.)
    1. Messianic Judaism. 2. Judaism—Customs and practices. 3. Judaism—History. 4. Judaism (Christian theology) 5. Jesus Christ—Jewish interpretations. I. Title.
BR158.B76 2007
289.9—dc22   2007025324

In keeping with biblical principles of creation stewardship, Baker Publishing Group advocates the responsible use of our natural resources. As a member of the Green Press Initiative, our company uses recycled paper when possible. The text paper of this book is comprised of 30% post-consumer waste.

Contents

Part 2   The Jewish People and Jewish History

Preface

For many years now, as a Jewish believer in Jesus with an academic background in Hebrew and Jewish studies, I have often been approached by Christians with all kinds of "Jewish" questions. Over the last few years, with the launching of an improved ministry website (www.icnministries.org), along with a website devoted to Jewish outreach alone (www.realmessiah.org), the volume of questions has increased dramatically.

Some have asked, "Should Christians observe the Sabbath?" Others have inquired, "Was the New Testament originally written in Hebrew?" Still others have asked if I could explain the background and significance of a particular traditional Jewish practice, while others have wondered out loud about the latest "Jewish" fad in the Church today.

Unfortunately, as the questions increased, the time necessary to answer these many questions did not increase, and so the idea was birthed of answering them all in a book. In fact, seeking to be proactive, I thought it wise to answer many other questions that would inevitably be asked, thereby allowing me (I hope!) to say in the future, "I already answered that in my book."

To be sure, I have now written more than 1,500 pages of material responding to Jewish objections to Jesus (published by Baker in the multivolume series *Answering Jewish Objections to Jesus*). The questions I address here are primarily *Christian* questions about Jewish-related issues. So the overlap between these studies is minimal, and the vast majority of the questions treated here are not treated in my apologetics series at all.

There has been, however, an additional motivation in writing this book, and that is my concern over the ever-growing number of bizarre and sometimes heretical teachings coming from the fringes of the Jewish roots movement. As readers of this present book will recognize at once, I am deeply committed to the Church's recovering her severed and often forgotten Jewish roots. But I am even more committed to seeing all believers, Jewish and Gentile alike, maintain a Jesus-focused lifestyle, one that is free from many of the secondary and (to repeat) at times heretical emphases put forth by these fringe groups.

This book, then, intends to be both informative and practical; and, with regard to the doctrinal and practical issues discussed, I have done my best to condense more than 35 years of careful study of the Scriptures into the pages of this book.

On a final, personal note (which is what a preface is for), I confess that I initially underestimated the amount of work that would be involved in writing this book, thinking that it would be a "fun" project not requiring much research. (In the unique parlance of an American political figure, I "misunderestimated.") Once I began to write, however, I was constantly prodded by my scholarly side, reminding me that some documentation was needed here and an additional endnote was needed there. The end result, then, is a nontechnical book written for a popular audience, but with nearly three hundred endnotes, and one that summarizes many years of study and reflection. It is my prayer that readers will find the pages that follow both enjoyable and edifying.

My appreciation to Jane Campbell and the terrific editorial team at Chosen Books, along with Timothy Beals, who also assisted greatly in the final editing of the material.

May Yeshua-Jesus, the Messiah of Israel and the Savior of the world, be greatly exalted in the earth today!

Michael L. Brown
April 2007

Part 1

Judaism and Jewish Practice

1. Are there Jewish denominations?
2. What is Hasidic Judaism?
3. What is the Oral Law?
4. What is the Tanakh?
5. What exactly is meant by the term *Torah*?
6. What is the Masoretic text?
7. What are the holy books of Judaism?
8. What are the main differences between Judaism and Christianity?
9. What do Jewish people think about Jesus?
10. Do the Jewish people expect a literal Messiah?
11. Do Jews refer to God by the name of Jehovah?
12. What is meant by the term *kosher*?
13. Why do traditional Jews have separate dishes in their kitchens for meat products and dairy products?

14. Why do traditional Jews light candles at the beginning of the Sabbath?
15. Why don't traditional Jews drive on the Sabbath?
16. Why do traditional Jewish men wear a skullcap (called *yarmulke* or, in Hebrew, *kippah*)?
17. Why do traditional Jewish women wear wigs (or even shave their heads)?
18. Why do some Jewish men grow long side curls?
19. Why do some Jewish men wear white fringes outside of their shirts?
20. Why do traditional Jewish men pray with black boxes (called phylacteries or, in Hebrew, *tefillin*) on their heads and arms?
21. What are the little boxes (mezuzahs) on the doorways of Orthodox Jewish homes?
22. Why do some religious Jewish men wear long black coats?
23. Why do traditional Jews claim that Jewish descent is matrilineal (i.e., coming through the mother) rather than patrilineal (i.e., coming through the father)?
24. Are there really 613 commandments in the Torah?
25. What are the seven laws of Noah?

1

Are there Jewish denominations?

Jewish denominations do not exist in exactly the same way that Christian denominations exist. There are, however, three main branches of Judaism: Reform, Conservative and Orthodox, Reform being the most liberal and Orthodox being the most traditional. Further subdivisions include Reconstructionist Judaism, which is to the left of Reform Judaism, and ultra-Orthodox Judaism (including Hasidic Judaism), which is the right wing of Orthodox Judaism.

Before comparing the beliefs and practices of the three main branches of Judaism, let us take a moment to review the historical development of Orthodox, Conservative and Reform Judaism. Although each of these three branches claims to be true to the spirit of the ancient rabbis (just as the various Christian groups claim to be true to the spirit of Jesus and the apostles), from a historical perspective, Reform Judaism, which is sometimes called Liberal or Progressive Judaism, emerged as a distinct, somewhat humanistic reaction against Orthodox Judaism roughly two hundred years ago, while Conservative Judaism developed out of Orthodox Judaism roughly one hundred years ago, but in clear contrast with Reform Judaism.

To briefly sketch the history of these three movements, Reform Judaism arose in Germany in the early 1800s as Jews began to break away from traditional practices, believing that these were now antiquated and irrelevant. As noted in *The Oxford Dictionary of the Jewish Religion*, "Its historic origins were motivated less by theological or ideological attitudes than by a desire for a more attractive form of service that would appeal to Jews who were in danger of dropping out of Judaism completely."[1]

In the eyes of the early Reform leaders, Judaism had to make itself relevant to an enlightened people living in an enlightened age, and rather than risk the complete assimilation of their people, a new expression of Judaism had to be developed, one that incorporated numerous changes. These changes included synagogues being called temples; prayer books using the vernacular language and not just Hebrew; sermons being preached in German; and musical (specifically, organ) accompaniment being added to public worship—all of which constituted *radical* departures from the traditions, traditions that were considered sacrosanct by the religious Jewish community. Such innovations, therefore, were strongly opposed.

Not surprisingly, within a fairly short period of time, deeper theological and ideological differences began to arise, and Reform Jews began to distinguish between what they felt were the eternal, truly inspired aspects of the Bible and rabbinic traditions, such as the ethical teaching of the prophets and the importance of the Jewish calendar, and those laws and customs that they considered to be "products of a particular age"[2]—and were therefore outmoded, outdated and potentially embarrassing—such as the biblical purity laws, wearing head coverings and the absolute submission to rabbinic authority. In keeping with this, the Reform motto, speaking in terms of the biblical commandments, eventually became "guidance, not governance," reflecting the Reform position that biblical and rabbinic law must be evaluated by human judgment and contemporary methods of study (such as the critical reading of sacred texts).

And, whereas traditional Judaism often functioned best when isolated from modern culture, Reform Judaism sought to interact with and even learn from modern culture. The Jews were coming out of the ghetto now, and they had to get in step with the spirit of the age. In fact, even the idea of being the chosen people whose homeland was in Israel was considered offensive to many, since it made them superior to the nations (as opposed to sent with a mission to the nations), as well as aliens in their own country. In fact, a foundational document of Reform Judaism, the Pittsburgh Platform of 1885, stated that the mission of Judaism was to "solve on the basis of righteousness and justice the problems presented by . . . the present organization of society."[3]

The Reform leaders taught that the Jewish people should live as permanent citizens in their countries rather than as aliens longing for their ancestral land, abandoning many of those ritual elements that marked them out from others.[4] In short, this was "a religious movement advocating the modifying of Orthodox tradition in conforming with the exigencies of contemporary life and thought."[5] Some Reform congregations even went as far as worshiping on Sunday rather than Saturday!

All this was met with absolute scorn by traditional Jewish leaders, who not only opposed these innovations but sought to outlaw the opening of Reform houses of worship. It would not be hard to imagine how the traditional Jewish community reacted to the news that a dinner in conjunction with the graduation ceremony of the first Reform seminary in America in 1883 included *shrimp*— something absolutely forbidden by Jewish dietary laws (see #12).[6] This was the horror of horrors.

It is therefore understandable that, in the days leading up to the Holocaust, when anti-Jewish laws were being passed, some Orthodox rabbis actually pointed to Reform Judaism as a primary cause of the disaster, arguing that the Reform movement, birthed in Germany, had led to the assimilation of many Jews into secular culture and to the abandoning of time-honored practices such as Sabbath observance. As expressed in the 1930s in *The Israelit* newspaper:

> We ourselves are to blame that we have any problems. When the ghetto gates fell [meaning when Jews could readily become part of the society at large] . . . it was our duty to demonstrate that Jews remain aware of their special character even when they are granted the opportunity to pursue the development of their external circumstances of life unimpeded—that they do not abandon the way of life based on the teachings and precepts of the Torah. Jews could have shown the entire world that it is certainly possible to acquire the treasures of culture such as art and science without abandoning the Jewish way of life. We have missed that opportunity of attaining a synthesis between Judaism and its eternal forms on the one hand, and the cultural assets of the surrounding world on the other.[7]

This indicates clearly how passionately Orthodox Jews felt about forsaking their traditions. For them, it spelled nothing less than death and destruction.

Conservative Judaism was far less reactionary than Reform Judaism, seeking "to conserve tradition in the modern setting, hence the name of the movement, Conservative Judaism."[8] As explained by Loel M. Weiss, a Conservative rabbi, "Conservative (Positive-Historical) Judaism began, not as a break with traditional practice but rather with a break with the traditional way of looking at our historical texts."[9] So, Jewish law was considered to be of great importance, but since scholars were now reading the Bible and the classic Jewish texts through critical eyes, the traditions did not carry the same weight for Conservative Jews as for Orthodox Jews. Everything, in a sense, had to be processed through the lens of historical, critical scholarship. As explained in *The Oxford Dictionary of the Jewish Religion*, "Since the Conservative movement saw Judaism as a dynamic, developing tradition practiced by a people, it hesitated, in contrast to the Reform movement, which, in 1885 and 1937 issued platforms, to draw sharp ideological lines . . . [that] would not only be counterproductive but untrue to the historical realities of tradition."[10]

So then, in contrast with Reform Judaism, the Conservative movement recognized the sanctity of the traditions but argued that they had more of a historical, human, albeit divinely guided development—which meant more of an *ongoing, flexible* development. And from the viewpoint of Conservative Jews, Orthodox tradition had become too rigid and inflexible, failing to adapt the ancient traditions to the modern world and failing to read critically the ancient, sacred texts. As expressed by Rabbi Joseph Telushkin,

> To this day, Conservative Judaism strikes a middle road between Reform and Orthodox Judaism. Unlike Reform, it considers itself bound by almost all Torah rituals as well as Torah ethics; unlike Orthodoxy, it considers itself free to introduce innovations in Jewish law, particularly the laws formulated in the Talmud.[11]

In contrast, from the viewpoint of Orthodox Jews, there has always been and there remains today only one true Judaism, the Judaism they believe was handed down in unbroken form through the generations from Moses until today (see #3). Orthodox Jews would argue that they alone faithfully adhere to the ancient traditions, which they accept as binding and not optional, also noting that before the rise of Reform Judaism, there was no such thing as "Orthodox." In other words, either you were a religious Jew or you were not. And if you were religious, you followed the rabbinic traditions, meaning that, from an Orthodox perspective, all past religious Jews, including the ancient rabbis, were "Orthodox."

Even within Orthodox Judaism, however, there is a right wing and a left wing, the former refusing to yield in any way to modern "enlightened" thinking, and the latter adhering strictly to all the foundations of Orthodoxy (such as Sabbath observance and the dietary laws) but being much more incorporated into the larger culture. The right wing is called ultra-Orthodox or *Haredi* (meaning "trembling before God"[12]) while the left wing is called Modern Orthodox. The right wing does not recognize either Conservative or Reform Judaism as legitimate expressions of Judaism in any way. For the strong pronouncement of the ultra-Orthodox rabbinic association called Agudath Israel, see #57.

What are the differences in the beliefs and practices of Orthodox, Conservative and Reform Jews? To highlight the differences, I will draw the contrast between key areas that divide Orthodox and Reform (understanding that Conservative Judaism takes a somewhat middle position, although in practice, it is closer to Reform), describing things in generalized terms.

Scripture

> **Orthodox**: The *Tanakh* (what Christians call the Old Testament) is God's perfect, inspired, authoritative Word, with the Torah occupying the highest level of authority. What God commands, to the extent it can be followed today, is required of all Jews. (In other words, observance is mandatory.)
>
> **Reform**: The Tanakh is an inspired yet imperfect human product, of special importance in moral and ethical matters. The Scriptures help shape our national identity and calling as Jews, but the Torah commands provide guidance rather than governance. (In other words, observance is optional.)

Rabbinic Authority

> **Orthodox**: God gave Moses a Written Law and an Oral Law, and this Oral Law has been passed on in a living way through

each generation of rabbinic leaders, whose rulings and teachings are to be closely followed. Contemporary rabbis function as the community leaders, giving application to the Torah's requirements for our day.

Reform: The rabbis of past generations should be respected and honored, but their teachings should not be followed in a slavish way. Today's rabbis provide moral and inspirational leadership for their congregations but do not legislate behavior.

Observance

Orthodox: Every aspect of Jewish life is mapped out, including when to pray, what prayers to say every day and on every occasion, what texts to study, how to observe the Sabbath and holy days, what to eat, family relations and laws of purity, etc. Orthodox Jews are expected to be fully observant. The more religious the community, the more synagogue attendance is constant through the year.

Reform: The ethical and moral commands of the Torah and Prophets should be followed, and a Jewish life cycle (circumcision, bar mitzvah, worship on the Sabbath, celebrating the holy days) is encouraged but not required. Dietary laws and other nonmoral laws are a matter of personal choice. In a typical Reform congregation, attendance swells dramatically during the major holy days as opposed to other times of the year.

God

Orthodox: The Lord is the Creator of the universe and the King of the world, omnipotent, omniscient, omnipresent and completely noncorporeal. Absolute faith in Him is both required and assumed. He rewards and punishes and is active in the world today, responding to the prayers and petitions of His people.

Reform: Officially, God is viewed as the noncorporeal Creator of the world, but most Reform rabbis are not at home with literal concepts of the deity, and one Reform leader explains:

> Like Maimonides, we are unable to accept a God who is, essentially, a bigger and better version of a human being—who operates the cosmos the way a conductor leads an orchestra. As a whole, we embrace metaphor. We imagine a God who is revealed in the experiences of loving relationships, of hope against despair, and of obligation to that which is beyond ourselves. . . . We are believers, though, who take the idea of belief quite seriously. I never have met a Reform rabbi who did not feel that something cosmically important was happening in the moment that he or she led Jews in declaring themselves before their God.[13]

Human Nature and Holiness

Orthodox: The human race is created by God, and every human being battles between the good inclination and the evil inclination. Every Jew, in particular, has a divine spark within him that, when ignited, will bring him into traditional Jewish observance. There is a tremendous emphasis put on keeping the commandments and walking in purity, both ritually and morally.

Reform: Human beings are the product of evolution, with great potential, even to usher in a Messianic era, and every human being has a divine spark. Sin is viewed primarily in social terms rather than measured against standards of holiness or, even more emphatically, laws of ritual purity.

Messiah and the Messianic Age

See #10 for details.

The discerning reader will recognize that, within the framework of Judaism, and given the distinctions between Judaism and Christianity (see #8), the differences between Orthodox and Reform Jews would parallel the differences between committed Christians and nominal Christians. The former take the Bible as God's infallible Word and seek to order their lives accordingly, taking the words of Jesus as binding, taking personal sin seriously, attending church services and Bible studies on a consistent, year-round basis and seeking to live in a God-conscious state all the time. The latter attend church sporadically, virtually never read their Bibles, tend to be seasonal Christians (baptism, Communion, Easter, Christmas) and identify themselves as Christian by religion but not by having a quality, ongoing relationship with the Lord. The former look at the latter as compromised and not reflecting the truth of the Gospel; the latter look at the former as fanatical, close-minded and even dangerous. The same can be said of Orthodox (especially ultra-Orthodox) views of Reform Judaism, and vice versa!

On a moral and ethical level, the subject of the acceptance of homosexuality provides a contemporary illustration of the differences between Orthodox, Conservative and Reform Judaism. For Orthodox Jews, the testimony of the Torah and the rabbinic tradition is clear, decisive and final: Homosexual practice is sinful and unacceptable, and practicing homosexuals can play no official religious role in the community. (Although Orthodox rabbis would state that compassion should be shown toward Orthodox Jews who struggle with same-sex desires, with rare exception, such Jews live very closeted lives in terms of their sexual struggles.) Reinforcing the prohibition of homosexual practice is the fact that traditional Judaism recognizes the words "Be fruitful and multiply" (Genesis 1:28, NASB) as the very first commandment given by God, hence the large Orthodox families, the most religious of whom do not practice birth control.

For Conservative Jews, the matter of homosexuality is the subject of serious, ongoing debate, with the ancient traditions needing to be freshly assessed and evaluated, although the primary Conservative view is shifting toward the acceptance of homosexual practice (specifically, recognizing civil unions and ordaining homosexual rabbis). Conservative rabbis also recognize that most of their congregants do not practice the fundamentals of Judaism in their private lives. As noted by Rabbi Weiss,

> We see it today throughout the Conservative Movement. Jews who don't observe *Kashrut* [dietary laws] or *Shabbat* [observing the Sabbath] or those who are intermarried are treated with the same honor and respect as those who follow these norms. In too many Conservative congregations, *Shabbat* and *Kashrut* are things to be observed in the public arena, in synagogue, but not necessarily by individual Jews. In fact, despite all our educational attempts, our members continue to think that Jews who observe *Shabbat* and *Kashrut* are "Orthodox."[14]

Why then, should gay and lesbian Jews be treated any differently if they desire membership in a Conservative synagogue?

Not surprisingly, the primary school for the training of Conservative rabbis, the Jewish Theological Seminary in Manhattan, allowed one of its graduating speakers—a woman now serving as the associate rabbi at the world's largest gay and lesbian synagogue—to give an impassioned plea for the acceptance of homosexuality. And what is the affiliation of this gay and lesbian synagogue, called Beth Simchat Torah and boasting a membership of 3,500? As you might have guessed, it is a Reform Congregation, and Reform Judaism actually supports the concept of same-sex marriages (or civil unions) and is willing to ordain gay and lesbian rabbis.[15] This quote from a reform rabbi, with reference to his gay brother, is illustrative of Reform Jewish thinking:

> I know what the Torah says about homosexuality in this week's [Torah] portion; it's called "abomination punishable by death." But I don't believe a loving God could have written such a thing. It could only have come from well-meaning but ignorant humans who could not see that homosexuality was part of God's diverse plan for humanity. It could only have come from people who knew almost nothing of what we know today. It could only have come from people who did not know my brother Greg; your goodness and your deep Jewish soul.[16]

In keeping with this, the current president of the Union for Reform Judaism, Rabbi Eric Yoffie, has passionately denounced what he perceives to be antigay bigotry, sounding a warning against America's "religious right."[17]

Today, Reform Judaism claims the largest number of adherents in the United States (approximately 38 percent of American Jews), closely followed by Conservative Judaism's 35 percent. Orthodox Judaism represents about 6 percent of American Jews and over 15 percent of Jews in Israel, where it is seeing its most rapid growth in terms of percentage of the overall Jewish population, since the ultra-Orthodox families have very large families (eight to twelve children are common) while the secular Israeli families have small families (fewer than two children per household).

Because of its modern, "enlightened" approach to Jewish life and law, Reform Judaism claims that it is the best antidote against Jewish assimilation, helping Jews who reject the traditional faith to maintain some semblance of Jewish identity.[18] In contrast, Orthodox Judaism, especially in its right-wing forms, sees Reform Judaism as a major part of assimilation, also pointing to the modern Orthodox "revival" in the last few decades, as many nonreligious Jews have become traditional. (Such a person is called a *baal teshuvah*, literally, "a master of repentance," but simply meaning someone who returns to traditional Judaism, the premise being that this is the proper and original faith for all Jews, hence the concept of "return.") This Orthodox revival has also been evidenced by some major publishing ventures in which numerous classic works of Judaism (see #7) have been translated into contemporary English and beautifully produced in parallel, Hebrew-English versions with extensive commentaries. Most notable in this genre is the 72-volume *Schottenstein Talmud*, published by ArtScroll.[19]

As for the major institutions of the three main branches of Judaism, the ultra-Orthodox have none, studying instead in yeshivas for many years, ideally throughout their entire lives, as work and family schedules allow. Their learning is voluminous, but narrowly focused. The vast majority of Modern Orthodox rabbis have been trained at Yeshiva University in New York City, although there are some schools in Israel now as well. The vast majority of Conservative rabbis have been trained at Jewish Theological Seminary, also in New York City, while the vast majority of Reform rabbis have been trained at Hebrew Union College and Jewish Institute of Religion, based in Cincinnati but with branch schools in New York City, Los Angeles and Jerusalem.

On a light note, there are a number of Jewish jokes that highlight the differences between Orthodox, Conservative and Reform, such as: The Orthodox are crazy (being considered too strict and fundamentalist in their practice and interpretation of the law), the Conservative are hazy (being considered unclear in their real convictions because of their middle-of-the-road approach) and the Reform are lazy (referring to their extreme laxness in terms of Jewish observance). Another joke is that the Orthodox say, *adonoy* (referring to the Eastern European pronunciation of the word *Lord*); the Conservative say, *adonay* (referring to the Middle Eastern pronunciation of *Lord*); and the Reform say,

"I-don'-know" (referring to their alleged ignorance of Hebrew and real Judaism).[20]

2

What is Hasidic Judaism?

"Hasidic Judaism developed during a period of intense misery for most Jews in eastern Europe. By the middle of the eighteenth century, the Jewish populations of Poland and the Ukraine had endured a century of intermittent poverty, persecution, and pogroms."[21] It was against this backdrop that the Hasidic movement began, and its origins in the eighteenth century can be traced directly to a highly charismatic, Ukranian-Jewish mystic, born as Israel ben Eliezer, but later known as the *Baal Shem Tov* (meaning, "Master of the Good Name," or, according to some, "Good Master of the Name"). Born in 1698 and orphaned as a very poor, young child, his life is shrouded in legend. According to tradition, even as a boy, he would go out by himself into the fields and woods to get alone with God—this was not a common Jewish practice—but from all reports, it seems that he was not recognized as a Jewish leader of note—in fact, he seems not to have impressed people at all—until 1734 when, according to his followers, he "revealed himself" by working miracles and demonstrating his holiness. (The title given to him, the Baal Shem Tov—abbreviated as the *Besht*—referred to his use of the divine name to work miracles.)

As his fame grew, he began to attract a wide range of disciples, both learned and unlearned, but his reputation was primarily that of a miracle worker and mystic rather than a scholar, and his teachings emphasized joyful relationship with God more than erudition. In this, he made a break with much of the traditional Jewish focus in his day, which placed a disproportionate emphasis on excelling in Torah study. (By Torah study, I refer here primarily to the study of the oral traditions; see #3 and #7.) In contrast, the Baal Shem Tov taught that even the most ignorant Jewish peasant could experience divine intimacy, even encouraging some level of deviation from the detailed, fixed system of Jewish daily prayers.

According to Dr. Gerhard Falk,

> The Baal Shem Tov taught that G-d is everywhere, not only in synagogues. He taught that G-d wants us to approach Him and His Torah with joy and gladness. . . . The poor and ignorant Jews of Russia . . . were astonished to hear this message. The Baal Shem Tov was happy in his poverty. He rejected the formalities of his opponents ([called] Misnagdim) and emphasized Jewish optimism and joy. . . .
>
> Believing that the highest form of prayer was an attitude of joy and happiness, of singing and dancing, he taught his followers that a good deed was worth more than all the adherence to the 613 Mitzvoth [commandments]. He also taught that the humble and the ignorant have a better chance of enjoying the World to Come than the arrogant and the learned.
>
> These lectures created great excitement among the miserable masses of Slavic Jews. Treated worse than the blacks in Mississippi before the civil rights movement, the Jews of Europe had no joy. Yet, the Besht taught them optimism and laughter amidst pogroms [organized, violent attacks on the Jewish people] and hatred. He literally rose above the content of daily life and became an enormous inspiration to his people. His movement was called Hasidism or Piety. Nearly one half of all Jews [meaning, in that part of the world] subscribed to his message despite the opposition of the formalists in Lithuania and elsewhere.[22]

These formalists, however, still constituted the communal majority in most all of the major Jewish cities—in terms of social status, influence and recognized Jewish leadership—and the greatest scholar of the era, an extraordinary genius, Rabbi Elijah, the *Vilna Gaon* (that is, "the genius of Vilna"), pronounced a ban on Hasidic

Jews in the harshest of terms. This caused them much suffering, and it is believed that upon the Vilna Gaon's death—remember that he was *the* greatest Jewish scholar of his day—many Hasidim danced on his grave in jubilation. This underscores how intense the initial conflict was!

The teachings of the Baal Shem Tov were passed on through his leading disciples, and over time, as Hasidic Jews increasingly came in line with traditional Jewish practices, even becoming famous for their exceptional devotion, the animosity between the opponents (called *Misnagdim* or *Mitnagdim* in Hebrew) and the Hasidic Jews lessened dramatically, although it still exists today. Their emphasis on mysticism stands out among other Orthodox and ultra-Orthodox Jews, but it is not entirely unique, in that study of the Zohar and other mystical texts is considered to be part of mainstream, traditional Judaism.

One of the most unique aspects of Hasidic Judaism—indeed, it is found only among Hasidic Jews—is the mystical importance placed on the person of the rebbe, the grand rabbi of the Hasidic community, and with that, the importance of having a spiritual connection with the rebbe. The rebbe, whose position is generally passed on in direct descent to the eldest son—hence, the reference to "Hasidic dynasties"—is believed to have a special and unique relationship with God and to be a miracle worker, a man whose blessings are to be coveted and whose guidance is sought by the members of his community, some of whom revere their rebbe out of all human proportion. In fact, in some Hasidic circles, telling stories about one's rebbe is considered a form of worship.

I can remember meeting some Hasidic Jews in New York in the 1970s who informed me that the only sin their rebbe ever committed was causing his mother pain in childbirth, although they assured me that he had since taken care of that issue. I kid you not![23] Other Hasidim I have met emphasized the great learning of their rebbe, while others pointed to their rebbe's alleged supernatural knowledge of people, places and events (received, it is believed, by divine revelation). Not surprisingly, it is common to see pictures of a community's rebbes (both past and present) prominently displayed in the homes of the Hasidim. This emphasis on the rebbe continues to draw criticism from other forms of Judaism, some of which see this as cultlike and, contrary to mainstream Jewish tradition, putting an overemphasis on man rather than God.

Although a large percentage of Hasidic Jews was slaughtered by the Nazis, a number of their leaders survived and reconstituted their movements in America, which remains the home of as many as several hundred thousand adherents. Hasidic groups are known by the place of their origin, the most prominent today being:

Lubavitch, from Lyubavichi in Belarussia. This movement, also known as Chabad, an acronym for *chokmah*, wisdom, *binah*, understanding and *daʿat*, knowledge, enjoyed exceptional growth under the leadership of Rabbi Menachem Mendel Schneerson (1902–94), the seventh and last in his dynastic succession (he had no children), and hailed by many of his followers as the Messiah. Schneerson, who led this movement from Brooklyn and never set foot in Israel, developed a worldwide Jewish outreach program devoted to calling nonobservant Jews back to traditional Judaism, establishing a massive network of children's schools and adult outreach centers. His success and his teachings about the nearing of the age of redemption, bolstered by some of the mystical beliefs of the Lubavitcher Hasidim, helped create the "Rebbe is the Messiah" movement, and to this day, billboards proclaiming him as King Messiah can be seen in many parts of Israel. Those directly or loosely affiliated with Lubavitch number as many as 200,000 and, contrary to popular expectations, Lubavitch has enjoyed significant growth since the death of their rebbe, who has not been succeeded.[24] Note, however, that the actual number of committed Lubavitch Hasidim is far below 200,000.

Satmar, from Satu Mare (meaning "Saint Mary"!) in Romania (originally, Szatmarnemeti, Hungary). The Satmar are more strict in their observance than the Lubavitchers—in fact, they have had numerous interfamily clashes over the years—and, in distinct contrast with Lubavitchers, they are completely ingrown, commonly speaking Yiddish and Hungarian before English, despite being based primarily in Brooklyn and upstate New York. A "model" Satmar community, called Kiryas Joel and located in the town of Monroe, "is a community where traditional values and the centrality of family are still the guiding principles of community life. It is a place where parents and children participate jointly in the beautiful ritual and customs of Hasidic and Orthodox Jewish life. To preserve these unadulterated values, Kiryas Joel is a community without television or radio. A few weeklies and other periodicals, published in Yiddish, are sold in the Village."[25] Satmar's most prominent rebbe was Yoel Teitelbaum (1887–1979), after whom Kiryas Joel is named. A heroic survivor of Auschwitz, where he lost most of his family, he was an ardent opponent of the modern state of Israel, believing that it was a nation founded by irreligious and atheistic Jews and that its presence stood in the way of the Messianic age, since it was the Messiah alone who was to regather the exiles and reestablish the nation of Israel. The Satmar number approximately 120,000, making them the largest Hasidic movement in terms of adherents from birth (whereas many Lubavitchers are either loosely affiliated or recent converts to Hasidic Judaism).

Breslov, from Bratslav, in the Ukraine. This was founded by Rebbe Nachman of Breslov (1772–1810), who was a great-grandson of the Baal Shem Tov. What makes this Hasidic movement unique is that they have been a community without a rebbe for almost two hundred years, basing themselves on their rebbe's teachings (including many parables and stories) and legendary accounts, along with the teachings of his disciples and their disciples. They are known for their outwardly joyous worship (common to all Hasidic worship is an intense expression of joy and fervor) and can be seen in Israel publicly dancing in the streets, part of their "outreach" to the secular community.[26] Their influence is dispro-portionate to their small numbers.

Other significant groups include Bobov, now headquartered in Borough Park, Brooklyn. It is perhaps the second-largest Ha-sidic group in America, after Satmar. In Israel, significant Hasidic groups include Ger, Vishnitz and Beltz.

A note about the term *Hasidic*: The Hebrew word *hasid* means "pious one, godly one," and it occurs 34 times in the Hebrew Bible, sometimes with reference to the Lord (see Psalm 145:17; Jeremiah 3:12) but normally with reference to godly people (see 1 Samuel 2:9; 2 Samuel 22:26; Micah 7:2; the word occurs most frequently in the Psalms; see Psalms 4:4; 12:2; 16:10; 37:28; 85:9; 116:15; 145:1, 5, 9). In the second century B.C., the godly Jews who opposed the onslaught of Hellenism were called *Hasideans*, or "godly ones." Until the 1700s, however, the term *Hasid* was, for the most part, used to describe godly individuals rather than specific Jewish groups, and there was no such thing as "Hasidic Judaism." Note also that an alternative spelling is *Chasidic*, reflect-ing the pronunciation of the opening Hebrew letter, *heth*, which is guttural, similar to the Scottish *ch* in *Loch Ness*. Also found are the spellings *Hassidic* (or *Chassidic*). The noun *Hasidut* (or *Chasidut*) refers to the practice of Hasidic Judaism.

3

What is the Oral Law?

According to traditional Judaism, when God gave Moses the writ-ten Torah on Mount Sinai, He also gave him an oral Torah, which contains explanations of the written Torah, along with principles of interpretation through which the Written Law can be under-stood. Moses then allegedly passed this Oral Law on to Joshua, who then passed it on to the elders of the next generation, then to the prophets, then to the leaders of what is called the Great Assembly (beginning in Ezra's day), then to specific pairs of leaders in the centuries before Jesus and then to whole generations of leaders in the subsequent centuries. (For the classic rabbinic formulation, see m. Avot chap. 1.)

Why was there a need for an Oral Law? The rabbis would say that without further oral explanation, many, if not all, of the biblical commandments are unintelligible. For example, God commanded the Israelites not to work on the Sabbath, with a death penalty legislated against those who broke the commandment. But nowhere does the Torah define exactly what constitutes work. How then could there be a death penalty for violation of an unclear commandment? According to traditional Judaism, God gave further explanation to Moses in the Oral Law, detailing the so-called 39 subdivisions of labor that were prohibited on the Sabbath.[27]

Another example of an allegedly unclear commandment is found in Deuteronomy 6:6–9, where Moses said to Israel:

> These commandments that I give you today are to be upon your hearts. Impress them on your children. Talk about them when you sit at home and when you walk along the road, when you lie down and when you get up. Tie them as symbols on your hands and bind them on your foreheads. Write them on the doorframes of your houses and on your gates.

What, exactly, does it mean to "tie [the commandments] as symbols on your hands and bind them on your foreheads"? What does it mean to "write them on the doorframes of your houses and on your gates"? The rabbis claim to have the explanation for this as well, interpreting these verses literally with reference to phylacteries and the mezuzah (see #20 and #21).

Dozens of other examples could be given, but the pattern is the same: Traditional Judaism claims that the Written Law cannot be understood without the Oral Law.

Why then is there little or no direct evidence in the Scriptures for this Oral Law? The rabbis would say that direct evidence is unnecessary, since there has been an unbroken chain of transmission through the generations—from Sinai until this day—and so there is no doubt about the reliability of the traditions. And, they would argue, an oral tradition is presupposed throughout the Hebrew Scriptures.

"But," you might protest, "is it not true that God based His covenant with Israel on the written Word?" (see Exodus 24:3–8; 34:27, among many other verses). The rabbis would agree with this statement to an extent, but they would emphasize that without the oral traditions, the written covenant cannot be understood. They would therefore state emphatically that there had to be an Oral Law in order for the written covenant to have been binding and applicable, both in ancient Israel and to this day. They would also argue that since the Oral Law was unwritten, one should not expect to find direct evidence of an unwritten law in written texts! (Does this sound slightly circular?)[28]

According to traditional Jews, it is the Oral Law that separates them from other religious faiths that also claim the Hebrew Bible as sacred Scripture—specifically, Christians—and it is the Oral Law that is especially beloved. As explained by Dr. Immanuel Jakobovitz, former Chief Rabbi of the United Kingdom:

> When our Sages asserted that "the Holy One, Blessed be He, did not make His covenant with Israel except by virtue of the Oral Law" (Gittin 60B), they not only propounded a cardinal Jewish belief, they also expressed a truth as evident today as it was in Talmudic times. The true character of Judaism cannot be appreciated except by an intimate acquaintance with the Oral Law. The Written Law, that is the Five Books of Moses, and even the rest of the Hebrew Bible, we share with other faiths. What makes us and our faith distinct and unique is the oral tradition as the authentic key to an understanding of the written text we call the Torah.[29]

Simply stated, there is no traditional Judaism without the traditions and no rabbinic Judaism without the rabbis.

Now, there is no reason to deny that traditions existed and developed in the life of ancient Israel—in fact, that is taken for granted and there is ample evidence to support this—but it is another thing entirely to argue that these traditions were divinely inspired, that they were given by God on Mount Sinai and that they were handed down in unbroken, authoritative form through the generations. That is a theory accepted only by Orthodox Jews. In fact, it is only ultra-Orthodox Jews who accept this concept in its literal totality.

What is ironic is that, eventually, the *oral* traditions were put in *writing*, and it is in their written form that they have been preserved. What makes this all the more ironic is that the Talmud stated that the written Torah was not to be transmitted orally and the oral Torah was not to be transmitted in writing (b. Gittin 60b). Nonetheless, as the oral traditions grew and as the living conditions of the Jewish people became more difficult—including persecution and dispersion—it was inevitable that these oral traditions were put into writing, and thus the Oral Law has been preserved through books. Orthodox Jews, however, would emphasize that even though the oral traditions have been put in writing for the last 1,800 years—and they continue to be put in writing—it is only in the context of a living community that these traditions can be fully experienced and understood, hence the need for ongoing oral instruction, explanation and example.

The many books of the Oral Law (see #7) contain discussion and amplification of the Torah laws; legal deliberations; new laws, customs and enactments; commentaries on the Torah and other portions of Scripture; folklore, parables, stories; and everything else that relates to virtually all aspects of Jewish life—all grounded in a rabbinic perspective.

According to traditional Jews, during the last two to three centuries B.C., the primary transmitters of the Oral Law were called the *zugot*, or "pairs," referring to two prominent leaders in each generation. They were followed by the Tannaim, who lived in the first two centuries of this era (the singular *Tanna* means "repeater" or "teacher"; these teachers transmitted the primary traditions that were being passed down and developed). These were followed by the Amoraim, who lived in the third to fifth centuries (*Amora* means "sayer"; these teachers continued to develop the traditions and sought to integrate them further with the biblical text). Next were the Saboraim in the sixth century (*Sabora* means "reasoner"; these men were the final editors of the Babylonian Talmud). From the seventh to the tenth centuries were the Gaonim (referring to the leaders of the Babylonian academies); next were the Rishonim, in the eleventh to fifteenth centuries. (The term *Rishonim* literally means "earlier ones," who were responsible for the major biblical and Talmudic commentaries, along with the development of the law codes.) From the sixteenth century until today are the Achronim (literally, "later ones," in contrast with the Rishonim).

Traditional Jews believe that, generally speaking, there is a spiritual decline in every century, since each new generation stands at a further distance from the revelation at Sinai, as stated in the Talmud, "If the former generation was like angels, we are like men; if they were like men, we are like donkeys" (b. Shabbat 112b). This means that an interpretation, ruling or custom that was established by a previous generation—especially from the generation of the Tannaim or Amoraim—becomes virtually sacrosanct in the following generations.

4

What is the Tanakh?

Tanakh is the Jewish name for the Hebrew Scriptures, what Christians call the Old Testament. The word itself is an acronym standing for three words: *Torah* (the Pentateuch), *Nevi'im*

(Prophets, pronounced *n'-vee-eem*) and *Ketuvim* (Writings, pronounced *k'-tu-veem*). The last two sections, Nevi'im and Ketuvim, can be called *Nakh*, but this term is primarily used in religious Jewish circles.

Although the contents of the Tanakh are identical to the contents of the Old Testament, the books are organized differently, following slightly different conceptual lines. The order of the books that is familiar to most Christian readers follows the Septuagint tradition and is divided as follows: Law (the five books of Moses); History (Joshua–Esther); Poetry and Wisdom (Job–Song of Solomon) and Prophets (Isaiah–Malachi, including Daniel and Lamentations).

The order of the biblical books in the Tanakh is broken down into three main categories:

Torah: The five books of Moses; this is identical to the "Old Testament" order, but the books are named after the opening word of each book, and so Genesis is *Bereshit*, pronounced *b'-rey-sheet*; Exodus is *Shemot*, pronounced *shey-moht*, taken from the second word of the text, *names*; Leviticus is *Vayikra*, pronounced *va-yik-rah*; Numbers is *Bamidbar*, pronounced *bah-mid-bar*; and Deuteronomy is *Debarim*, pronounced *d'-vah-reem*, taken from the second word of the text, *words*. For more discussion of the term *Torah*, see #5.

Prophets: This section is divided into the "Former Prophets"— referring to Joshua, Judges, 1–2 Samuel and 1–2 Kings, based on the belief that these books were all written by prophets— and the "Latter Prophets"—referring to Isaiah, Jeremiah, Ezekiel and Hosea–Malachi, called "The Twelve."

Writings: This includes all the remaining books, generally in the following order: Psalms, Job, Proverbs, Ruth, Song of Solomon (normally called "Song of Songs," and based on the opening verse), Ecclesiastes (normally called *Koheleth*, meaning "the preacher" or "convener," based on the opening verse), Lamentations (called *Eichah*, meaning "how, alas," which is the opening word of the book), Esther, Daniel, Ezra, Nehemiah and 1–2 Chronicles.

Reading through portions of the Scriptures is a fixed part of Jewish liturgy, with the greatest emphasis put on the Torah, which is read through in its entirety in the synagogues over the course of every year. This is supplemented each week by a reading from the Nevi'im (Prophets), called the *Haftarah* (meaning "supplement," commonly pronounced *Haftorah*), while other portions of Scripture, especially the Psalms, are included in the daily prayers.

This is the annual cycle of readings from the Torah and Prophets, beginning afresh every fall, which means that religious Jews are all reading the same Torah portions each week. Each Torah portion is called a *parasha* or *parsha* and is named after the opening word of each section. (The numbers in parentheses refer to differences between the Hebrew verse numbers and the verse numbers in most English translations.)

Genesis (*Bereshit*)

Bereshit	1:1–6:8	Isaiah 42:5–43:10
Noah	6:9–11:32	Isaiah 54:1–55:5
Lekh Lekha	12:1–17:27	Isaiah 40:27–41:16
Va-yera'	18:1–22:24	2 Kings 4:1–37
Hayyei Sarah	23:1–25:18	1 Kings 1:1–31
Toledot	25:19–28:9	Malachi 1:1–2:7
Va-yetse'	28:10–32:3(2)	Hosea 12:12–14:10(9)
Va-yishlah	32:4(3)–36:43	Hosea 11:7–12:12
Va-yeshev	37:1–40:23	Amos 2:6–3:8
Mikkets	41:1–44:17	1 Kings 3:15–4:1
Va-yigash	44:18–47:27	Ezekiel 37:15–28
Va-yehi	47:28–50:26	1 Kings 2:1–12

Exodus (*Shemot*)

Shemot	1:1–6:1	Isaiah 27:6–28:13; 29:22–23
Va-'era'	6:2–9:35	Ezekiel 28:25–29:21
Bo	10:1–13:16	Jeremiah 46:13–28
Be-shalah	13:17–17:16	Judges 4:4–5:31
Yitro	18:1–20:23(26)	Isaiah 6:1–7:6; 9:5–6(6–7)
Mishpatim	21:1–24:18	Jeremiah 34:8–22; 33:25–26
Terumah	25:1–27:19	1 Kings 5:26 (4:29)–6:13
Tetsavveh	27:20–30:10	Ezekiel 43:10–27
Ki Tissa'	30:11–34:35	1 Kings 18:1–39
Vayakhel	35:1–38:20	1 Kings 7:40–50
Pekudei	38:21–40:38	1 Kings 7:51–8:21

Leviticus (*Vayikra*)

Vayikra	1:1–5:26 (6:7)	Isaiah 43:21–44:23
Tsav	6:1(8)–8:36	Jeremiah 7:21–8:3; 9:22–23(23–24)
Shemini	9:1–11:47	2 Samuel 6:1–7:17
Tazria'	12:1–13:59	2 Kings 4:42–5:19
Metsora'	14:1–15:33	2 Kings 7:3–20
'Aharei Mot	16:1–18:30	Ezekiel 22:1–19
Kedoshim	19:1–20:27	Amos 9:7–15
'Emor	21:1–24:23	Ezekiel 44:15–31
Behar	25:1–62	Jeremiah 32:6–27
Bechukotai	26:1–27:34	Jeremiah 16:19–17:14

Numbers (*Bamidbar*)

Bamidbar	1:1–4:20	Hosea 2:1–22
Nasso'	4:21–7:89	Judges 13:2–25
Beha'alotha	8:1–12:16	Zechariah 2:14(10)–4:7
Shelach	13:1–15:41	Joshua 2:1–24
Korah	16:1–18:32	1 Samuel 11:14–12:22

continued

Hukkat	19:1–22:1	Judges 11:1–33
Balak	22:2–25:9	Micah 5:6–6:8
Pinchas	25:10–30:1(29:40)	1 Kings 18:46–19:21
Mattot	30:2(1)–32:42	Jeremiah 1:1–2:3
Mass'ei	33:1–36:13	Jeremiah 2:4–28, 3:4

Deuteronomy (Debarim)		
Debarim	1:1–3:22	Isaiah 1:1–27
Va'etchanan	3:23–7:11	Isaiah 40:1–26
'Ekev	7:12–11:25	Isaiah 49:14–51:3
Re'eh	11:26–16:17	Isaiah 54:11–55:5
Shoftim	16:18–21:9	Isaiah 51:12–52:12
Ki Tetze'	21:10–25:19	Isaiah 54:1–10
Ki Tavo'	26:1–29:8(9)	Isaiah 60:1–22
Nitzavim	29:9(10)–31:30	Isaiah 61:10–63:9
Ha'azinu	32:1–52	2 Samuel 22:1–22:51
Vezot Ha'Bracha	33:1–34:12	Joshua 1:1–18

There are other, special readings for various holy days, most notably the reading of what are called the Five Scrolls (Hebrew, *chamesh megillot*) on five of the major holy days. The Five Scrolls are the Song of Songs (or Song of Solomon), which is read on Passover (*pesach*) to commemorate God's love relationship with His people; Ruth, which is read on Shavuot (Pentecost) because of the harvest imagery; Lamentations (called *Eichah*, based on the opening word, *How*), which is read on Tisha b'Ab (the Ninth of Av, the ultimate day of mourning on the Jewish calendar); Ecclesiastes (called *Kohelet*, based on the Hebrew word found in Ecclesiastes 1:1, meaning, "the preacher" or "the convener," and translated "teacher" in the NIV), which is read on Sukkot, Tabernacles, in recognition of the transitory nature of life; and Esther, which is read on Purim, whose background is given in Esther 9:26–32.

Because the majority of Jews worldwide today are not observant (in fact, roughly 90 percent are *not* Orthodox; see #1), most of them are not familiar with their own Scriptures. In contrast, observant Jews tend to be very familiar with the portions of the Tanakh that are part of their liturgical and study cycle, but not as familiar with other portions of the Tanakh, since they primarily study the Talmud and related legal literature (see #3).

As for the use of acronyms (as in Tanakh), it should be noted that there are literally hundreds of such acronyms in Judaism, and so Rabbi Moses ben Maimon (Maimonides) is called *Rambam* (based on the letters R-M-B-M) and Rabbi Moses ben Nachman (Nachmanides) is called *Ramban* (based on the letters R-M-B-N). Similarly, Rabbi David Kimchi is called *Radak* (based on the letters R-D-K) and Rabbi Levi ben Gershom is called *Ralbag* (based on the letters R-L-B-G).

5
What exactly is meant by the term *Torah*?

The Hebrew word *torah* means "instruction, teaching, law." In some cases, it primarily means "instructive precept, law," as in Exodus 12:49, "The same law [*torah*] applies to the native-born and to the alien living among you." Similar to this is the usage of *torah* in verses such as Leviticus 6:9(2), rendered in the New Jewish Version with, "Command Aaron and his sons thus: This is the ritual (*torah*) of the burnt offering" (cf. NASB, which renders this, "Command Aaron and his sons, saying, 'This is the law for the burnt offering'"; NIV has "regulations" instead of "law"). In other cases, *torah* primarily means "instruction, teaching," as in Proverbs 3:1, "My son, do not forget my teaching [*torah*], but keep my commands in your heart." But even here, when *torah* means "teaching," it carries with it a note of authority, as indicated by the second half of the verse, which makes reference to "my commands." So then, when God gave *the*

Torah to Israel, He was not simply giving His people a set of laws, nor was He merely giving them divine revelation. Rather, He was giving them His binding instruction, His covenantal commands, His divine directions. He was telling them, "This is how you are to live before Me, and these are the consequences of obedience or disobedience. This is what I require of you."

To convey this, the NJPSV sometimes renders *torah* as "Teaching" (with a capital T), as in Joshua 1:8, "Let not this Book of the Teaching cease from your lips, but recite it day and night, so that you may observe faithfully all that is written in it. Only then will you prosper in your undertakings and only then will you be successful." In this context, Torah refers to divinely given, divinely binding direction. It is filled with laws, but it is not exclusively law. It is divine revelation.

In the process of time, however, *torah* became especially connected with the concept of God's Law for Israel, and so when the Septuagint translators rendered the word *torah* (the Septuagint was translated in the third to second centuries B.C.), they generally translated it with the Greek *nomos*, which primarily means "law, custom, ordinance," but which lacks the nuance of "teaching." Similarly, the New Testament authors, writing in Greek, followed this established convention and used the word *nomos* when referring to the Torah, as in Luke 24:44; Romans 6:14; 1 Corinthians 9:8–9; and scores of other passages.[30]

Jewish scholars have rightly objected to the strict association of *torah* with "law," feeling that this association contributes to a wrong concept of Judaism as primarily a religion of laws. This is certainly a valid objection, since to equate *torah* with "law" is to narrow its meaning. When rightly understood, however, the Torah can be thought of as God's holy standard, His definitive word to ancient Israel, His authoritative instruction—and this comports well with the concept of the divine Law. I also find it interesting that the same scholars and rabbis who state that *torah* should not be translated as "law" actually refer to the Oral Law and the Written Law, even though the Hebrew phrases speak of an oral *torah* and a written *torah*. Why then translate these terms with "Oral Law/Written Law" if *torah* does not mean this at all?

It is also fair to ask why traditional Judaism produced major law codes (see #7) that are studied daily and adhered to punctiliously if *torah* is wrongly understood as "law." And why is the Talmud itself *filled* with head-spinning legal discussions—all considered to be an essential part of Torah study—if *torah* does not mean "law"? And don't portions of Scripture such as Psalm 119, full of praise for the Torah's commandments, point to an association between the Torah and Law?

My point in raising these questions, however, is *not* to advocate that the word *torah* be rendered primarily as "law." In fact, thinking *only* of "law" *does* bring a wrong association to mind. Rather, my point is to emphasize that there is legitimacy to thinking of the Torah as the Law of God, recognizing that His Law contains much more than just laws. Having said that, it is interesting to observe how the use of *nomos* in Greek is influenced and stretched by the concept of *torah*. A good example of this is found in John 10:34, where Jesus makes reference to "your Law [*nomos*]," but His quote is not from the Pentateuch but from the Psalms. Similarly, in the Koran, *tawrah* primarily refers to the Old Testament as a whole (while *injil*, "gospel," refers to the entire New Testament).

Returning to traditional Judaism—*the* Torah-centered religion—the word *torah* becomes all-inclusive in its meaning. Torah study means the study of all religious Jewish texts, and the highest form of worship is *talmud torah lishmah*, study of Torah for its own sake, traditionally applied primarily to Talmud study. And *torah* becomes the Jewish way of life, as illustrated by this famous story from the Talmud:

> It has been taught: R. Akiba said: Once I went in after R. Joshua to a privy, and I learnt from him three things. I learnt that one

does not sit east and west but north and south; I learnt that one evacuates not standing but sitting; and I learnt that it is proper to wipe with the left hand and not with the right. Said Ben Azzai to him: Did you dare to take such liberties with your master? He replied: It was a matter of Torah, and I required to learn. It has been taught: Ben Azzai said: Once I went in after R. Akiba to a privy, and I learnt from him three things. I learnt that one does not evacuate east and west but north and south. I also learnt that one evacuates sitting and not standing. I also learnt it is proper to wipe with the left hand and not with the right. Said R. Judah to him: Did you dare to take such liberties with your master?—He replied: It was a matter of Torah, and I required to learn. R. Kahana once went in and hid under Rab's bed. He heard him chatting [with his wife] and joking and doing what he required. He said to him: One would think that Abba's mouth had never sipped the dish before! He said to him: Kahana, are you here? Go out, because it is rude. He replied: It is a matter of Torah, and I required to learn.

b. Berachot 62a

So, even the way a rabbinic teacher has sexual relations with his wife is a matter of Torah! This gives a hint to the expansive use of the term *torah* in Judaism.

As for the etymology of the word *torah* in Hebrew, there are several possible explanations. Some have traced it back to the Akkadian word *tertu*, a "divine oracle." (Akkadian refers to the language of the ancient Assyrians and Babylonians.) A more popular explanation is to derive *torah* from the Hebrew root *y-r-h*, either in the sense of "to teach" or in the sense of "to shoot an arrow."

6

What is the Masoretic text?

I have often heard Christians boast that the translation of the Old Testament they use is "based on the Masoretic text." In point of fact, virtually every translation of the Tanakh into any language is based on the Masoretic text, since this is the only complete text of the Hebrew Scriptures that we have. The only exceptions would be variant Hebrew readings preserved in the Dead Sea Scrolls or variants in the ancient versions—in particular, the Septuagint—that seem to reflect a different Hebrew original. Otherwise, every translation of the Hebrew Scriptures can use one text and one text only: the Masoretic text!

What, then, is the Masoretic text (commonly abbreviated MT)? Actually, it is more accurate to speak of the Masoretic textual tradition, since there are literally thousands of medieval manuscripts of the Hebrew Scriptures that were copied and preserved by the Jewish scribes whom we call the *Masoretes* (literally, "the transmitters"), and there are thousands of very minor variants in these manuscripts. In other words, there is not one "master" text of the Hebrew Bible, but the scribes were so careful in their transmission methods that the differences in the Masoretic manuscripts are, for the most part, of extremely minor consequence.

The work of the Masoretes is generally dated from the sixth to the eleventh centuries A.D., but the oldest complete copy of the Hebrew Bible we have today dates to the eleventh century (it is called the Leningrad B19a). What happened to the earlier copies? And how reliable can an eleventh-century text be? That is more than thirteen centuries after the last book of the Tanakh was written! In contrast, the oldest complete copy of the Greek New Testament dates to less than three centuries after the writing of the last book of the New Testament.

Those who questioned the accuracy of the Masoretic manuscripts were in for a surprise when the Dead Sea Scrolls were discovered in the late 1940s. Here were Hebrew manuscripts that were more than *one thousand years* older than the oldest Masoretic texts, and yet some of the Dead Sea texts agreed with the Masoretic texts word for word and letter for letter. What a testimony to the careful work of these Jewish scribes! Of course, there were other scrolls that deviated extensively from the Masoretic manuscripts—especially in spelling conventions—but these deviations reflected one of two things: either the popular spelling style that was often used at that time (meaning that these ancient scrolls were *less* accurate than the medieval manuscripts) or a different, ancient textual tradition was preserved (meaning that the question is not the accuracy of the transmission but the origin of the tradition).

What, then, became of all the manuscripts between the time of the Dead Sea Scrolls and the eleventh-century B19a manuscript? Because the biblical texts were considered sacred, they could not be destroyed, so they were either buried when they were no longer usable or else stored away in special rooms that functioned like a hidden warehouse, sometimes in the back of a synagogue. (One of the most famous Hebrew manuscript treasure troves was discovered in one such synagogue room, called the Cairo Genizah. The word *genizah* means "a storage room." It should also be remembered that the Dead Sea Scrolls were hidden away for safekeeping, only to be discovered nineteen centuries later.)

How was it, then, that the Jewish scribes, both before and after the Masoretes, were able to preserve the biblical text with such accuracy? First, it is clear that God willed that His Word would be preserved for His people through the ages, which is the biggest reason that the biblical text of the Hebrew and Greek Scriptures has been so wonderfully and even miraculously kept through the ages. Second, because the scribes believed that they were handling sacred texts, they were scrupulous in their transmission methods, counting the letters, words and sentences in each book of the Tanakh, making note of the middle letter, middle word and middle sentence of each book (or of the Torah as a whole). Can you imagine how painstaking this work was? And just think: If the manuscript was off by one single letter, it would not be used. That's scribal accuracy!

Third, because Judaism put a tremendous emphasis on study and on the memorization of the sacred texts (meaning the Tanakh and the rabbinic literature; see #7), the scribes were specially equipped for their task, having an extreme familiarity with the biblical texts and a high level of academic discipline.

The Masoretes were also responsible for developing the vowel system used in Hebrew Bibles today. (Hebrew vowels, for the most part, are not represented by letters—as they are, for example, in English. Instead, they are represented by series of dots or short lines placed beneath, above or to the side of the consonants.) The Masoretes also developed an elaborate (and somewhat esoteric) system of marginal notes, in which they commented on every kind of textual phenomenon and variant.

7
What are the holy books of Judaism?

The Jewish people are not only the "people of the Book" (meaning the Bible); they are the people of *many* books, some of which represent collections totaling millions of words. And it is through these other books—and their accompanying traditions—that religious Jews interpret the Bible.

The ultimate holy book of Judaism—in terms of being the inspired Word of God—is the Tanakh (the Old Testament; see #4), with the Torah having the preeminence in the Tanakh, since traditional Jews believe that God literally dictated the contents of the Torah to Moses on Mount Sinai, supplementing this written Torah with thousands of oral explanations and principles. These oral traditions, customs, laws and interpretations were eventually put in writing, beginning around A.D. 200 (see #3; again, this represents the traditional Jewish viewpoint).

Although there were many Jewish writings produced between the end of the Tanakh and the early centuries of this era—some of which are preserved in the Apocrypha, which is considered to be part of the Bible by Catholics, and others of which have been discovered among the Dead Sea Scrolls—none of these books is considered sacred in traditional Judaism. To be sure, some of them, such as the Book of Enoch (included in what is called the Pseudepigrapha) or the Temple Scroll (from the Dead Sea Scrolls), were considered to be sacred in certain Jewish circles roughly two thousand years ago. But since those Jewish expressions—called "Judaisms" by many scholars today—did not continue to thrive after the destruction of the Temple in A.D. 70, and since Pharisaic Judaism, which developed into Rabbinic Judaism, eventually prevailed, traditional Jews today place virtually no importance on these ancient writings, writings they would consider "external" or heretical. (For traditional Jews, the New Testament would also fall into the category of an external, heretical document.) As far as the authority of "holy books" in Judaism, the closer the book to Mount Sinai, the more authority it has (for further explanation of this, see #3).

How do traditional Jews relate to their holy books? These books are certainly considered sacred, and to study them is to study Torah (see #5), to learn the ways and the will of God, to participate in the spiritual life of the nation, thereby bridging the generations. And in a real sense, the holy books are seen as continuations of the Sinai revelation, the outworking of divine truth and practice through the chosen nation. On the other hand, traditional Jews do not relate to their holy books—outside of the Bible itself and, on some level, the Talmud—in the same way that Christians relate to the New Testament. That is to say, because traditional Judaism is, by its very nature, a religion based on tradition, not every word of the holy books has to be taken as direct, infallible truth. That also means that to this day, "holy books" can be written by religious Jews—part of the ongoing chain of tradition—but again, they would not carry the same authority as the foundational books of Judaism.

These foundational books can be divided into legal material (called *halakha*) and biblical, interpretive material (called *haggada*), although the Talmud contains much of both, and some of the interpretive material is legal in its emphasis. Here is a glossary describing the most important books (or collections of books) in Judaism:

Babylonian Talmud—The foundational text for Jewish religious study, it consists of 2.5 million words of Hebrew and Aramaic commentary and expansion on the *Mishnah*. It includes much *Halakha* as well as *Haggada*, and thus it touches on virtually every area of life, religion, custom, folklore and law. It reached its final form between A.D. 500 and 600, and it is mainly the product of the Babylonian sages. See also *Palestinian Talmud*.

Haggada (sometimes spelled *Aggada*)—Nonlegal (i.e., nonbinding) rabbinic stories, sermons and commentaries relating to the Tanakh and Jewish life. See also *Halakha* and *Midrash*.

Halakha—A specific legal ruling ("What is the *halakha* in this case?"); or rabbinic legal material in general. The word *Halakha* is interpreted as meaning "the way to go." See also *Haggada*.

Humash (pronounced *KHU-mash*)—Another name for the five books of Moses. It literally means "fifth," short for the "five-fifths of the Torah."

Jerusalem Talmud—See *Palestinian Talmud*.

Kabbalah—The general term for Jewish mystical writings and traditions. It literally means "that which has been received." See also *Zohar*.

Midrash—Rabbinic commentaries on a verse, chapter or whole book of the Tanakh, marked by creativity and interpretive skill. The best-known collection is called *Midrash Rabba*, covering the five books of Moses as well as the Five Scrolls (see #4).

Mishnah—The first written collection of legal material relating to the laws of the *Torah* and the ordinances of the sages. It provides the starting point for all subsequent *Halakha*. It was compiled about A.D. 200 by Rabbi Judah HaNasi (which means "the Prince") and especially emphasizes the traditions of the rabbis who flourished from A.D. 70 to 200. See *Talmud* and *Halakha*.

Mishneh Torah—Systematic compilation of all Jewish law by Moses Maimonides (also called Rambam; A.D. 1135–1204). It remains a standard legal text to this day. See also *Shulkhan Arukh*.

Palestinian Talmud—Similar to the *Babylonian Talmud* but based primarily on the work of the sages in Israel. It is shorter in scope, less authoritative and therefore studied less than the *Babylonian Talmud*. It reached its final form in Israel about A.D. 400.

Responsa Literature—A major source of *Halakha* from A.D. 600 until today, it consists of the answers to specific legal questions posed to leading rabbinic authorities in every generation.

Shulkhan Arukh—The standard and most authoritative Jewish law code, compiled by Rabbi Joseph Karo (A.D. 1488–1575). See also *Mishneh Torah*.

Siddur—The traditional Jewish prayer book, containing selections from the Tanakh, as well as prayers composed by the rabbis.

Talmud—See *Babylonian Talmud* and *Palestinian Talmud* (or *Jerusalem Talmud*).

Tanakh—Acronym for <u>T</u>orah, <u>N</u>evi'im, <u>K</u>etuvim, the Jewish name for the Old Testament in its entirety. Although the order of the books is different from that of a Christian Old

Testament, the contents are exactly the same. For details, see #4.

Targum—Literally, "translation." This refers to the expansive Aramaic translations of the Hebrew Bible that were read in the synagogues where biblical Hebrew was no longer understood. They were put in written form between A.D. 300 and 1200. The most important *Targums* are *Targum Onkelos* to the five books of Moses and *Targum Jonathan* to the *Nevi'im* (Prophets).

Zohar—The foundational book of Jewish mysticism. It was composed in the thirteenth century A.D., although mystical tradition dates it to the second century A.D. The general term for Jewish mystical writings and traditions is *kabbalah*, known today in a popularized and somewhat distorted form. *Kabbalah* literally means "that which has been received."

An older but extremely useful introduction to the most sacred books of Judaism is Barry W. Holtz, ed., *Back to the Sources: Reading the Classic Jewish Texts* (reprint, New York: Simon & Schuster, 1986). See also Barry W. Holtz, ed., *The Schocken Guide to Jewish Books* (New York: Schocken, 1992).

8

What are the main differences between Judaism and Christianity?

Although Judaism and Christianity have the Tanakh (Old Testament) in common, and although "Christianity" was, in fact, a first-century Jewish sect—note the title of the popular book by Edith Schaeffer, *Christianity Is Jewish*[31]—there are a number of fundamental differences between the New Testament Messianic faith and the Talmudic rabbinic faith. I will reduce these differences to their most fundamental levels, understanding that there is much oversimplification in the process, including using the terms "Judaism" and "Christianity" as if they were mutually exclusive. Note also that when referring to Judaism and Christianity, I am referring especially to traditional Judaism and to those basic Christian beliefs that are, by and large, universally held. My intent is to show areas of contrast rather than to describe fully what "Judaism" and "Christianity" believe.

God—Judaism believes in God's absolute unity; Christianity believes in God's tri-unity. Judaism believes that it is acceptable for Gentiles to worship God as Trinity but states that for a Jew, it is idolatrous, especially since this includes the worship of Jesus. Judaism emphasizes God's complete incorporeality (i.e., that He has no bodily form of any kind); Christianity puts less emphasis on His incorporeal nature.

Messiah—Judaism believes that the Messiah, who will be fully human, is yet to come, although there are Jewish traditions that indicate that there is a potential Messiah in each generation. This Messiah will regather the Jewish exiles, fight the wars of the Lord, rebuild the Temple in Jerusalem and bring about universal peace and the knowledge of God (see further #10). Christianity believes that the Messiah, who was both fully human and fully divine—the Word incarnate, the Son of God—came two thousand years ago to die for our sins, rising from the dead and sending God's Spirit to the earth to continue His mission. He will return at the end of the age to establish His Kingdom on the earth, destroy God's enemies and bring about universal peace and the knowledge of God.

Sin—Judaism believes that every human being has a battle between the good inclination (the *yetzer hatov*) and the evil inclination (the *yetzer hara*'), but it does not believe in the doctrine of "original sin," emphasizing instead that

Having summarized some of the fundamental differences between "Judaism" and "Christianity," it is important to remember that there are many areas of commonality, and many Christians today are committed to rediscovering the Jewish roots of their faith—not trying to become Orthodox Jews (though, unfortunately, some are!), but rather recognizing that many church traditions over the years have obscured the biblical, Jewish foundations on which faith in Yeshua the Messiah was originally built. (For more on this, see #43.)

9
What do Jewish people think about Jesus?

There is not a simple answer to this question, given the great diversity in beliefs and perspectives among the Jewish people. And, for the most part, Jewish people do not spend a lot of time thinking about Jesus in a serious way. That is to say, outside of Christmas celebrations or concerns about the religious right or the latest media fad—like the *Da Vinci Code* furor in 2006 or the *Passion of the Christ* uproar in 2004—the person of Jesus is not a topic of discussion or thought in most Jewish households. After all, they would say, we are Jews, not Christians, and Jesus is for the Christians (i.e., Gentiles).

For the most part, then, Jesus is not viewed as a directly relevant religious figure by the great majority of Jewish people. It is true that more Jews now recognize that Jesus—Yeshua!—was Jewish, something that I did not realize until I was close to thirteen years old. When I happened to discover this fact, I cracked a joke to my Jewish schoolmates, asking them, "When did Jesus become Catholic? After He rose from the dead?" That reflects how we thought of things! In light of these kinds of perceptions, it is not surprising that most Jews would not immediately connect "Christ" with "Messiah," seeing it primarily as part of Jesus' name.

through the power of repentance, the evil inclination can be overcome. Christianity believes that Adam's fall affected the entire human race (this, too, is believed by Judaism, but not in as radical a way), that the best of us fall infinitely short of God's glory and perfection and only through the blood of Jesus, the Messiah, can we be spiritually transformed.

Salvation—Judaism does not hold to the concept of individual salvation, and in the late 1970s, when a major Christian organization launched the evangelistic "I Found It" campaign, an Orthodox Jewish rabbi—with whom I attended graduate school classes at New York University—launched the "We Never Lost It" campaign. Judaism thinks more corporately than does Christianity, and even though the concept of forgiveness of sins and atonement is important (see the next paragraph), there is no such concept of "being saved" or "getting saved" in Judaism, and there is much less emphasis on the afterlife (see also the next two entries).

Atonement—Although traditional Jews pray daily for the rebuilding of the Temple and the restoration of animal sacrifices (Reform Jews have removed such petitions from their prayer book), Judaism does not believe that blood atonement is essential for personal atonement. Rather, repentance, good deeds, prayer and personal suffering (seen, at times, as a payment for sin) take the place of sacrifices; partial support for this is found in 2 Chronicles 7:14, among other verses. Christianity teaches that atonement can only come through the substitutionary death of the Messiah and that true saving faith includes repentance (see Acts 2:38; 20:21; 26:20).

Afterlife—While Judaism recognizes that this world is the vestibule to the world to come, and while there is daily prayer for the coming of the Messiah and the Messianic age, the primary emphasis in Judaism is on the present world, the here and now, in keeping with the emphasis in the Tanakh. Christianity sees the world to come—specifically, heaven and hell—as being of paramount importance, to the point that the way we are called to live in this world can only make complete sense in the light of eternity. While there is a wholesome appreciation of life in this world, it is not to be separated from the world to come.

Creed vs. Deed—Judaism has basic creeds—most notably Moses Maimonides's Thirteen Principles of Faith, although some of these were hotly disputed in his day—and there are fundamental, essential beliefs in Judaism. The greater emphasis, however, is put on deeds—specifically, observing the commandments of the Torah, as understood and passed on through the traditions. Christianity puts a tremendous emphasis on good works and stresses the importance of a transformed life, but its greater emphasis is put on holding to the essentials of the faith, from which a transformed life and good works will naturally emanate. Thus it is sometimes said that Judaism emphasizes orthopraxy; Christianity emphasizes orthodoxy. Or, put another way, Judaism is the religion of the deed, Christianity the religion of the creed. These statements are, however, somewhat exaggerated.[32]

Mission—Both Jews and Christians feel a calling to be a light to the world and to make God known, but that sense of mission is worked out very differently in Judaism and Christianity. The former places its emphasis on being faithful to the Jewish calling, meaning living according to the Torah and rabbinic traditions, praying the communal prayers and studying the sacred texts. In so doing, the example of the Jewish people will ultimately enlighten the world. Christianity feels a sacred calling to make the message of salvation known through all available means, including living a life deeply devoted to the Lord (and thereby being an example and hastening

redemption) and, quite pointedly, sharing the Good News about Jesus to everyone. Thus, Christianity has always had "missionaries," while that has not been the norm for more than 1,900 years in Judaism. (For Jewish missionaries to Jews, see #2, on Lubavitch.)

Calendar—Judaism is much more committed to a daily, weekly and annual life cycle than is Christianity, and therefore Jewish life revolves around the calendar more than does Christianity, which puts a greater emphasis on individual relationship with God and life in the Spirit (in the context of a community of believers) than on the ordered lifestyle of a religious community. (This statement would be modified somewhat in liturgical church traditions.) In Judaism, the Sabbath is central to the weekly schedule, with the seasons of the holy days being major focal points of religious activity during the year (in the fall, *Rosh HaShanah*, or the New Year, but called Trumpets in the Torah; *Yom Kippur*, the Day of Atonement; and *Sukkot*, Tabernacles; in the spring, *Pesach*, Passover; and *Shavuot*, Weeks or Pentecost, with intervening holy days in between). In Christianity, Sunday is viewed as the Sabbath by many Christians, but not in the comprehensive, strict way that the Sabbath is practiced in Judaism, while for many other Christians, Sunday is simply the primary day for corporate worship. (For the question of the Sabbath, see #49.) In liturgical churches, the major holidays, such as Easter and Christmas, are part of a sacred, traditional cycle of days, but again, not with the emphasis or comprehensive nature that is found in Judaism. In non-liturgical churches, Easter, or Resurrection Sunday, is a special day of celebration and even evangelism, but not much more, while for many Christians, Christmas is not of deep religious significance.

When Jews do have opinions about Jesus, they are quite diverse. In the eyes of the ultra-Orthodox, Jesus is an apostate Jew and an archenemy of the Jewish people, the founder of a destructive religion that has brought untold hardship and persecution on us through the generations. Some believe that He actually said what the New Testament attributes to Him—not that they would have read it for themselves—while others believe that His followers were the primary ones responsible for deviating from the path. (Paul comes in for special criticism here; see #44.) Either way, to the extent they believe that the Talmud and rabbinic writings actually speak about this same Jesus (whom they know as Yeshu; see #38), they would regard Him as a deceiver of the masses.[33]

Jews who are less religious and who have actually given thought to the person of Jesus tend to be more positive in their assessment, although there remains a wide range of opinion. Some view Jesus as a great rabbi who was either misunderstood or misrepresented by His followers in the next generations, leading to the birth of Christianity. Some see Him as a wise man and even a prophet; some consider Him to be a brave figure standing against the tyranny of Rome; others view Him as a mystic or guru figure (in many cases, projecting back on Jesus what they themselves feel are spiritually positive qualities). Still others feel that we cannot know much about Him, questioning the validity of the sources we have at our disposal, in keeping with critical, skeptical scholarship as reflected in the Jesus Seminar.

As divergent as these views are—deceiver, rabbi, prophet, teacher, mystic—they all have this in common: With the exception of Jewish believers in Yeshua, the Jewish people do *not* recognize Jesus as the Messiah and, more emphatically, they do *not* recognize Him as God incarnate. So, He might be a great rabbi or even a noble revolutionary, but certainly not the Redeemer. Perhaps He's an enlightened guru, but definitely not God!

In the last few decades, there has been an increasing desire to reclaim Jesus the Jew by Jewish scholars, some of whom are Orthodox, and although this reclamation stops short of reclaiming Him as Messiah and Lord, it is still a step in the right direction.[34] And in Israel, schoolchildren learn something about Yeshua as well (they, too, know Him as Yeshu; see again #38), although, to repeat, they do *not* learn about Him as Savior or Redeemer.

A challenging recent study, written by a Jewish academic and reflecting Jewish problems with the Christian Jesus, is Professor Amy Jill-Levine's *The Misunderstood Jew: The Scandal of the Jewish Jesus*.[35] I do not concur with a number of her key premises, and her ecumenical desire to affirm fully both Judaism and Christianity is not tenable (see #60). (As I have repeatedly stated, if Jesus is not the Messiah of Israel—which is a foundational truth of the New Testament—then no one should follow Him. Put another way, either Jesus is the Messiah of everyone or the Messiah of no one.) Nonetheless, her book helps give the Christian reader insight into some of the issues that the Jewish people have with Jesus, providing many valuable insights.

On a more personal, anecdotal level, a Messianic Jewish leader recently told me that his congregation has enjoyed extensive interaction with the Jewish community where he lives, even holding joint meetings with the Conservative synagogue—this is almost unprecedented for a Messianic Jewish group—and going on a tour of Israel together. Quality interaction like this has actually gone on now for several years. And yet this leader commented to me with sadness that after all the time these two groups have spent together, it simply hasn't dawned on the members of the Conservative Jewish congregation that Yeshua has any relevance for them.

This remains typical for the great majority of Jews worldwide, and to this day, when I tell a Jewish person that I'm a believer in Jesus, the typical response is, "So, you *were* Jewish but now you believe in Jesus?" or, "How can you be Jewish and believe in Jesus?" The two seem incompatible to them, as stated by the Jewish comedian (and rabbi) Jackie Mason: "There's no such thing as a Jew for Jesus. It is like saying a black man is for the KKK. You can't be a table and a chair. You're either a Jew or a Gentile."[36]

So, it looks like we still have a lot of work to do in terms of getting the Jewish people to understand that Jesus-Yeshua is one of them and that embracing Him as the Messiah is the most Jewish thing they can do. But progress is being made, and it is also common to get this response when I tell a Jewish person about my faith: "So, you're a Jew for Jesus!" At least they've heard of the concept! Best of all, there is a wonderful promise in the Word about the glorious spiritual destiny of the Jewish people (see #59).

10
Do the Jewish people expect a literal Messiah?

Traditional Jews expect a literal Messiah, the son of David, who will do many of the things that Christians expect Jesus to do upon His return. At that time, passages such as Isaiah 2:1–4 or Isaiah 11 will be fulfilled; see also Jeremiah 23:5–6.

According to Moses Maimonides (A.D. 1135–1204), the great codifier and organizer of Jewish laws and beliefs, this is how the Messiah will be known:

> If a king will arise from the House of David who is learned in Torah and observant of the mitzvot [the Torah's commandments], as prescribed by the written law and the oral law, as David his ancestor was, and will compel all of Israel to walk in [the way of the Torah] and reinforce the breaches [in its observance]; and fight the wars of G-d, we may, with assurance, consider him the Messiah.

If he succeeds in the above, builds the Temple in its place, and gathers the dispersed of Israel, he is definitely the Messiah.

If he did not succeed to this degree or he was killed, he surely is not [the redeemer] promised by the Torah. [Rather,] he should be considered as all the other proper and complete kings of the Davidic dynasty who died. G-d only caused him to arise in order to test the many, as [Daniel 11:35] states; "and some of the wise men will stumble, to try them, to refine, and to clarify until the appointed time, because the set time is in the future."[37]

The Messiah, according to Maimonides, whose view is considered authoritative by most traditional Jews, will not be a miracle worker and he will certainly not die and then rise from the dead. Instead, he will be an extraordinarily gifted human being who will lead Israel and the nations back to God.

There is a tradition dating back to the Talmud that mentions a second Messianic figure, called the "Messiah son of Joseph," although the origins of this belief are very difficult to trace.[38] According to some traditions, he will only come if the Jewish people are not yet worthy of Messiah son of David. (These figures are called *Messiah ben David* and *Messiah ben Yoseph*; traditional Jews say *Moshiach* rather than Messiah.) He will perform many of the Messianic functions before getting cut down in battle in the last great war, at which point Messiah son of David will raise him from the dead, perform the remaining Messianic functions and establish God's kingdom on the earth. His death, however, is not viewed in vicarious, substitutionary terms—like the death of Jesus for our sins—and so this Messiah son of Joseph *is* a suffering Messiah but *not* a redeeming Messiah.[39]

There are many mystical beliefs associated with the coming of the Messiah, along with the belief that in every generation there is a potential Messiah waiting to be revealed. Thus it is that some of the most influential Jews of past generations—especially those steeped in mysticism—have been viewed after their death as the potential Messiahs of their respective generations, but their respective generations were not considered worthy and so this potential Messiah was never revealed. (For the Messianic expectations of the Lubavitcher Hasidim, see #2.)

This again underscores the traditional Jewish belief that the Messiah will be fully human, also explaining Talmudic traditions that state that if the people of Israel were to observe one Sabbath (or, according to other traditions, two consecutive Sabbaths), the Messiah would be revealed. (In other words, he is here in every generation but not recognized as Messiah and not revealed in his full glory or potential.) In keeping with this, and as formulated by Maimonides, traditional Jews pray and confess daily, "I believe in perfect faith in the coming of the Messiah, and even though he delay, I will wait for him every day that he will come."

This account in the Talmud has always moved me:

When R. Joshua ben Levi found the prophet Elijah standing by the entrance to the cave in which R. Simeon ben Yohai was buried, he asked him, "Will I be allowed to enter the world-to-come?" Elijah answered, "If this master here desires it." R. Joshua later said, "I saw two [Elijah and myself] but I heard the voice of a third." He then asked Elijah, "When will the Messiah come?" "Go and ask him yourself," was his reply. "Where is he sitting?" "At the entrance to the city [of Rome]." "And by what sign may I recognize him?" "He is sitting among the poor who are stricken with illnesses; all of whom untie and retie all the bandages over their sores at the same time, whereas he unties and reties each bandage separately, saying to himself: Should I be wanted, I must not be delayed."

So R. Joshua went to the Messiah and greeted him: "Peace be upon you, my master and teacher." "Peace be upon you, son of Levi," the Messiah replied. R. Joshua: "When will you come, O master?" "Today," was the Messiah's answer.

When R. Joshua came back to Elijah, the latter asked him, "What did he say to you?" R. Joshua: "Peace be upon you, son of Levi." Elijah observed, "By that he assured you and your father of a portion in the world-to-come." R. Joshua: "[How can I believe him, seeing that] he spoke falsely to me, for he told me that he would come today, yet he has not come." Elijah: "When he told you, 'Today,' he was quoting the first word of a verse that goes on to say, 'If you will hear His voice'" (Ps. 95:6).[40]

While teaching a Ph.D. class on rabbinic interpretation of Messianic prophecy as a visiting professor at Trinity Evangelical Divinity School in 1998, I read this passage with the small class of students, almost breaking down in tears as my heart was torn for the redemption of our people. It was quite unexpected in an academic setting like that! The Messiah, seen here in his suffering, was so eager to redeem his people—"Should I be wanted, I must not be delayed"—but we were not ready.

Conservative Jews still expect a literal Messiah, but Reform Judaism, in its classical form, has put a greater emphasis on the Messianic era that will be realized through the mission of the Jewish people and the self-improvement of the human race. This is in keeping with the somewhat humanistic, antisupernatural outlook of Reform Judaism but is certainly out of step with historic Jewish beliefs.

It should be remembered, however, that the majority of Jews today—both in America and worldwide—are not deeply religious and therefore belief in a Messiah is not something on the minds of a great many Jews. For them, the concept of God must become central in their lives before they will give much thought to the idea of a Messiah.

11
Do Jews refer to God by the name of Jehovah?

The name *Jehovah* is actually based on a mistaken reading of the biblical text by medieval Christian scholars who were educated in the Hebrew language but were not aware of certain Jewish through the power of repentance, the evil inclination can be overcome. Christianity believes that Adam's fall affected the entire human race (this, too, is believed by Judaism, but not in as radical a way), that the best of us fall infinitely short of God's glory and perfection and only through the blood of Jesus, the Messiah, can we be spiritually transformed.

Salvation—Judaism does not hold to the concept of individual salvation, and in the late 1970s, when a major Christian organization launched the evangelistic "I Found It" campaign, an Orthodox Jewish rabbi—with whom I attended graduate school classes at New York University—launched the "We Never Lost It" campaign. Judaism thinks more corporately than does Christianity, and even though the concept of forgiveness of sins and atonement is important (see the next paragraph), there is no such concept of "being saved" or "getting saved" in Judaism, and there is much less emphasis on the afterlife (see also the next two entries).

Atonement—Although traditional Jews pray daily for the rebuilding of the Temple and the restoration of animal sacrifices (Reform Jews have removed such petitions from their prayer book), Judaism does not believe that blood atonement is essential for personal atonement. Rather, repentance, good deeds, prayer and personal suffering (seen, at times, as a payment for sin) take the place of sacrifices; partial support for this is found in 2 Chronicles 7:14, among other verses. Christianity teaches that atonement can only come through the substitutionary death of the Messiah and that true saving faith includes repentance (see Acts 2:38; 20:21; 26:20).

Afterlife—While Judaism recognizes that this world is the vestibule to the world to come, and while there is daily prayer for the coming of the Messiah and the Messianic age, the primary emphasis in Judaism is on the present world, the here and now, in keeping with the emphasis in the Tanakh. Christianity sees the world to come—specifically, heaven and hell—as being of paramount importance, to the point that the way we are called to live in this world can only make complete sense in the light of eternity. While there is a wholesome appreciation of life in this world, it is not to be separated from the world to come.

Creed vs. Deed—Judaism has basic creeds—most notably Moses Maimonides's Thirteen Principles of Faith, although some of these were hotly disputed in his day—and there are fundamental, essential beliefs in Judaism. The greater emphasis, however, is put on deeds—specifically, observing the commandments of the Torah, as understood and passed on through the traditions. Christianity puts a tremendous emphasis on good works and stresses the importance of a transformed life, but its greater emphasis is put on holding to the essentials of the faith, from which a transformed life and good works will naturally emanate. Thus it is sometimes said that Judaism emphasizes orthopraxy; Christianity emphasizes orthodoxy. Or, put another way, Judaism is the religion of the deed, Christianity the religion of the creed. These statements are, however, somewhat exaggerated.[32]

Mission—Both Jews and Christians feel a calling to be a light to the world and to make God known, but that sense of mission is worked out very differently in Judaism and Christianity. The former places its emphasis on being faithful to the Jewish calling, meaning living according to the Torah and rabbinic traditions, praying the communal prayers and studying the sacred texts. In so doing, the example of the Jewish people will ultimately enlighten the world. Christianity feels a sacred calling to make the message of salvation known through all available means, including living a life deeply devoted to the Lord (and thereby being an example and hastening redemption) and, quite pointedly, sharing the Good News about Jesus to everyone. Thus, Christianity has always had "missionaries," while that has not been the norm for more than 1,900 years in Judaism. (For Jewish missionaries to Jews, see #2, on Lubavitch.)

Calendar—Judaism is much more committed to a daily, weekly and annual life cycle than is Christianity, and therefore Jewish life revolves around the calendar more than does Christianity, which puts a greater emphasis on individual relationship with God and life in the Spirit (in the context of a community of believers) than on the ordered lifestyle of a religious community. (This statement would be modified somewhat in liturgical church traditions.) In Judaism, the Sabbath is central to the weekly schedule, with the seasons of the holy days being major focal points of religious activity during the year (in the fall, *Rosh HaShanah*, or the New Year, but called Trumpets in the Torah; *Yom Kippur*, the Day of Atonement; and *Sukkot*, Tabernacles; in the spring, *Pesach*, Passover; and *Shavuot*, Weeks or Pentecost, with intervening holy days in between). In Christianity, Sunday is viewed as the Sabbath by many Christians, but not in the comprehensive, strict way that the Sabbath is practiced in Judaism, while for many other Christians, Sunday is simply the primary day for corporate worship. (For the question of the Sabbath, see #49.) In liturgical churches, the major holidays, such as Easter and Christmas, are part of a sacred, traditional cycle of days, but again, not with the emphasis or comprehensive nature that is found in Judaism. In non-liturgical churches, Easter, or Resurrection Sunday, is a special day of celebration and even evangelism, but not much more, while for many Christians, Christmas is not of deep religious significance.

Having summarized some of the fundamental differences between "Judaism" and "Christianity," it is important to remember that there are many areas of commonality, and many Christians today are committed to rediscovering the Jewish roots of their faith—not trying to become Orthodox Jews (though, unfortunately, some are!), but rather recognizing that many church traditions over the years have obscured the biblical, Jewish foundations on which faith in Yeshua the Messiah was originally built. (For more on this, see #43.)

9
What do Jewish people think about Jesus?

There is not a simple answer to this question, given the great diversity in beliefs and perspectives among the Jewish people. And, for the most part, Jewish people do not spend a lot of time thinking about Jesus in a serious way. That is to say, outside of Christmas celebrations or concerns about the religious right or the latest media fad—like the *Da Vinci Code* furor in 2006 or the *Passion of the Christ* uproar in 2004—the person of Jesus is not a topic of discussion or thought in most Jewish households. After all, they would say, we are Jews, not Christians, and Jesus is for the Christians (i.e., Gentiles).

For the most part, then, Jesus is not viewed as a directly relevant religious figure by the great majority of Jewish people. It is true that more Jews now recognize that Jesus—Yeshua!—was Jewish, something that I did not realize until I was close to thirteen years old. When I happened to discover this fact, I cracked a joke to my Jewish schoolmates, asking them, "When did Jesus become Catholic? After He rose from the dead?" That reflects how we thought of things! In light of these kinds of perceptions, it is not surprising that most Jews would not immediately connect "Christ" with "Messiah," seeing it primarily as part of Jesus' name.

When Jews do have opinions about Jesus, they are quite diverse. In the eyes of the ultra-Orthodox, Jesus is an apostate Jew and an archenemy of the Jewish people, the founder of a destructive religion that has brought untold hardship and persecution on us through the generations. Some believe that He actually said what the New Testament attributes to Him—not that they would have read it for themselves—while others believe that His followers were the primary ones responsible for deviating from the path. (Paul comes in for special criticism here; see #44.) Either way, to the extent they believe that the Talmud and rabbinic writings actually speak about this same Jesus (whom they know as Yeshu; see #38), they would regard Him as a deceiver of the masses.[33]

Jews who are less religious and who have actually given thought to the person of Jesus tend to be more positive in their assessment, although there remains a wide range of opinion. Some view Jesus as a great rabbi who was either misunderstood or misrepresented by His followers in the next generations, leading to the birth of Christianity. Some see Him as a wise man and even a prophet; some consider Him to be a brave figure standing against the tyranny of Rome; others view Him as a mystic or guru figure (in many cases, projecting back on Jesus what they themselves feel are spiritually positive qualities). Still others feel that we cannot know much about Him, questioning the validity of the sources we have at our disposal, in keeping with critical, skeptical scholarship as reflected in the Jesus Seminar.

As divergent as these views are—deceiver, rabbi, prophet, teacher, mystic—they all have this in common: With the exception of Jewish believers in Yeshua, the Jewish people do *not* recognize Jesus as the Messiah and, more emphatically, they do *not* recognize Him as God incarnate. So, He might be a great rabbi or even a noble revolutionary, but certainly not the Redeemer. Perhaps He's an enlightened guru, but definitely not God!

In the last few decades, there has been an increasing desire to reclaim Jesus the Jew by Jewish scholars, some of whom are Orthodox, and although this reclamation stops short of reclaiming Him as Messiah and Lord, it is still a step in the right direction.[34] And in Israel, schoolchildren learn something about Yeshua as well (they, too, know Him as Yeshu; see again #38), although, to repeat, they do *not* learn about Him as Savior or Redeemer.

A challenging recent study, written by a Jewish academic and reflecting Jewish problems with the Christian Jesus, is Professor Amy Jill-Levine's *The Misunderstood Jew: The Scandal of the Jewish Jesus*.[35] I do not concur with a number of her key premises, and her ecumenical desire to affirm fully both Judaism and Christianity is not tenable (see #60). (As I have repeatedly stated, if Jesus is not the Messiah of Israel—which is a foundational truth of the New Testament—then no one should follow Him. Put another way, either Jesus is the Messiah of everyone or the Messiah of no one.) Nonetheless, her book helps give the Christian reader insight into some of the issues that the Jewish people have with Jesus, providing many valuable insights.

On a more personal, anecdotal level, a Messianic Jewish leader recently told me that his congregation has enjoyed extensive interaction with the Jewish community where he lives, even holding joint meetings with the Conservative synagogue—this is almost unprecedented for a Messianic Jewish group—and going on a tour of Israel together. Quality interaction like this has actually gone on now for several years. And yet this leader commented to me with sadness that after all the time these two groups have spent together, it simply hasn't dawned on the members of the Conservative Jewish congregation that Yeshua has any relevance for them.

This remains typical for the great majority of Jews worldwide, and to this day, when I tell a Jewish person that I'm a believer in Jesus, the typical response is, "So, you *were* Jewish but now you believe in Jesus?" or, "How can you be Jewish and believe in Jesus?" The two seem incompatible to them, as stated by the Jewish comedian (and rabbi) Jackie Mason: "There's no such thing as a Jew for Jesus. It is like saying a black man is for the KKK. You can't be a table and a chair. You're either a Jew or a Gentile."[36]

So, it looks like we still have a lot of work to do in terms of getting the Jewish people to understand that Jesus-Yeshua is one of them and that embracing Him as the Messiah is the most Jewish thing they can do. But progress is being made, and it is also common to get this response when I tell a Jewish person about my faith: "So, you're a Jew for Jesus!" At least they've heard of the concept! Best of all, there is a wonderful promise in the Word about the glorious spiritual destiny of the Jewish people (see #59).

10

Do the Jewish people expect a literal Messiah?

Traditional Jews expect a literal Messiah, the son of David, who will do many of the things that Christians expect Jesus to do upon His return. At that time, passages such as Isaiah 2:1–4 or Isaiah 11 will be fulfilled; see also Jeremiah 23:5–6.

According to Moses Maimonides (A.D. 1135–1204), the great codifier and organizer of Jewish laws and beliefs, this is how the Messiah will be known:

> If a king will arise from the House of David who is learned in Torah and observant of the mitzvot [the Torah's commandments], as prescribed by the written law and the oral law, as David his ancestor was, and will compel all of Israel to walk in [the way of the Torah] and reinforce the breaches [in its observance]; and fight the wars of G-d, we may, with assurance, consider him the Messiah.

If he succeeds in the above, builds the Temple in its place, and gathers the dispersed of Israel, he is definitely the Messiah.

If he did not succeed to this degree or he was killed, he surely is not [the redeemer] promised by the Torah. [Rather,] he should be considered as all the other proper and complete kings of the Davidic dynasty who died. G-d only caused him to arise in order to test the many, as [Daniel 11:35] states; "and some of the wise men will stumble, to try them, to refine, and to clarify until the appointed time, because the set time is in the future."[37]

The Messiah, according to Maimonides, whose view is considered authoritative by most traditional Jews, will not be a miracle worker and he will certainly not die and then rise from the dead. Instead, he will be an extraordinarily gifted human being who will lead Israel and the nations back to God.

There is a tradition dating back to the Talmud that mentions a second Messianic figure, called the "Messiah son of Joseph," although the origins of this belief are very difficult to trace.[38] According to some traditions, he will only come if the Jewish people are not yet worthy of Messiah son of David. (These figures are called *Messiah ben David* and *Messiah ben Yoseph*; traditional Jews say *Moshiach* rather than Messiah.) He will perform many of the Messianic functions before getting cut down in battle in the last great war, at which point Messiah son of David will raise him from the dead, perform the remaining Messianic functions and establish God's kingdom on the earth. His death, however, is not viewed in vicarious, substitutionary terms—like the death of Jesus for our sins—and so this Messiah son of Joseph *is* a suffering Messiah but *not* a redeeming Messiah.[39]

There are many mystical beliefs associated with the coming of the Messiah, along with the belief that in every generation there is a potential Messiah waiting to be revealed. Thus it is that some of the most influential Jews of past generations—especially those steeped in mysticism—have been viewed after their death as the potential Messiahs of their respective generations, but their respective generations were not considered worthy and so this potential Messiah was never revealed. (For the Messianic expectations of the Lubavitcher Hasidim, see #2.)

This again underscores the traditional Jewish belief that the Messiah will be fully human, also explaining Talmudic traditions that state that if the people of Israel were to observe one Sabbath (or, according to other traditions, two consecutive Sabbaths), the Messiah would be revealed. (In other words, he is here in every generation but not recognized as Messiah and not revealed in his full glory or potential.) In keeping with this, and as formulated by Maimonides, traditional Jews pray and confess daily, "I believe in perfect faith in the coming of the Messiah, and even though he delay, I will wait for him every day that he will come."

This account in the Talmud has always moved me:

When R. Joshua ben Levi found the prophet Elijah standing by the entrance to the cave in which R. Simeon ben Yohai was buried, he asked him, "Will I be allowed to enter the world-to-come?" Elijah answered, "If this master here desires it." R. Joshua later said, "I saw two [Elijah and myself] but I heard the voice of a third." He then asked Elijah, "When will the Messiah come?" "Go and ask him yourself," was his reply. "Where is he sitting?" "At the entrance to the city [of Rome]." "And by what sign may I recognize him?" "He is sitting among the poor who are stricken with illnesses; all of whom untie and retie all the bandages over their sores at the same time, whereas he unties and reties each bandage separately, saying to himself: Should I be wanted, I must not be delayed."

So R. Joshua went to the Messiah and greeted him: "Peace be upon you, my master and teacher." "Peace be upon you, son of Levi," the Messiah replied. R. Joshua: "When will you come, O master?" "Today," was the Messiah's answer.

When R. Joshua came back to Elijah, the latter asked him, "What did he say to you?" R. Joshua: "Peace be upon you, son of Levi." Elijah observed, "By that he assured you and your father of

59

a portion in the world-to-come." R. Joshua: "[How can I believe him, seeing that] he spoke falsely to me, for he told me that he would come today, yet he has not come." Elijah: "When he told you, 'Today,' he was quoting the first word of a verse that goes on to say, 'If you will hear His voice'" (Ps. 95:6).[40]

While teaching a Ph.D. class on rabbinic interpretation of Messianic prophecy as a visiting professor at Trinity Evangelical Divinity School in 1998, I read this passage with the small class of students, almost breaking down in tears as my heart was torn for the redemption of our people. It was quite unexpected in an academic setting like that! The Messiah, seen here in his suffering, was so eager to redeem his people—"Should I be wanted, I must not be delayed"—but we were not ready.

Conservative Jews still expect a literal Messiah, but Reform Judaism, in its classical form, has put a greater emphasis on the Messianic era that will be realized through the mission of the Jewish people and the self-improvement of the human race. This is in keeping with the somewhat humanistic, antisupernatural outlook of Reform Judaism but is certainly out of step with historic Jewish beliefs.

It should be remembered, however, that the majority of Jews today—both in America and worldwide—are not deeply religious and therefore belief in a Messiah is not something on the minds of a great many Jews. For them, the concept of God must become central in their lives before they will give much thought to the idea of a Messiah.

11
Do Jews refer to God by the name of Jehovah?

The name *Jehovah* is actually based on a mistaken reading of the biblical text by medieval Christian scholars who were educated in the Hebrew language but were not aware of certain Jewish scribal customs. In short, they did not realize that it was a Jewish tradition to write the vowels for the word 'adonai, "Lord," with the consonants for the name Yahweh, known as the tetragrammaton, and they wrongly read this hybrid word as *Yehowah*, or Jehovah in English. That is to say, *the name Jehovah (or Yehowah) did not exist in Israel*—despite the popularity of this name in English-speaking Christian circles, and despite religious organizations like Jehovah's Witnesses.

Before getting into more specifics about the original pronunciation of God's name, YHWH, let me explain the Jewish scribal custom known as *qere-ketiv* (pronounced *q'rey*, *k'teev*), Aramaic for "read" and "it is written." This practice included several different scribal customs, including: (1) the practice of not reading certain words that were considered objectionable in the biblical Hebrew text and replacing them with less offensive words in their place; and (2) the practice of replacing one reading of a word with a variant reading of that same word, normally reflecting a minor difference in spelling or grammar. An example of the former would be the reading of the verb "lie with" (Hebrew *shakab*) for the verb "ravish" (Hebrew *shagal*). This occurs four times in the Tanakh, Deuteronomy 28:30; Isaiah 13:16; Jeremiah 3:2; and Zechariah 14:2, which is why the NIV translates with "ravish" (as written in the Hebrew text) but in an ancient synagogue, the marginal text with "lie with" would have been read. In this case, "ravish" would be the *ketiv*, what is written in the main Hebrew text, while "lie with" would be the *qere*, the word to be read in place of what is written. An example of the latter would be the substitution of the plural form of a word for the singular form, or, to use English as an example, substituting the spelling "color" for "colour." These types of substitutions occur frequently. Again, the substituted form is the *qere* while the replaced form is the *ketiv*.

How did the Jewish scribes indicate this? In some manuscripts, the word to be replaced (the *ketiv*, the word written in the main text) would be left without vowels, which would be quite conspicuous. (As noted in #6, Hebrew vowels are expressed with short lines and dots under, next to or above the consonants.) Then, in the margin of the text, the *qere* would be written in full (that is, with both consonants and vowels). In other manuscripts, the consonants of the word in the text (*ketiv*) would be preserved but the vowels of the word to be read in its place (*qere*) would be substituted, creating a hybrid form, while the consonants of the *qere* word would be written in the margin.

Re-creating this in English—this is only for the purpose of illustration, since the languages are very different—I will substitute the Hebrew name Miryam for the name Mary, using the two methods just mentioned.

The first method would look like this, where the vowels would be left out from the word in question in the main text (the *ketiv*) and the word to be read in its place (the *qere*) would be written out in full:

The virgin's name was Mry.   Miryam

The second method would look like this, where the vowels from the marginal text (the *qere*) would be inserted into the word in the main text (the *ketiv*), creating a hybrid, nonexistent form in the main text, while the word in the margin would be written without vowels.

The virgin's name was Miriya.   Mrym

In both cases, any English reader would recognize at once that there was something wrong with the form in the main text (either *Mry* or *Miriya*), looking at once to the margin to see the replacement word. How then was it that the Christian scholars who began studying Hebrew in the late Middle Ages missed the fact that the

Hebrew form *yehowah* was a combination of the consonants for *yahweh* and the vowels for *'adonai*?

It is very simple. In the case of the divine name *yhwh*, which occurs roughly 6,800 times in the Hebrew Bible, the scribes did not write the *qere* form, *'adonai*, in the margins, so these scholars had no idea that they were actually looking at a hybrid form, similar to the make-believe *Miriya* just used as an illustration.

It had been a Jewish belief for many centuries that the Lord's name was too sacred to be pronounced and so, whenever it occurred in the text, Jews would say "the Lord" (*'adonai*) in its place. This is reflected as far back as the Septuagint, the Greek translation of the Hebrew Scriptures made by Jewish scholars in the third to second centuries B.C., in which the Greek word *kurios*, "lord," was substituted for the name *yahweh*. It may also be reflected in the scribal practice found in the Dead Sea Scrolls in which a different script was used when writing out the consonants *y-h-w-h*.

There was no need, then, for later Jewish scribes to constantly indicate in the margins that *y'howah* was not the original reading, since this was universally known to all literate Jews. It was not known, however, to the Christian scholars who were newcomers to Hebrew and who mistakenly took the hybrid form of the name to be the original form of the name.[41]

What then was the original pronunciation of the Lord's name? It is best reconstructed as *yahweh*, a causative form of the root "to be" and meaning, "He who causes things to be; he who makes things happen." (The Hebrew for the famous words "I am that I am" in Exodus 3:14 is *'eh'yeh 'asher 'eh'yeh*, with the word *'eh'yeh* being a play on words with *yahweh*, also coming from the same root, "to be.") This reconstruction is also based on the short form *yah*, which occurs in the word "Hallelujah" (from the Hebrew words *hall'lu* [praise] *yah*), as well as in names such as Elijah (from the Hebrew *'eliyahu*, short for "my God is Yahweh").

Religious Jews would not think of referring to God by either the wrong name Jehovah or the right name Yahweh, since the former is basically meaningless to them and the latter would be considered too sacred to pronounce. To them, He would be called God or the Lord or *HaShem* (literally, the Name; in popular practice, then, HaShem becomes the Lord's new name). However, when words such as *God* or *Lord* are written by religious Jews, they are not written in full—hence the common forms G-d or L-rd—since they are considered too sacred even to write out, except in official, sacred texts, such as the Bible or prayer book.

Interestingly, while all of us have become familiar with the (wrong) form Jehovah, and while some of us are also familiar with the (correct) form Yahweh, the English way of saying *yahweh* would be actually "Jahveh"—which sounds quite odd to our ears. Yet that is far closer to the Lord's self-revealed name than is Jehovah! Thankfully, our heavenly Father is pleased if we walk with Him in close, intimate fellowship, and He is not put off by being called Jehovah, nor is He bothered if we do not relate to Him well as Yahweh, although increasingly, it seems that His people are worshiping Him by the name He chose to use when revealing Himself to His people.

12

What is meant by the term *kosher*?

The term *kosher* is derived from the Hebrew root *k-sh-r*, meaning "suitable" or "fit for use."[42] In Judaism, its first reference is to the dietary laws, describing food that is acceptable (*kosher*) for a religious Jew to eat, as in the question, "Is this kosher?" meaning, "Can I as an observant Jew eat this food? Does it meet the rabbinic requirements?" Based on this usage, the word has become popularized and is used even in non-Jewish circles with reference to all kinds of nondietary subjects with the meaning "okay, acceptable, lawful, above board." An example of this would be if someone offered you an incredible business deal, one that sounded too good to be true, causing you to wonder if it was really on the up-and-up, leading you to ask, "Is this kosher?" In that context, you certainly would not mean, "Has this been approved by the rabbis?"

Returning, however, to the primary meaning of *kosher*, Christians tend to be ignorant of the extent of the Jewish dietary laws, generally knowing that religious Jews don't eat pork products, shrimp or lobster. Kosher laws go far beyond that, speaking of a whole way of life. As noted by Christian Old Testament scholar John Hartley, pointing back to the biblical dietary laws, laws that have been greatly expanded by the rabbis:

> In following these dietary laws, the Israelites obeyed God's instructions several times each day, developing deep in their consciousness an attitude of obedience to God. That all the people observed these laws at every meal was a mighty force of solidarity, uniting the people as God's special treasure (Exodus 19:5). It separated the Israelites from their polytheistic neighbors and became a distinguishing mark of their national identity. The importance of these dietary laws increased when the Jews became dispersed among the nations. They have become a significant force in preserving Jewish identity. They erect a high barrier against assimilation and amalgamation of the Jewish people, which would lead to the loss of their racial identity. Today, keeping kosher is a distinguishing mark of a very devout Jew and communicates the understanding that that person belongs to the chosen people of God.[43]

The primary biblical passages outlining the dietary laws are Leviticus 11 and Deuteronomy 14:3–21 (other relevant passages will be discussed below). Note carefully that the passage in Deuteronomy follows on the heels of Deuteronomy 14:1–2: "You are the children of the LORD your God. Do not cut yourselves or shave the front of your heads for the dead, for you are a people holy to the LORD your God. Out of all the peoples on the face of the earth, the LORD has chosen you to be his treasured possession." So, the dietary laws were an essential part of God's calling on His people Israel to be His very own children, holy and set apart.

Just think of how many activities take place around a meal—family time, Christian fellowship, meeting with friends, building a relationship, talking about business plans—and then think of what would happen if you could not sit down and eat with someone because of dietary restrictions. That would produce real separation, which was one of the purposes of the dietary laws. Others have argued that the dietary laws were also given for health purposes (due to hygienic issues with the eating of pork, shellfish and the like), while others have suggested that there were other factors behind the divine selection of which foods could be eaten.

Over the course of time, the rabbinic interpretation of a number of other verses—most importantly, Exodus 23:19; 34:26; Deuteronomy 14:21, which forbade boiling a baby goat in its mother's milk, and Deuteronomy 12:21, which allegedly spoke of a divinely given form of ritual slaughter—led to a much more intricate development of the dietary laws, which included the prohibition of eating milk products with meat products (see further, #13) and the requirement of rabbinic supervision of the process of animal slaughter (called *shechitah*; a ritual slaughterer is called a *shochet*).[44] In addition to this, since the later rabbis were not entirely sure of the exact identity of every single animal listed in Leviticus 11 and Deuteronomy 14, they broadened the list of forbidden animals, just to play it safe.

There are many comical—and sometimes painful—stories relating to Christian ignorance of or insensitivity to the *kosher* laws and customs. For example, based on the belief that the New Testament abolished the dietary laws, some Christians have "tested" the orthodoxy and spiritual freedom of new Jewish believers by asking—or even requiring—them to eat a pork sandwich! More tragically, some medieval baptismal formulas required Jews to confess that they would learn to acquire a taste for pork, even if they had previously avoided it all their lives. Can you imagine the arrogance and ignorance behind such a formula?[45]

On a lighter note, in 2006, some evangelical Christians in Italy with a real love for Israel decided to reach out to Messianic Jews in their country, inviting them to a day of fellowship and interaction. At every meal—quite unintentionally, to be sure—pork products were prominently (and unavoidably) featured. They wanted to make the meals special, and they had no idea that, either through life habit or spiritual choice (out of solidarity with their Jewish roots), many of these Jewish believers would prefer not to eat pork. Thankfully, it caused no lasting offense, but it did show that these dear Christians had a lot to learn!

13

Why do traditional Jews have separate dishes in their kitchens for meat products and dairy products?

The practice of having separate dishes for meat and dairy products (respectively called *fleisch* and *milch* in Yiddish, which is close to German)—indeed, of having the kitchen itself divided between meat and dairy use—is based on a rabbinic interpretation of the prohibition in the Torah that forbids boiling a young goat in its mother's milk. This prohibition is found three times (see Exodus 23:19; 34:26; Deuteronomy 14:21).

What are the origins of the prohibition? Jewish biblical scholar Nahum Sarna outlines the history of Jewish interpretation of this prohibition, the explanation of which "largely remains an enigma." Citing the opinions of different Jewish scholars, he writes:

Its importance may be measured by its being repeated twice more in the Torah, in Exodus 34:26 and Deuteronomy 14:21. In this latter source the prohibition appears in the context of the dietary laws, but the other two sources indicate that its origin lies in the overall context of the festivals. The juxtaposition of this rule with the law of the first fruits led Menahem ibn Saruq (10th cent.) to interpret *gedi* not as a kid of the goats but as "berries." This eccentric explanation was taken up by Menahem ben Solomon (first half 12th cent.), who took "mother's milk" to be figurative for the juice of the bud that contains the berry. The entire passage conveyed to him a proscription on bringing the first fruits before they are ripe. Many scholars, medieval and modern, follow the suggestion of Maimonides that this law prohibits some pagan rite—although no such rite is presently known.

Rashbam, Bekhor Shor, Ibn Ezra, and Abravanel all, in various ways, adduce a humanitarian motivation akin [see also Exodus 22:29]. Rashbam further suggests that because festivals were celebrated with feasts of meat, and because goats are generally multiparous and have a high yield of milk, it was customary to slaughter one of the kids of a fresh litter and to cook it in its mother's milk. The Torah looks upon such a practice as exhibiting insensitivity to the animal's feelings. The explanation of Rashbam has been buttressed by the modern observation that in biblical times goats were far more plentiful than sheep in the Land of Israel and were the main source of milk. The flesh of the young kid is more tender and more delicate in flavor than lamb. Also, since the estrous cycle of goats occurs during the summer months and parturition takes place in the rainy season, the earliest litter would be produced just around the time of Sukkot. This injunction, therefore, regulates the festivities at the Festival of the Ingathering of the Harvest.[46]

There is debate, then, about the *rationale* behind the law, but its application seems fairly straightforward: Do not boil a kid in its mother's milk. The Talmudic rabbis, however, expanded greatly on this, as explained by biblical and Semitic scholar Jeffrey H. Tigay:

The text specifies only boiling the flesh of a kid in its own mother's milk. Halakhic [Jewish legal] exegesis interpreted the rule more broadly, prohibiting the cooking or eating of any domestic cattle with the milk or milk products of any domestic cattle, or deriving any benefit from such mixtures. Supplementary regulations also prohibited eating fowl or game with milk and required the use of separate utensils for milk and meat, including their products. This broad interpretation is presumably based on the desire to prevent inadvertent violation of the original prohibition. In a society of small settlements where dairy and cattle farming were not kept separate, there was considerable likelihood that if a young animal was boiled in milk, the milk would come from its own mother. Furthermore, milk and meat from different types of animals are similar in appearance, and small pieces of food can adhere to most types of utensils. The halakhah minimizes the possibility of errors due to these factors.[47]

Thus, as summarized by Sarna,

The interdiction of boiling a kid in its mother's milk was generalized to outlaw the mixing of all meat and milk (meaning all dairy products). Its threefold repetition in the Torah was explained by Rabbi Simeon bar Yohai as indicative of three aspects of the prohibition: cooking such a mixture, eating it, and deriving any benefit from it. [b. Hullin 115b.][48]

Put another way, the threefold repetition of this law in the Torah meant that Jews were prohibited from eating, tasting or enjoying milk and meat together, prompting a sarcastic rejoinder from a nineteenth-century nonreligious Jew who argued that, because the explicit prohibition against adultery is found but twice in the Torah, that means that Jews can eat it and taste it but not enjoy it!

For religious Jews, however, this is anything but a laughing matter. As explained on the Judaism 101 website:

This separation [of milk and meat] includes not only the foods themselves, but the utensils, pots and pans with which they are cooked, the plates and flatware from which they are eaten, the dishwashers or dishpans in which they are cleaned, and the towels on which they are dried. A kosher household will have at least two sets of pots, pans and dishes: one for meat and one for dairy. . . .

One must wait a significant amount of time between eating meat and dairy. Opinions differ, and vary from three to six hours. This is because fatty residues and meat particles tend to cling to the mouth. From dairy to meat, however, one need only rinse one's mouth and eat a neutral solid like bread, unless the dairy product in question is also of a type that tends to stick in the mouth.

Note that even the smallest quantity of dairy (or meat) in something renders it entirely dairy (or meat) for purposes of kashrut. For example, most margarines are dairy for kosher purposes, because they contain a small quantity of whey or other dairy products to give it a dairy-like taste.[49]

So, the simple prohibition not to boil a kid in its own mother's milk—either based on humanitarian grounds or in reaction to pagan practices—became the basis for an elaborate system of dietary laws, requiring different sets of kitchen utensils—indeed, a dual kitchen—not to mention minutely detailed rabbinic specifications of exactly what can be eaten and when.

Not surprisingly, verses such as Genesis 18:8 have caused considerable difficulty for the rabbinic interpreters who claim that Abraham kept both the oral and written Torahs. The verse states that Abraham "brought some curds and milk and the calf that had been prepared, and set these before [his guests]. While they ate, he stood near them under a tree." So then, did Abraham violate the rabbinic law by serving milk and meat together? One rabbinic explanation is that, being angels, the guests did not really eat but only appeared to. (Presumably, that is why Abraham felt free to violate the rabbinic laws, since he knew they would not eat!) Another explanation is that, contrary to what the text seems to say, Abraham followed the rabbinic law and waited several hours to serve the meat after serving the dairy products. (After all, he had to give the guests something to eat, and it took a long time to prepare and cook the goat!)

Reform Jewish scholar Gunther Plaut, who, as a liberal rabbi, does not accept these Orthodox interpretations that project the later, rabbinic customs back on to the biblical text, notes:

> Traditional [Jewish] interpreters experience great difficulties here [meaning Genesis 18]. If the three are divine messengers, why do they eat? According to the Midrash, they merely appeared to eat. According to Rashi, they pretended out of courtesy. The text of course is oblivious of later Jewish dietary laws which forbade serving milk and meat at the same meal.[50]

Certainly, Plaut is correct, and Abraham never heard of the rabbinic rules calling for the separation of milk and meat products. But for an ultra-Orthodox Jew, these are sacred commandments, going back to patriarchal times and clearly legislated at Sinai. This is also part of what rabbinic Judaism refers to as "making a fence [*seyag*] around the Torah" (see m. Avot 1:1), the rough equivalent of enforcing a 70-mile-per-hour speed limit by making a new, 55-mile-per-hour rule—just to make it easier for people to keep the law. This is similar to a host of rabbinic laws, such as the rule that Sabbath candles must be lit at least eighteen minutes before sundown, a custom discussed in the next answer.

14
Why do traditional Jews light candles at the beginning of the Sabbath?

Traditional Jews light candles at the beginning of the Sabbath for both practical and spiritual reasons. Let us take a look at the practical reasons first, reasons that were relevant in past centuries but are no longer relevant for almost all Jews worldwide today.

In Exodus 35:3, after reiterating some of the Sabbath laws (see Exodus 35:1–2), the divine command is then given: "Do not light a fire in any of your dwellings on the Sabbath day." What exactly does this signify? This commandment is found only here in the Bible, and various interpretations have been given to it. One Christian commentator states that "there is added here [in Exodus 35:1–3] a prohibition against building a fire on the sabbath, one definition of what is meant by customary work on the sabbath, quite possibly one having to do with the preparation of food (cf. [Exodus] 16:22–30)."[51] Another Christian commentator notes, "Although the prohibition against lighting a fire on the Sabbath (v. 3) is not mentioned elsewhere, it is implied in part in 16:23," a verse which also speaks of preparing food on the Sabbath.[52]

Without further information, the full import of this verse is subject to debate. What we do know is that later Jews applied the injunction in a sweeping and literal way, and when we remember that, until the twentieth century, only candles or oil lamps were used to illuminate the homes at night, this commandment presented a problem. How could you function in your home at night with no lights? Because of this, the custom developed to light candles or oil lamps before the onset of the Sabbath, thereby providing light for a few hours, since the Talmudic rabbis taught that, as long as the light is ignited before the Sabbath begins (note that the Jewish day is measured from sundown to sundown rather than from sunrise to sunrise), the fire can continue to burn.

There is some historic debate, however, about how this custom became such a religious fixture in Judaism, to the point that traditional Jews for close to two thousand years have believed that it was actually a divine command to light the Sabbath candles. Commenting on Exodus 35:3, Professor Nahum Sarna explains:

72

The manner in which the prohibition against kindling fire on the Sabbath is worded led the rabbis of the Talmud to understand that fire may not be kindled on the Sabbath itself; however, fire lit before the Sabbath and not refueled on the Sabbath is permitted. The Jewish sectarians known as Karaites rejected this interpretation and spent the day in darkness, although some later adherents did accept the rabbinic practice. It was probably to demonstrate opposition to the early Karaite view that the kindling of lights on the eve of Sabbath gradually became obligatory. To this end, the geonim, the post-Talmudic heads of the Babylonian academies, instituted the recital of a blessing over them.[53]

Thus Jewish women who light the Sabbath candles each week recite this blessing, which says: "Blessed are You, Lord, our God, King of the Universe, who sanctifies us with His commandments, and *commands us to light the candles of Shabbat*" (my emphasis).

When did God command this? If you look in the Scriptures, you will find no such commandment—not so much as a hint of it—and traditional Jews would not argue this point. They would say that this is one of the seven rabbinic commandments that are followed as if they were one of the 613 commandments of the Torah (see #24).

Historians offer additional insight into what actually led to the formal establishing of the custom:

> It has been suggested that the custom arose to protest against the Babylonian belief in the Sabbath as an unlucky and gloomy day when no fire or light was lit. In Roman times, the lighting of the Sabbath lamps was a distinguishing feature of Jewish homes, and the younger Seneca [an important Roman author] condemned Romans for imitating this custom (*Epistalue* 95:47).[54]

Of course, traditional Jews, who project many of their practices back into biblical times, believe that the patriarchs and their wives lit the Sabbath lights as well. As claimed by Rabbi Naftali Silberberg:

> This Mitzvah [commandment] finds its origins with the very first Jewish woman, our Matriarch Sarah, whose Shabbat candles would miraculously remain lit every Friday afternoon until the next. When Isaac saw that the candles of his new wife Rebecca exhibited the same miraculous quality, he realized that he had indeed found a worthy successor to his righteous mother.[55]

Ultra-Orthodox Jews believe this with the utmost seriousness, as far-fetched as it sounds and as anachronistic as it is.

What we do know is that, over the course of time, a number of corollary, spiritually interpreted customs became somewhat fixed, including: lighting two candles, which, according to tradition, represent the twofold injunction to remember and observe the Sabbath (Exodus 20:8; Deuteronomy 5:12); the covering of the woman's eyes while she recites the blessing (but after she lights the candles); and the waving of her hands in circular motions over the candles, normally three times.

Why does the woman cover her eyes? According to Rabbi Shraga Simmons,

> From the Code of Jewish Law it would appear that the custom is just to put the hand in front of the candles, so as not to see them before the blessing. Usually we make a blessing and then do the thing (like eat challah or blow the shofar). But when lighting Shabbat candles, once we make the blessing it would be considered Shabbat and then too late to light fire, which is prohibited on Shabbat. So in this case, we light first, but cover our eyes until after the blessing, thus recreating the "lighting" after the blessing.[56]

Did you follow that? Normally the recitation of the blessing precedes the doing of a thing—similar to Christians saying grace before they eat—but in this case, if the blessing was recited first, it would inaugurate the Sabbath, after which it is forbidden to light a fire. And so, the fire is lit, the eyes covered (so as not to see the light), the blessing recited and then the eyes opened! This may sound convoluted, but it is typical of rabbinic thinking, and it has not stopped traditional Jews from zealously keeping the Sabbath through the centuries.

In an interesting twist, Messianic Jews who follow the rabbinic tradition of lighting the Sabbath candles sometimes modify the rabbinic prayer, since, in reality, the lighting of the candles has nothing to do with the biblical Sabbath commandment. Hence some of them recite their own version of the blessing, one which thanks God for giving us Yeshua, the Light of the world, and acknowledges our calling to be a light to the nations. So, Messianic Jews take a rabbinic tradition and then create a new and (for them) more meaningful tradition of their own.

Why do the women wave their hands over the Sabbath candles? There are a number of different opinions, including: the woman is gathering the light and warmth to herself; or she is motioning toward the candles to indicate that she is about to pronounce a blessing over the candles. None of this is certain, however, and it appears impossible to trace the origin of this tradition.

There are also a number of very curious customs that have developed as a result of the rabbinic interpretation about not kindling a fire on the Sabbath (which, by extension, includes turning on or off electrical appliances, including lights; for the prohibition on driving, see #15). Thus, many traditional Jews now have timers for their electrical appliances—in other words, if a Jewish *person* doesn't actually perform the act of shutting off the oven or turning off the light, it is okay—and there is even something called the Shabbat Elevator, timed to stop at every floor (since a religious Jew cannot press the elevator button on the Sabbath). I have been on such elevators in high-rise hotels in Israel, and it makes for a long ride!

Traditional Jews also remove or unscrew the light in the refrigerator, lest by opening or closing the door, they inadvertently turn on (or off) the light. This, too, is the subject of rabbinic law, and a modern, widely used compendium of Sabbath laws has this to say:

> If, upon opening an electric refrigerator on Shabbath or Yom Tov [holy day], one finds that the internal light has automatically been switched on,
>   a. this does not make it forbidden to eat the food inside, but
>   b. one should consult a qualified rabbinical authority about what to do with regard to closing the door of the refrigerator again.[57]

For many reasons, I am quite sure that God never intended such regulations to be associated with the observance of the Sabbath. On the other hand, traditional Jews would tell you that: (1) they find holiness in the details; (2) having grown up with these customs, it is a natural way of life for them; and (3) they take great delight in the Sabbath (see Isaiah 58:13). Indeed, traditional Jews will often invite a nontraditional Jew to their homes on Friday night so he or she can enjoy the beauty of the Sabbath with them. This is a common method of outreach among groups like Chabad (Lubavitch; see #2).

Other Jews have found these many Sabbath laws to be onerous and oppressive. This is most common among Jews not raised in observant homes who then became observant before leaving the Orthodox lifestyle. For them, each new regulation seemed to add a new restriction, completely unrelated to the spirit of the day. There are also Jews who were raised Orthodox and found hypocrisy and legalism in their community's Sabbath observance, helping to turn them away from tradition. This, however, is not the norm, and for the great majority of traditional Jews, the Sabbath is welcomed with joy and expectation every week.

The most recent Sabbath invention of interest is the Kosher-Lamp, the top of which can be twisted to cover the light. With this a traditional Jew can even read in bed on Friday night (called 'erev shabbat, "Sabbath eve"), simply twisting the top when it is time to go to sleep. What an invention![58] The designers proudly announce on their website that this meets with stringent Torah law and is approved by the leading rabbis.

Rabbi Shlomo Eliyahu Miller of Toronto was one of the lamp's supporters, and his official endorsement revolves around the rabbinic concept of *muktzeh* (or *muktza*), which refers to objects that cannot be moved or handled on the Sabbath or holy days, or objects that are unprepared for use on these days. Rabbi Miller writes:

> I was asked by Rabbi Shmuel Veffer concerning an electric lamp he invented called "KosherLamp™."
>
> With respect to "moving *muktza*," the body of the lamp is *muktza*, however the upper portion of the lamp [the top and inner cylinder] is a separate part and is a "*kli heter*" (permitted vessel) whose purpose is to shade the light. When light is desired, one turns it [the top] to expose the light. All this is called "*kli heter*," (permitted vessel) but one should be careful when turning the top not to move the base of the lamp. However touching or holding the bottom of the lamp without moving it is also permitted.[59]

Yes, this is rabbinic law! Rabbi Yehoshua Y. Neuwirth, editor of the previously mentioned Sabbath-law compendium, is also cited in support:

> All authorities would permit twisting the shade on Shabbos. It is similar to opening or closing a closet door in which there is a light burning on Shabbos. This is even the case where the shade forms part of the lamp. R. Neuwirth writes explicitly in Shemiras Shabbos [his compendium on observing the Sabbath]:

A shade which is made to direct the light or to cover it up altogether may be adjusted on Shabbath, even if it is made in such a way that it forms part of the lamp.[60]

Michael Kress, in an article in the *Dallas Morning News*, November 27, 2004, entitled "Lighter Duty," reported on this invention, also noting that "Jewish observance has always been difficult, but today's Jew can rely on technology and product engineering to make life a little easier. The KosherLamp is one of several new products geared toward easing the rigors of the traditional Jewish lifestyle."[61]

Kress also lists a number of "holy gadgets," describing some of the latest:

Some high-end ovens come with a "Sabbath mode," which ensures that opening it on Shabbat will not cause any forbidden activities, such as turning on lights, changing digital displays, or triggering the heating mechanism. In Sabbath mode, the oven won't shut off automatically after several hours, like it usually does, so it can be left on throughout the Sabbath. (Cooking is forbidden on Shabbat, but pre-prepared food may be heated.)

For those without a Shabbat-friendly oven, the British company Vikron makes a stand-alone warming device for food that looks like a piece of furniture.

And General Electric and others have recently introduced a device for refrigerators that disables the light and ice maker, ensuring that opening the door will not cause a Sabbath desecration.

Sukkot is the autumn festival during which Jews eat and sometimes sleep in temporary huts. In the past, the huts, called sukkot, had to be built from scratch or from kits that required tools and significant construction time. Today, Jews can buy snap-together sukkot that assemble in minutes, no tools needed.[62]

Do you think you've heard it all? There's more!

Many of the inventions were developed in Israel, where rabbis are constantly working to ensure that the country's health and defense systems can function without breaking Shabbat.

One example: the Shabbat pen, which circumvents the rule against writing on the Sabbath by taking advantage of a provision in Jewish law that an action is only prohibited if it is permanent. This pen's ink disappears after a few hours, so observant doctors, soldiers and others on weekend duty can write quick notes, then rewrite them after Shabbat in permanent ink. . . .

Aside from whether a gizmo is technically permissible, observant Jews must grapple with another question, Rabbi Shafran said: "Does this in some sense undermine the spirit of the law?" For example, even many rabbis who are OK with timers disapprove of using them to watch television on the Sabbath.

But most experts see no problem with most of the products.[63]

While such inventions are welcomed with amusement by many nontraditional Jews—as if this were a further proof of traditional Jewish hypocrisy and legal casuistry—traditional Jews rightly point out that nontraditional Jews tend to ignore the Sabbath almost completely. And so the debate goes on, showing no signs of abating.

15
Why don't traditional Jews drive on the Sabbath?

The primary reason that traditional Jews don't drive on the Sabbath is related to Exodus 35:3, discussed immediately above, the prohibition against kindling a fire on the Sabbath. Since the process of ignition is considered to be equivalent to starting a fire—which is also considered a "creative" act, something also prohibited by the rabbis on the Sabbath—to start a car engine would be considered a clear violation of the Sabbath.

As stated on the *Ask Moses* website:

> Turning a key in a car sets the ignition on—which creates a spark—a fire. Not the kind of fire of banging two stones together, but a fire, nevertheless—a human being creating when G-d commands that he rest from all creative acts.
>
> Granted, some of these are so routine and ordinary, with no "work" involved, and don't seem to involve any genuine creative efforts, but that is the challenge of observing the Shabbat to the letter of the law.[64]

A corollary issue is the Sabbath commandment found in Exodus 16:29 not to go out of one's "place" on the Sabbath (NASB). This command was given in the context of the gathering of manna: On the sixth day there would be double manna, and it would not rot overnight (in contrast with the other days of the week, in which the manna could not be kept overnight; see Exodus 16:14–26). And so the Israelites did not need to go out and gather manna on the seventh day. Instead it was to be a day of rest (see Exodus 16:27–29).

The ancient rabbis understood this prohibition in a general sense, as opposed to applying it only in terms of not going out to gather manna, making certain loopholes for Sabbath travel within closely proscribed limits (cf. Acts 1:12), but otherwise having the effect of keeping the Jewish people in and around their homes and neighborhoods on the Sabbath. Thus, driving a car would violate this concept in both the spirit and letter of these laws—according to rabbinic interpretation, that is—and for these reasons, traditional Jews do not drive cars on the Sabbath.[65]

Because of this, Orthodox Jews tend to live in close proximity to one another, within walking distance of the synagogue, where they all gather together with their families, thereby putting certain limitations on where exactly they can live. Customs such as this, coupled with the various restrictions that dietary laws place on Orthodox Jews, mean that religious Jews have a number of safeguards against assimilation, along with a fairly strong community base.

In contrast with this, Conservative and Reform Jews do not feel bound by such restrictions, and in the Conservative Jewish community in which I grew up, where the synagogue was about one mile from most of our homes, only the rabbi walked to and from synagogue. As our religious leader, this seemed only appropriate! Some of the men, however, so as to give the appearance of honoring the Sabbath, actually drove to the Sabbath service but parked about one block away, walking the rest of the distance.

It is practices such as these that have caused Orthodox rabbis—in particular, the ultra-Orthodox—to scorn non-Orthodox forms of Judaism (see #1). Some non-Orthodox Jews, however, would point to what, in their minds, constitutes an endless series of loopholes made by the traditional rabbis in order to make their impossibly rigid rules livable. In keeping with this would be the recently developed "KosherLamp" for the Sabbath, discussed earlier (see #14).

16

Why do traditional Jewish men wear a skullcap (called *yarmulke* or, in Hebrew, *kippah*)?

Although it would be unthinkable for a religious Jewish man today to walk around with his head uncovered, there is no explicit biblical support for this custom, while in Jesus' day, there is little or no evidence that it was a religious custom for Jewish men to cover their heads.

Traditional Judaism teaches that it is forbidden for a man to walk even a few feet without covering his head (with exceptions, such as taking a shower), and so immediately, upon rising from bed, a traditional Jewish man will put his yarmulke on, often wearing a hat over his yarmulke when he goes out. Nontraditional Jews tend not to wear a yarmulke except at religious gatherings (such as synagogue services) or ceremonies (such as a wedding), and to facilitate this, Conservative synagogues have a box with yarmulkes and prayer shawls at the door. This practice is followed by some Reform synagogues as well, although for many decades, Reform Jews proudly worshiped in their synagogues with their heads uncovered. (For head coverings and the practices of traditional Jewish women, see #17.)

The origins of the yarmulke are unclear, since there is nothing in the Torah that would relate to this (other than the fact that the high priest wore a certain kind of head covering), and there is scant mention in the Talmud about this practice, aside from the reference to an exceptionally pious man who would not walk more than a few feet without covering his head "since the Divine Presence is above my head" (b. Kiddushin 31a). What is clear is that, over the centuries, "covering the head became a sign of reverence and awe and an acknowledgement of the omnipresence of God"[66]—especially when praying and studying. Indeed, this has become such a sign of piety that for a Jewish man *not* to cover his head would be to loudly proclaim his *impiety*. In keeping with this, a famous twentieth-century rabbi was once chastised by his mother when, as a little boy, he was not quick enough in putting his yarmulke back on his head after it had fallen off. How, she asked, could he be so irreverent?

This practice, which did not become fixed until the late Middle Ages, is then projected back to biblical times by traditional Jews. In fact, a rabbi told me a traditional Jewish joke that claims that we can prove from the Torah that Isaac covered his head. The text cited is Genesis 24:63, stating that Isaac went into the field to meditate. The "proof" is this: "You mean to tell me that Isaac would pray and meditate without covering his head?"

On a more serious, historical note, Christians should be aware that any depiction of Jesus wearing a yarmulke would be anachronistic, since there is no proof of any kind that this was the custom of the day—especially in the form of a traditional skullcap. In modern times, the "orthodoxy" of a Jewish man can be partially gauged by the nature of his skullcap (assuming he wears it all day): If it is small and knitted, he is probably a modern Orthodox or a committed Conservative; if it is larger and black (and not knitted) he is Orthodox; and if he wears a hat over his yarmulke, he is ultra-Orthodox. On festive occasions, including Sabbaths and holy days, ultra-Orthodox Jews (especially Hasidic) wear what is called a *streimel* (or *shtreimel*), a fur hat costing several thousand dollars and most commonly made of sable.

As for the Yiddish word *yarmulke* (also spelled *yarmulka* or *yarmelke*), it is of uncertain origin, although a minority view is that it is derived from the Hebrew/Aramaic words *yarei malka*, meaning "fearers of the King."

Interestingly, it is common in other religions as well for men—in particular, the religious leaders—to cover their heads, including Islam and segments of Christianity. Rabbi Joseph Telushkin notes:

> A funny caption to a photograph is reputed to have appeared in the *Jerusalem Post* in 1964—I have not seen the original—when Pope Paul VI visited Israel. He was met by the Israeli president [who was not a religious Jew, and therefore was not wearing a *yarmulke*], and the caption under the photograph read: "The Pope is the one wearing the *yarmulka!*"[67]

It is common to see Messianic Jews wearing head coverings in their services, either as a demonstration to visiting Jews that it is, in fact, Jewish to believe in Jesus, or as something meaningful in their own lives before God. Does this contradict Paul's words in 1 Corinthians 11:4? He writes there: "Every man who prays or prophesies with his head covered dishonors his head." For more on that, see the very next question.

17
Why do traditional Jewish women wear wigs (or even shave their heads)?

According to *The Oxford Dictionary of the Jewish Religion*, "For married women, the obligation to cover the head goes back to ancient times (see *Is.* 3.17; *B.Q.* 8:6) and [according to the Mishnah] a wife's public bareheadedness was grounds for divorce (*Ket.* 7:6)."[68] This may also be related to ancient Near Eastern culture, where, "In Mesopotamia shaving off half the hair was used as a punishment intended to bring public humiliation."[69] Paul also writes that "every woman who prays or prophesies with her head uncovered dishonors her head—it is just as though her head were shaved. If a woman does not cover her head, she should have her hair cut off; and if it is a disgrace for a woman to have her hair cut or shaved off, she should cover her head" (1 Corinthians 11:5–6). New Testament scholar Craig Keener explains:

> Women's hair was a common object of lust in antiquity, and in much of the eastern Mediterranean women were expected to cover their hair. To fail to cover their hair was thought to provoke male lust as a bathing suit is thought to provoke it in some cultures today. Head covering prevailed in Jewish Palestine (where it extended even to a face veil) and elsewhere, but upper-class women eager to show off their fashionable hairstyles did not practice it. Thus Paul must address a clash of culture in the church between upper-class fashion and lower-class concern that sexual propriety is being violated.[70]

So, Paul's words here are in harmony with the ancient Jewish view of the importance of a woman—in particular a married woman—having her hair covered. Just one verse earlier, however, he seemed to contradict what has become the traditional Jewish practice of men always covering their heads, especially in prayer and worship, stating: "Every man who prays or prophesies with his head covered dishonors his head" (verse 4). How do Messianic Jews explain this, since many of them wear a yarmulke in worship and prayer (see #16)?

Messianic Jewish commentator David Stern writes:

> Wearing something down over his head. This is the literal translation [of 1 Corinthians 11:4], and it is used here to show that Sha'ul [Paul] is talking about wearing a veil, not a hat. The usual translation, "with his head covered" obscures this fact, and as a result an issue has arisen in Messianic Judaism that should never have come up at all, namely, whether it is proper for a Messianic Jewish man to wear a *kippah* . . . in public worship. Of course it is proper, since objection to it is based only on a mis-translation of this verse.[71]

Returning to the question at hand regarding women covering their hair, *The Oxford Dictionary of the Jewish Religion* notes that "in modern times, Orthodox married women cover their heads with a wig or head scarf when in public,"[72] and not to do so would be considered an affront to both God and one's husband. It is a matter of modesty and purity, since, among men outside of the immediate family, only the woman's husband should have the privilege of seeing her real hair. It is also common for traditional Jewish girls and unmarried women to cover their hair with a scarf, again as a matter of modesty, just like Amish or Mennonite girls and women cover their hair. And since Judaism encourages women to dress up and look beautiful (but with modesty), covering their hair with a nice wig is not considered demeaning or negative.

The custom in many Hasidic communities, however, is harder to understand, since "women cut off all their hair before marriage and thereafter wear a head scarf" (called in Yiddish a *tikhel*).[73] This practice seemingly takes the practice of modesty to a ridiculous extreme, actually robbing the wife of her dignity, and I have no desire to defend this at all. It is certainly not biblical (note that the rabbinic commentators put a negative, nonattractive connotation on the shaving of the head of a woman captured in war; see Deuteronomy 21:10–14; b. Yevamot 48a), and it violates the spirit of Paul's words—which, of course, carry no weight for a Hasidic Jew—that long hair is given to a woman as a covering and for her glory (see 1 Corinthians 11:15–16).

Why then is this practiced? It is actually not widely practiced in traditional Judaism—in fact, it is almost exclusively found today among Hasidic Jews of Hungarian origin (this would primarily include the Satmar)—and its rationale and background are disputed. One view is that, while living in Hungary, the women shaved their heads so as not to be taken by the Gentile nobles. Another view is based on a traditional practice in Jewish mysticism in which women would clip off a piece of their hair before going to the ritual bath (*mikveh*), and this developed into the custom of shaving the head entirely. Whatever the origins of this unappealing tradition, it is striking that it took hold in some circles to the point of becoming a fixed practice for devout Jewish women, standing as a testament to the power of tradition and custom in Judaism.[74]

18
Why do some Jewish men grow long side curls?

The growing of side curls, called *pe'ot*, literally "corners" (in traditional pronunciation, *peyos*, which sounds like PEY-us), is based on the prohibition in Leviticus 19:27 (cf. also Leviticus 21:5): "Do not cut the hair at the sides of your head or clip off the edges of your beard." (Note that the same Hebrew word *pe'ah*, the singular for *pe'ot*, is translated in the NIV in this verse as "sides" and "edges.") See also Deuteronomy 14:1: "You are the children of the LORD your God. Do not cut yourselves or shave the front of your heads for the dead." (Readers will remember this verse from the earlier discussion of kosher laws in #12.)

Now, it is clear from the contexts that these prohibitions refer primarily to acts that disfigure or damage—note the ban on cutting oneself in Deuteronomy 14:1, especially in the context of mourning for the dead, and see Leviticus 19:28, which follows the command in Leviticus 19:27—and that is in keeping with the explanation of Rashi, the foremost Jewish biblical commentator, of Deuteronomy 14:1: "Do not make cuts and incisions in your flesh [to mourn] for the dead, in the manner that the Amorites do, because you are the children of the Omnipresent and it is appropriate for you to be handsome and not to be cut or have your hair torn out."

The rabbis, however, did not simply interpret these verses as prohibitions against disfiguring practices. They understood them in the context of God's calling on Israel to be a separate people, as emphasized in Deuteronomy 14:2: "For you are a people holy to the LORD your God. Out of all the peoples on the face of the earth, the LORD has chosen you to be his treasured possession." We saw above, in #12, that this was a major reason for the dietary laws. In fact, being separated is part of the definition of holiness: to be separated *from* sin and impurity and to be separated *to* God.

Thus rabbinic Judaism understood Leviticus 19:27 in very specific ways (again, in keeping with the spirit of traditional Judaism that believes every area of life is legislated by divine law). This is Rashi's commentary on this verse. The bracketed references are to the Talmud and another foundational rabbinic document:

> You shall not round off the corner of your head. This refers to someone who [cuts his hair in such a way that he] makes [the hair on] his temples even with that behind his ear and on his forehead [i.e., the front hairline], thereby causing [the hairline] surrounding

his head to become a circle, since the main hairline behind the ears is at a much higher level than [the hair on] his temples. [*Makkot* 20b] the edge of your beard [meaning:] The end of the beard and its borders. And these are five: two on each cheek at the top [edge of the cheek] near the head, where [the cheek] is broad and has two "corners" [i.e., extremities—one near the temple and the other at the end of the cheek bone towards the center of the face]—and one below, on the chin—at the point where the two cheeks join together. [*Torath Kohanim* 19:74, *Makkot*. 20b][75]

Following these practices, then, produces side curls, which are then viewed in some circles as a matter of piety, primarily by the ultra-Orthodox, the only Jews to follow this practice today, although even among ultra-Orthodox Jews, there are differences (no surprise here!). The Lubavitch Hasidim wear their side curls behind their ears (and therefore in a less prominent way) while Satmar Hasidim allow their *peyos* to hang down naturally, albeit quite curled. (For more on these groups, see #2.) Thus some Satmars feel that the Lubavitchers have compromised. In Israel today, it is not uncommon to see young Jewish men with their heads almost completely shaved but with side curls more than one foot long—I have seen some almost waist length on occasion—and this is part of their devotion to God.

Oddly enough, the rabbinic application of the biblical command *not* to do strange things to our facial or head hair has resulted in a very strange look indeed, and there is no reason to think that Jews in the Old Testament period wore their hair like this, although I'm quite sure that an ultra-Orthodox Jew would beg to differ.

19
Why do some Jewish men wear white fringes outside of their shirts?

Generally speaking, the custom of wearing white fringes, called *tsitsit* in Hebrew, is only practiced by Orthodox Jews, and it is based on the biblical commandment found in Numbers 15:37–41 (see also Deuteronomy 22:12):

> The LORD said to Moses, "Speak to the Israelites and say to them: 'Throughout the generations to come you are to make tassels on the corners of your garments, with a blue cord on each tassel. You will have these tassels to look at and so you will remember all the commands of the LORD, that you may obey them and not prostitute yourselves by going after the lusts of your own hearts and eyes. Then you will remember to obey all my commands and will be consecrated to your God. I am the LORD your God, who brought you out of Egypt to be your God. I am the LORD your God.'"

In ancient times, the men wore long, four-cornered garments, as opposed to a shirt that is tucked into the pants. And it was often the custom of ancient Near Eastern royalty to wear a specific type of blue tassel on the corners of these garments. And so, when God commanded His people to wear garments with these same blue tassels, He was reminding them that they were a kingdom of priests (see Exodus 19:4–6), responsible to keep their King's commandments.

What made this blue color so significant? The Hebrew word for "blue" in Numbers 15 is *tekhelet*, often called "royal blue" (which some scholars believe was actually closer to violet or blue-purple), since the dye used to make this color came from a hard-to-find snail called the *chilazon*, a snail that was more than worth its weight in gold. Thus, this very color was a sign of wealth and royalty.

Why, then, do Jewish men today wear white fringes instead of blue? Over the process of time, the rabbis determined that the *chilazon* was no longer accessible, and rather than use a similar-looking blue dye, they decided to leave it out entirely, hence the white fringes seen today. Also, as customs of dress changed and Jewish men no longer wore these four-cornered garments, other adaptations were made. Thus, traditional Jewish men today wear what is called a *tallit katan* (a small *tallit*) under their shirts, somewhat like a T-shirt, except that it has white fringes hanging from the corners. (The prayer shawl that Jewish men wear while praying is called the *tallit* or *tallis*, depending upon the Jewish pronunciation. The *tallit* also has these same tassels, or fringes.)

Less-religious Orthodox Jews wear these fringes tucked into their clothes, but more observant Jews wear them out in order to fulfill more carefully the biblical commandment to *see* the fringes and be reminded of their obligation to keep the commandments of the Torah. In keeping with this, the rabbis developed various customs of tying these fringes into series of knots, also as a reminder of the commandments, which, according to rabbinic Judaism, number 613. (These knots are also tied into the fringes of the prayer shawl, the *tallit*, which explains the Jewish joke about the rabbi who brought his *tallit* into the dry cleaners, only to receive it back two weeks later with the note, "Rabbi, I apologize for the delay, but it took me forever to get out all those knots!")

Now, there are not actually 613 knots tied into the fringes—that would *really* be a lot of knots!—but they are tied into the fringes strategically, as explained by Professor Jacob Milgrom:

> The Hebrew numerical value of the consonants of the word *tsitsit* is 600. If five (for the sets of double knots) and eight (for the number of thread ends) be added, they yield a total of 613, which, according to rabbinic tradition, represents the number of biblical commandments of which the *tsitsit* are to remind the wearer.[76]

And so, whenever a Jewish man looks at any of these fringes, he is reminded of his obligation to keep all 613 commandments, and thus this specific commandment—to wear the fringes and look at them—became of great importance in rabbinic Judaism. In the words of the great legal codifier Moses Maimonides (A.D. 1135–1204):

> One should always be heedful of the commandment to wear *tsitsit*, for the Torah equated and connected all other *mitzvot* [commandments] with it, as it is written, "And you shall see it and remember all of the commandments of the Lord and you shall do them" (*Laws of Tsitsit*, 3:13).

Why is it that Orthodox Jewish women do not wear these fringes? According to rabbinic tradition, women are exempt from time-oriented commandments, primarily because of their household and family responsibilities. And so, because the text makes reference to *looking at* the fringes, which can only be done in the daytime, women are exempt from wearing the fringes according to rabbinic law.

Did Jesus Himself wear these fringes, which, in the first century, would have been blue? Since He was a Torah-observant Jew, we have every reason to believe that He did, although He denounced the ostentatious wearing of the fringes so as to be seen by man (see Matthew 23:5). Matthew 9:20 and Luke 8:44 also point in this direction, describing how the woman with the issue of blood reached out and touched the *fringe* of Yeshua's garment (see also Matthew 14:36; Mark 6:56 where the sick wanted to touch the fringe of His garment). Significantly, the Greek word translated "fringe" is *kraspedon*, and in the Septuagint, the ancient Jewish translation of the Scriptures into Greek, that same word is used to translate the Hebrew word for fringes (or tassels) in Numbers 15:38–39; Deuteronomy 22:12; Zechariah 8:23. It is also used in Matthew 23:5, where Jesus rebuked the religious hypocrites for making their tassels especially long. So, this would indicate that Jesus also wore a fringed garment, and it was this fringe—representing the utter extremity of His garment, and, according to a minority view, endued with special powers—that these sick people touched in faith, and all of them were healed.[77]

20
Why do traditional Jewish men pray with black boxes (called phylacteries or, in Hebrew, *tefillin*) on their heads and arms?

This custom was widely practiced in Yeshua's day—in fact, it is very possible that He Himself wore these—and the Lord made reference to this custom when denouncing some of the hypocritical religious leaders: "Everything they do is done for men to see: They make their phylacteries wide and the tassels on their garments long" (Matthew 23:5).

Notice, however, that Jesus did not criticize them for *wearing phylacteries*, traditionally known as *tefillin* (literally "prayers"), but for doing so in an ostentatious way. In fact, wearing tassels on the garments was a Torah command (see #19), so the Lord was certainly not criticizing people for wearing tassels but rather for their excessive public use so as to be seen by people.

What exactly was Jesus describing? The phylacteries were "small leather or parchment boxes containing a piece of vellum inscribed with four texts from the law (Exodus 13:2–10, 11–16; Deuteronomy 6:4–9; 11:13–21) and were worn on the arm or tied to the forehead (cf. Exodus 13:9, 16; Deuteronomy 6:8; 11:18). To show their piety to the world, these leaders made large, showy phylacteries."[78]

When did God command the Israelites to wear these boxes? Let us look at some of the Torah texts that were included within these leather boxes in Jesus' day and in our day as well. In Deuteronomy 6:6–9, Moses said to the people of Israel,

> These commandments that I give you today are to be upon your hearts. Impress them on your children. Talk about them when you sit at home and when you walk along the road, when you lie down and when you get up. Tie them as symbols on your hands and bind them on your foreheads. Write them on the doorframes of your houses and on your gates.

Similar language is used in Exodus 13:16, with reference to the redemption of the firstborn. There God says, "And it will be like a sign on your hand and a symbol on your forehead that the LORD brought us out of Egypt with his mighty hand."

What exactly did it mean to "tie [the commandments] as symbols on your hands and bind them on your foreheads"? How was the deliverance from Egypt to be commemorated "like a sign on your hand and a symbol on your forehead"?

There is evidence that some ancient Jewish groups, such as the Samaritans (see #28), did not interpret these verses literally, while it is noteworthy that the Septuagint translators, working two to three centuries before the time of Jesus, understood the verses metaphorically. And Rashbam, a famous medieval rabbinic commentator, agreed that the verses should be interpreted figuratively (cf. Proverbs 1:9; 3:3; 4:9; 6:21; 7:3; note, however, that he also stated that the practice of putting on phylacteries should be followed because it was taught by tradition).

On the other hand, we know that by the second century B.C. at the latest it was common in a number of Jewish circles to interpret these verses literally, as evidenced by the discovery of phylacteries in the Dead Sea Scroll archives, and these phylacteries closely resemble those described in detail in the rabbinic writings and worn today by religious Jews in morning prayer (with the exception of the Sabbath and certain holy days).[79]

Can it be demonstrated that God wanted His people to wear black leather boxes on their arms and foreheads? The rabbinic traditions claim that God specifically communicated the details of this commandment to Moses on Mount Sinai (see Oral Law), as explained by Rabbi Nathan Cardozo:

Nowhere does the written Torah describe this sign and ornament. The *tefillin* we use today are the result of the tradition of the orally transmitted Torah. Yet not only are the fragments of *tefillin* found in the Qumran excavations similar to our own; the order of the biblical passages written on these fragments indicates that the difference of opinion between Rashi (eleventh century) and Rabbenu Tam (twelfth century) dates back to the earliest moments of Jewish history, for *tefillin* of both types were found! Centuries later, as well, "in Nehardea and Jerusalem they found two sets of *tefillin*: one according to the order of Rashi, and the other according to Rabbenu Tam" (*Piskei Tosafot, Menachot* 34b).[80]

The Talmud also contains some extremely far-fetched explanations as to how the specific details of the phylacteries can be deduced from the biblical text, especially in b. Sanhedrin 4b, where an impossible linguistic derivation is put forth by the famous Rabbi Akiva.

In any case, whether God originally intended for His people to wear these black boxes—be it all day, as was the practice in Talmudic times, or primarily during morning prayer—the putting on of the *tefillin* (or, as traditional Jews refer to it, "laying *tefillin*") has become a much-loved traditional custom, the arm *tefillin* being close to the heart (since it is put on the left arm) and the head *tefillin* being close to the mind (since it is put on the forehead).

Although the evidence would strongly suggest that God did not literally command the ancient Israelites to make and wear phylacteries, contrary to the claims of traditional Judaism, it is clear that the wearing of phylacteries reflects a tradition more than two thousand years old, and this practice has taken on great meaning in the life of traditional Jews through the centuries, tying them in a very literal way to the Torah commands.

21

What are the little boxes (mezuzahs) on the doorways of Orthodox Jewish homes?

In the Bible, the word *mezuzah* simply meant "doorframe, threshold," occurring a total of eighteen times (see Exodus 12:22–23; 21:6; Deuteronomy 6:9; 11:20; Judges 16:3; 1 Samuel 1:9; 1 Kings 6:31, 33; 7:5; Isaiah 57:8; Ezekiel 41:21; 43:8 [twice]; 45:19 [twice]; 46:2; Proverbs 8:34; the plural of the word is *mezuzot*). Christians would be especially familiar with verses such as Exodus 12:22–23, where God commanded the Israelites in Egypt to put the blood of the sacrificial lamb on the door frames of their houses when the Passover was inaugurated. But these verses are not related to the mounting of mezuzahs in Jewish homes. Rather, the key verses are Deuteronomy 6:9 and 11:20, where God commanded the Israelites to write His commandments "on the doorframes of your houses and on your gates" (meaning, the gates of their cities; more fully, see Deuteronomy 6:4–9 and 11:18–20).

We cited these passages, above, when discussing the practice of putting on phylacteries, asking whether God commanded His people *literally* to keep His words before their eyes (see #20). The same question has to be asked with regard to Deuteronomy 6:9 and 11:20: Did God *literally* intend that His people write His words on the door frames of their houses and on their gates? It is not uncommon for Christians to have Scripture plaques in various rooms of their homes, reminding them of key promises or important ethical teachings, while believers even have a verse like Joshua 24:15, "As for me and my household, we will serve the Lord," hanging over their front door. Is this similar to what the Lord had in mind?

There is a fascinating example from ancient Israel where archaeologists discovered an inscription actually written on the door frames of a house. What is striking is that it was a prayer addressed to Yahweh and His female deity consort! The inscription, discovered in northern Israel in the mid-1970s in what is today called Kuntillet 'Ajrud, reads as follows: "Thus says . . . Say to Yehalle[lel], Yo'asa and . . . I bless you [or have blessed you] to/before Yahweh of Samaria and his asherah." This inscription reflects the rampant idolatry that existed in the northern kingdom of Samaria (see 2 Kings 17:7–17), and, in that light, it is highly unlikely that this inscription was written out of obedience to Yahweh's Torah commandment.[81] That would really be a stretch! But this inscription may reflect a custom that was not unusual in ancient Israel, and so the command to write God's words on the door frames or city gates could have been literally intended.

Traditional Jews, however, claim that God had something very specific in mind: They believe that the Lord wanted the Israelites to write out two key Torah passages on a tiny scroll (Deuteronomy 6:4–9; 11:13–21, two of the passages that are contained in the phylacteries) and to place these passages in a small container, called a mezuzah, which would be placed in a specific way on the door frame. This way, while the actual verses would not be seen, they would, in effect, be placed on the door frames of the houses, serving as a reminder of those verses and of God's presence.

In keeping with the spirit of traditional Judaism, which leaves little wiggle room in the application of the commandments, the mezuzah is required to be a certain size and is to be placed on the right door frame at a certain height and at a certain angle. When a traditional Jew walks through the doorway, he touches the mezuzah with his hand and kisses it. It is common to see the Hebrew letter *shin* on the mezuzah, standing for *Shaddai*, a biblical title of God, traditionally translated "Almighty."[82] Otherwise, the *shin* is placed on the back of the scroll within the mezuzah.

As to the question of why the mezuzah is affixed at an angle, the Judaism 101 website answers: "The rabbis could not decide whether it should be placed horizontally or vertically, so they compromised!"[83]

22

Why do some religious Jewish men wear long black coats?

I once asked this question to an ultra-Orthodox Jewish man, since it is mainly the ultra-Orthodox who wear long black coats. He responded, "We do it because our fathers did." That is the power of tradition in Judaism! He also stated that this would be in keeping with biblical practice, where people wore long robes rather than shorts, so this is also a matter of modesty, although religious Jews would not look to the Bible in specific support of wearing long black coats.

On another level, the particular type of dress in question—the specific kind of long black coat—is of relatively recent origin and is based on traditional European Jewish custom. In short, the style of dress that was common in certain traditional Jewish communities in Eastern Europe several centuries ago became fixed as time went on, again, a testament to the power of custom in Judaism. (It is even said that "the custom of the people is law.") In other words, if a community adopts a particular practice—whether in dress or in family life or in study habits—and that practice becomes customary to the point that "everyone is doing it," and if that practice then continues through the generations (with rabbinic approval, of course), then it becomes somewhat sacrosanct, not easily changed. Similar to this is the custom of Mennonite women who wear a certain type of head covering or the custom of Amish men to grow their beards but shave their mustaches.

Related to the power of custom—especially in Judaism—is the concept of the "good old days," meaning that the former generations were considered to be on a higher spiritual plane than the succeeding generations, and in certain eras, some of the Jewish communities were considered to be especially holy and devoted. Their practices, then, would be adhered to even more zealously, and that is exactly what happened with the customary dress of these Eastern European communities—the long coats, certain types of hats and even knickers. That is to say, some of this was not even Jewish in origin as much as it was the customary dress of the society at large. But so highly esteemed were these Jewish communities by the succeeding generations that even their dress was copied, to this very day. In fact, in some ultra-Orthodox communities in Israel, such as Mea Shearim in Jerusalem, the men can be identified by the outfits they wear, outfits associated with specific Eastern European Jewish communities. Thus, some of them still wear knickers and white coats; others wear knickers with black coats; others wear black coats and regular pants.

I once visited a yeshiva (a learning center for Orthodox rabbinic study) in Lakewood, New Jersey, at the invitation of an ultra-Orthodox Jewish friend of mine who studies there. (This yeshiva has roughly four thousand men studying there daily, making it the world's largest yeshiva.) Every man there wore black pants and a white shirt—without exception, and without it being a stated requirement for entry—and upon entering the yeshiva, my friend hung up his (black) hat and (black) coat, which became one of many (to my eyes) identical hats and coats, although my friend assured me that his was readily distinguishable to him.

In any case, there is no biblical basis for the custom of wearing long black coats, nor is such a basis claimed for the custom.

23

Why do traditional Jews claim that Jewish descent is matrilineal (i.e., coming through the mother) rather than patrilineal (i.e., coming through the father)?

To many readers of the Bible, it would seem that the opposite would be true and that one's Jewishness would be traced through the father rather than the mother. After all, biblical genealogies trace descent through the father, we speak of the patriarchs Abraham, Isaac and Jacob rather than the matriarchs Sarah, Rebecca, Rachel and Leah, and men in Bible days were known as the son of their father (e.g., *Simon Bar Jonah* means "Simon son of Jonah"). Why, then, does the Talmud claim that Jewish descent is traced through the mother? And why does this remain the primary determining factor in Jewish law today ("Is your mother Jewish?")? This is so established in Jewish culture that a Jew seeking to gain citizenship in Israel needs to prove that his or her mother was Jewish.

Many scholars believe today that this understanding was not fixed until the early centuries of this era, and some cite Acts 16:1–3 as a case in point. There we read that Paul met Timothy in Lystra, "whose mother was a Jewess and a believer, but whose father was a Greek. . . . Paul wanted to take him along on the journey, so he circumcised him because of the Jews who lived in that area, for they all knew that his father was a Greek." According to the Jewish historian Shaye Cohen, this points to the fact that Jewish identity through the mother was not universally fixed throughout the Jewish world at that time, which is why Timothy was not circumcised at birth. Paul, however, recognized him as Jewish, hence his willingness to circumcise him, whereas Titus was not circumcised, since he was a Gentile (see Galatians 2:3).[84]

Professor Cohen further notes:

Numerous Israelite heroes and kings married foreign women: for example, Judah married a Canaanite, Joseph an Egyptian, Moses a Midianite and an Ethiopian, David a Philistine, and Solomon women of every description. By her marriage with an Israelite man a foreign woman joined the clan, people, and religion of her husband. It never occurred to anyone in pre-exilic times to argue that such marriages were null and void, that foreign women must "convert" to Judaism, or that the off-spring of the marriage were not Israelite if the women did not convert.[85]

Traditional Jews, however, believe that the concept of matrilineal Jewish descent does, in fact, go back to the Bible, which would be in keeping with their view that the traditions they follow today have their ultimate origin in the Scriptures (as interpreted, of course, by the Oral Law). What, then, is the basis for this belief? Several Scriptures are offered in support, a few of which will be treated here.

The Talmud (b. Kiddushin 68a-b) points to Exodus 21:4: "If [a slave's] master gives him a wife and she bears him sons or daughters, the woman and her children shall belong to her master, and only the man shall go free," which is explained as follows: "This refers to a Gentile bondmaid given as wife to a Hebrew slave. The children remain slaves when their father is freed, shewing that they bear their mother's status."[86] (Notice that the Torah does *not* say that the woman is a Gentile; this is read into the text by the later rabbis.)

Another text cited in the Talmudic discussion is Deuteronomy 7:3–4:

Do not intermarry with them [the surrounding, pagan nations]. Do not give your daughters to their sons or take their daughters for your sons, for they will turn your sons away from following me to serve other gods, and the LORD's anger will burn against you and will quickly destroy you.

The Talmud then asks, "How do we know that her issue bears her status?—R. Johanan said on the authority of R. Simeon b. Yohai,

Because Scripture saith, For he will turn away thy son from following me: thy son by an Israelite woman is called thy son, but thy son by a heathen is not called thy son." This is typical of Talmudic reasoning: Every word in the Torah can take on special significance, hence this seemingly forced deduction here.

Two other, related passages cited by Orthodox Jews are Ezra 10 and Nehemiah 9, where the Jewish men were called to account for marrying foreign wives, being commanded to divorce their wives and send them off along with the children who had been born to them. This, too, would point to the non-Jewish status of these children. Otherwise, why were the fathers ordered to send them away?

These arguments, which are developed at greater length in the Talmud and rabbinic writings, are hardly compelling. In the case of Ezra and Nehemiah, the issue could have simply been pragmatic, since it was expected that the mother would raise the children rather than the father (there was no such thing as stay-at-home dads!). And the point of Professor Cohen, cited above, with regard to many Israelite men marrying Gentile women, is well taken: Their children were considered Israelites without any record of the wives formally converting to the Israelite faith. Nonetheless, only Jewish descent through the mother was recognized in Jewish communities for almost two thousand years until Reform Judaism decided in 1983 to accept the children of Jewish fathers (patrilineal descent), without any conversion process being required. Orthodox Jews, as expected, completely dismiss this viewpoint, although a very good case can be made for patrilineal descent.

Messianic Jewish leaders have also discussed this question, with no kind of universal viewpoint being adopted as of yet, although some have suggested this guideline: If someone had either a Jewish father or a Jewish mother and considers himself or herself to be Jewish, he or she should be accepted as such.

24
Are there really 613 commandments in the Torah?

There is no biblical reference to 613 commandments, although the later rabbinic leaders claimed that all 613 commandments are alluded to within the Ten Commandments. The first actual reference to 613 commandments is found in a lengthy Talmudic passage. There, Rabbi Simlai (third century A.D.) is quoted as saying, "Six hundred and thirteen precepts were communicated to Moses, three hundred and sixty-five negative precepts, corresponding to the number of solar days [in the year], and two hundred and forty-eight positive precepts, corresponding to the number of the members of man's body" (b. Makkot 23b–24a; we will return to this passage at the end of this answer). Based on this comment, medieval Jewish scholars sought to come to agreement as to the exact enumeration and delineation of the 613 commandments, since there is a good deal of ambiguity in counting.[87]

For example, would you count "Be fruitful and multiply," spoken in Genesis 1:28 and repeated in Genesis 9:1 (NASB), to be one of the 613 commandments? The rabbis did, recognizing it as the first word of command given to the human race. What about commandments that overlap each other? Should these be subdivided?

Questions such as these, among many others, caused these scholars to come up with slightly different counts—there was essential agreement about the vast majority of these commandments—and the most famous compilation of all, Maimonides' *Book of the Commandments*, actually counted only 606 explicit Torah commandments, the last seven consisting of *rabbinic* commandments, namely: (1) the command to wash the hands before eating (note the conflict over this already in Matthew 15 and Mark 7); (2) laws regarding the *Eruv*, a rabbinic concept that removed some Sabbath restrictions in very specific ways; (3) reciting a blessing before eating or partaking of any kind of pleasure; (4) lighting the candles on the Sabbath; (5) celebrating the holiday of Purim, which is referred to in the book of Esther but whose observance is not mandated there (see Esther 9:23–32); (6) celebrating Hanukkah, a holiday commemorating events that took place in the second century B.C., well after the Tanakh was already completed; and (7) reciting the Hallel prayer on certain occasions.

Although some Jewish leaders differed with Maimonides in including these rabbinic commandments in the count of 613, all traditional Jews recognize these seven commandments as divinely given through the authority of the rabbis. Thus, as noted earlier (#14), when a Jewish woman lights the Sabbath candles, she blesses God "who commanded us to kindle the Sabbath candles," even though this is not written in the Torah but rather comes from the rabbis.

The Hebrew acronym for 613 is *taryag*, as the Hebrew letter *t* equals 400, *r* equals 200, *y* equals 10 and *g* equals 3. Thus the 613 commandments are known in Hebrew as *taryag mitzvoth*. In keeping with Rabbi Simlai's statement, the commandments are divided into negative and positive precepts (that is, "Thou shalt not" and "Thou shalt"). Because of the destruction of the Temple and the lack of a functioning Temple priesthood, Jews today can observe, as written in the Torah, only 77 out of the 365 negative commandments and 194 out of 248 positive commandments. This is one of the major reasons that religious Jews pray three times daily for the rebuilding of the Temple and the redemption of their people: They are eager to perform the rest of the commandments!

I'll close this answer with the entire lengthy passage from the Talmud that I mentioned earlier (b. Makkot 23b–24a). You're in for a surprise!

> R. Simlai when preaching said: Six hundred and thirteen precepts were communicated to Moses, three hundred and sixty-five negative precepts, corresponding to the number of solar days [in

the year], and two hundred and forty-eight positive precepts, corresponding to the number of the members of man's body. Said R. Hamnuna: What is the [authentic] text for this? It is, Moses commanded us torah, an inheritance of the congregation of Jacob, 'torah' being in letter-value, equal to six hundred and eleven, 'I am' and 'Thou shalt have no [other Gods]' [not being reckoned, because] we heard from the mouth of the Might [Divine]. David came and reduced them to eleven [principles], as it is written, A Psalm of David. Lord, who shall sojourn in Thy tabernacle? Who shall dwell in Thy holy mountain?—[i] He that walketh uprightly, and [ii] worketh righteousness, and [iii] speaketh truth in his heart; that [iv] hath no slander upon his tongue, [v] nor doeth evil to his fellow, [vi] nor taketh up a reproach against his neighbour, [vii] in whose eyes a vile person is despised, but [viii] he honoureth them that fear the Lord, [ix] He sweareth to his own hurt and changeth not, [x] He putteth not out his money on interest, [xi] nor taketh a bribe against the innocent. He that doeth these things shall never be moved. 'He that walketh uprightly': that was Abraham, as it is written, Walk before Me and be thou whole-hearted. 'And worketh righteousness,' such as Abba Hilkiahu. 'Speaketh truth in his heart,' such as R. Safra. 'Hath no slander upon his tongue,' that was our Father Jacob, as it is written, My father peradventure will feel me and I shall seem to him as a deceiver. 'Nor doeth evil to his fellow,' that is he who does not set up in opposition to his fellow craftsman. 'Nor taketh up a reproach against his neighbour'; that is he who befriends his near ones [relatives]. 'In whose eyes a vile person is despised'; that was Hezekiah the king [of Judah] who dragged his father's bones on a rope truckle-bed. 'He honoureth them that fear the Lord'; that was Jehoshaphat king of Judah, who every time he beheld a scholar-disciple rose from his throne, and embraced and kissed him, calling him Father, Father; Rabbi, Rabbi; Mari, Mari! 'He sweareth to his own hurt and changeth not,' like R. Johanan; for R. Johanan [once] said: I shall remain fasting until I reach home. 'He putteth not out money on interest,' not even interest from a heathen. 'Nor taketh a bribe against the innocent,' such as R. Ishmael son of R. Jose. It is written [in conclusion], He that doeth these things shall never be moved. Whenever R. Gamaliel came to this passage he used to weep, saying: [Only] one who practised all these shall not be moved; but anyone falling short in any of these [virtues] would be moved! Said his colleagues to him: Is it written, 'He that doeth all these things [shall not fall]'? It reads, 'He that doeth these things', meaning even if only he practises one of these things [he shall not be moved]. For if you say otherwise, what of that other [similar] passage, Defile not ye yourselves in all these things? Are we to say that one who seeks contact with all these vices, he is become contaminated; but if only with one of those vices, he is not contaminated? [Surely,] it can only mean there, that if he seeks contact with any one of these vices he is become contaminated, and likewise here, if he practises even one of these virtues [he will not be moved].

Isaiah came and reduced them to six [principles], as it is written, [i] He that walketh righteously, and [ii] speaketh uprightly, [iii] He that despiseth the gain of oppressions, [iv] that shaketh his hand from holding of bribes, [v] that stoppeth his ear from hearing of blood, [vi] and shutteth his eyes from looking upon evil; he shall dwell on high. 'He that walketh righteously,' that was our Father Abraham, as it is written, For I have known him, to the end that he may command his children and his household after him, etc.; 'and speaketh uprightly,' that is one who does not put an affront on his fellow in public. 'He that despiseth the gain of oppressions,' as, for instance, R. Ishmael b. Elisha; 'that shaketh his hand from holding of bribes,' as, for instance, R. Ishmael son of Jose; 'that stoppeth his ear from hearing of blood,' one who hears not aspersions made against a rabbinic student and remains silent, as once did R. Eleazar son of R. Simeon; 'and shutteth his eyes from looking upon evil,' as R. Hiyya b. Abba [taught]; for R. Hiyya b. Abba said: This refers to one who does not peer at women as they stand washing clothes [in the court-yard] and [concerning such a man] it is written, He shall dwell on high.

Micah came and reduced them to three [principles], as it is written, It hath been told thee, O man, what is good, and what the Lord doth require of thee: [i] only to do justly, and [ii] to love

105

mercy and [iii] to walk humbly before thy God. 'To do justly,' that is, maintaining justice; and 'to love mercy,' that is, rendering every kind office; 'and walking humbly before thy God,' that is, walking in funeral and bridal processions. And do not these facts warrant an a fortiori conclusion that if in matters that are not generally performed in private the Torah enjoins 'walking humbly,' is it not ever so much more requisite in matters that usually call for modesty? Again came Isaiah and reduced them to two [principles], as it is said, Thus saith the Lord, [i] Keep ye justice and [ii] do righteousness [etc.]. Amos came and reduced them to one [principle], as it is said, For thus saith the Lord unto the house of Israel, Seek ye Me and live. To this R. Nahman b. Isaac demurred, saying: [Might it not be taken as,] Seek Me by observing the whole Torah and live?—But it is Habakuk who came and based them all on one [principle], as it is said, But the righteous shall live by his faith.

Yes, the concluding comment is that the 613 commandments were reduced to one, as expressed in Habakkuk 2:4, "The just shall live by his faith" (KJV)—a favorite text of Paul (see Romans 1:17; Galatians 3:11). Of course, this is *not* to say that the Talmudic rabbis were Christians, but it is to say that when Paul boiled everything down to the just living by faith, he was in good company.

25

What are the seven laws of Noah?

Jewish tradition believes that God has fundamental, universal requirements for the entire human race and specific, detailed requirements for the Jewish people. This would be in keeping with the opening chapters of the book of Amos, where the surrounding nations are rebuked by the Lord for sins of man against man—such as covenant breaking and cruelty—but the people of Israel and Judah are rebuked for violating the Torah of the Lord (beginning in Amos 2:4).

Since Genesis 9:1–7 contains the Lord's instructions to Noah and his family after the flood, the rabbis found here seven fundamental laws for the human race. As stated in the Talmud: "Our Rabbis taught: seven precepts were the sons of Noah commanded: social laws [meaning, the establishing of government and courts of justice]; to refrain from blasphemy, idolatry, adultery, bloodshed, robbery, and eating flesh cut from a living animal" (b. Sanhedrin 56a. The discussion continues into 56b, with other rabbis presenting slightly modified lists; for other Talmudic references to these Seven Noachide Laws, see b. Avodah Zarah 2a).

As explained in a footnote to the Soncino Talmud:

These commandments may be regarded as the foundations of all human and moral progress. Judaism has both a national and a universal outlook in life. In the former sense it is particularistic, setting up a people distinct and separate from others by its peculiar religious law. But in the latter, it recognises that moral progress and its concomitant Divine love and approval are the privilege and obligation of all mankind. And hence the Talmud lays down the seven Noachian precepts, by the observance of which all mankind may attain spiritual perfection, and without which moral death must inevitably ensue. That perhaps is the idea underlying the assertion . . . that a heathen is liable to death for the neglect of any of these. The last mentioned is particularly instructive as showing the great importance attached to the humane treatment of animals; so much so, that it is declared to be fundamental to human righteousness.[88]

Now, if you take a moment and read the verses in Genesis 9, you might scratch your head and wonder how the ancient rabbis found seven commandments here, since the text seems only to prohibit murder and the eating of meat with blood. Well, the rabbis were experts in reading their traditions back into the Scriptures, often seeing multiple layers of meaning in the Torah text and believing that every divine command that was included in the Oral Law (see

#3)—with the rarest of exceptions—could be tied in to some verse or phrase or word or unusual spelling phenomenon in the biblical text. In fact, many Talmudic discussions are devoted to this very subject, namely, how to find support for traditional practices in the Scriptures. This makes for some ingenious arguments.

In any case, regardless of the origin of these commandments, it is clear that by New Testament times, there were God-fearing Gentiles who attended the synagogues and worshiped the God of Israel and were expected to live by these basic requirements, without converting to Judaism. The book of Acts mentions them on several occasions (see 8:27; 10:2, 22; 13:26, 50; 17:4, 17), and in a number of cities, the first Gentiles to hear and believe the Good News about Jesus the Messiah were these God-fearers: "Some of the Jews were persuaded and joined Paul and Silas, as did a large number of God-fearing Greeks and not a few prominent women" (Acts 17:4). This message was good news indeed, as Paul explained to the Ephesians that "through the gospel the Gentiles are heirs together with Israel, members together of one body, and sharers together in the promise in [Messiah] Jesus" (Ephesians 3:6). So, the Gentiles became spiritual equals to the Jews without having to become Jews (see #54).

This, however, was troubling to some of the Jewish believers, who insisted that full membership in God's household required circumcision and full submission to the Torah, teaching that "the Gentiles must be circumcised and required to obey the law of Moses" (Acts 15:5; Paul's letter to the Galatians had to confront this teaching head-on). To the contrary, Peter stated that "No! We believe it is through the grace of our Lord Jesus that we are saved, just as they are" (verse 11), and the final apostolic verdict was simply this: "We should not make it difficult for the Gentiles who are turning to God. Instead we should write to them, telling them to abstain from food polluted by idols, from sexual immorality, from the meat of strangled animals and from blood" (verses

19–20; see further, #48). These requirements appear to parallel closely some of the seven Noachide laws, but they may simply reflect practical realities: If we are to live together and work together as believing Jews and Gentiles, at least these fundamentals must be practiced.

This does, however, shed light on the letters to the Gentile congregations in the New Testament: Paul teaches these believers the most fundamental things, such as moral purity, relational purity, work ethics and family ethics, since he does not assume that they knew these things before. On the other hand, he does not tell them, "Submit yourselves to the Torah!" As Gentiles, they were not required to do so, and as believers in Jesus who had entered the reality of the age to come—just like their fellow Jewish believers—they stood in an entirely different relationship to the Torah (see #48).

Returning, however, to the question at hand, today there is a growing Noachide movement, sometimes called the *B'nei Noah* ("sons of Noah"). This movement consists of Gentiles who find Judaism beautiful and attractive but who choose not to convert to Judaism, and many of these Gentiles were former Christians who, for a number of reasons, including the mistaken belief that Trinitarian beliefs are idolatrous, have renounced their Christian faith.[89]

Yet there's more to the story. One of the leaders in this Noachide movement is Dr. Vendyl Jones, who has been searching for the Ark of the Covenant for decades, and who claimed to be the inspiration behind the Indiana Jones movie series. This claim, however, was denied by both Steven Spielberg and George Lucas.[90]

The only Jewish group actively involved in spreading the Seven Laws of Noah to the Gentile world—and in a fairly minor way at that—is the Hasidic sect called Lubavitch (see #2), the primary Jewish group active in missionary work to bring nonreligious Jews into traditional observance. This, then, is in keeping with their missionary emphasis, and just as they call Jews to follow the rabbinic traditions, they call on Gentiles to follow the so-called Seven Laws of Noah.

A number of books have been written about the Noachide movement in recent years. See Chaim Clorfene and Yaakov Rogalsky, *The Path of the Righteous Gentile: An Introduction to the Seven Laws of the Children of Noah* (New York: Philip Feldheim, 1987); Kimberly E. Hanke, *Turning to Torah: The Emerging Noachide Movement* (Northvale, NJ: Jason Aronson, 1995); Rabbi Yirmeyahu Bindman, *Seven Colors of the Rainbow* (New York: Philip Feldheim, 2000); Michael Ellias Dallen, *The Rainbow Covenant: Torah and the Seven Universal Laws* (Springdale, AR: Lightcatcher Books, 2003).[91]

Part 2

The Jewish People
and Jewish History

111

26

What is the origin of the term *Jew*, and can Jews today really trace their lineage back to the Jewish people of the Bible?

The English word *Jew* is derived from the Hebrew word *y'hudi* (*y'-hoo-dee*), which is derived from *y'hudah* (*y'-hoo-dah*), or Judah.

Judah was the name of the fourth son of Jacob (see Genesis 29:35), and subsequently his descendants were called the tribe of Judah. After that, Judah became the name of the southern kingdom (the northern kingdom was called Israel), before becoming the name of the province of Judah after the Babylonian exile. A native of the territory of Judah (or, later, the province of Judah) was called a Judean, which in Greek was transliterated *Ioudaios*, which came into Latin as *Iudaeus*, and ultimately into Middle English as *Iewe*, from which we get the word *Jew*.

This means that, technically speaking, Abraham was not a Jew (or, for that matter, an Israelite), Moses was not a Jew (although he was an Israelite), and famous biblical leaders from northern Israel like Elijah, Elisha, Amos and Hosea—to name just a few—were not Jews (although again, all of them were Israelites). Yet historically, since *Jew* became the name of the people as a whole, all of these figures are viewed as part of Jewish history, and for a

Jew, Abraham is "our father" (*avinu*) and Moses is "our teacher" (*rabbenu*).

Can all of today's Jews be traced back to the province of Judah? To a great extent, yes, but it is important to remember that: (1) even in the province of Judah, there were Israelites from the other tribes who had previously joined with the "Judeans"; (2) even the earlier, southern kingdom of Judah consisted primarily of the tribes of Judah, Benjamin and Levi; (3) there were Israelites who had been exiled in previous generations who ultimately integrated with other Judean exiles; and (4) throughout Jewish history, until this very day, Gentiles have converted to Judaism and have become fully integrated into the Jewish community. In fact, one of the most famous Talmudic leaders, Rabbi Akiva, was the son of a convert to Judaism. (For further discussion on Jewish origins, see #27.)

There is a myth that today's Jews (especially Ashkenazi Jews) are not really Jews but instead are descended from the Khazars, who converted en masse to Judaism more than one thousand years ago. There was even a Jewish author, Arthur Koestler, who advocated this view in his book *The Thirteenth Tribe*, and when he was found dead of an apparent suicide, there were claims that he had been killed by other Jews because of his views![1] But lack of evidence has never stopped wild theories from spreading, and as of January 2007, a Google search of "thirteenth tribe" yielded 41,000 hits—including anti-Semitic websites such as RadioIslam. org, which states:

> Khazar Jews. The revelation of another Jewish hoax. Finally Available To ALL—Absolute Historical Proof: Jews are not originate from Palestine! They are not "descendants" of the mythic Jews of the Bible! The information that the Zionists wants to put the lid on! The fact that over 90 percent of those today calling themselves "Jews," are actually descendants of the *Khazar* people, originating from *southern Russia*.[2]

113

Some years ago, I was confronted with a similar myth when I encountered a group of Black Hebrews on the streets of New York City. This cult, which is to be distinguished from Ethiopian Jews or blacks who have converted to Judaism, believes that the white man is the manifestation of Satan and that they, the black Hebrews, are the real Jews.

These men were preaching on a street corner in Manhattan with a loud sound system, wearing striking apparel, best described as a mix between biblical outfits and Star Trek costumes. After listening to them preach for a while—they quoted everything from the Bible to the Apocrypha and beyond—I asked, "If we are really not Jews, then why did Hitler try to wipe us out?"

The main speaker looked at me with scorn and then cited an alleged Hitler quote to the effect that Hitler also knew that we were not really Jews! The scene was absurd beyond words. He then proceeded to make reference to a Hebrew verb that spoke of the Jews being "darkened" or "blackened" according to the Scriptures (to his credit, he rightly pronounced the Hebrew and even knew the term *Tanakh*). Somehow, he overlooked the verse that said that Judah's princes were "brighter than snow and whiter than milk"—see Lamentations 4:7—and he failed to understand that the verb he cited, *qadar*, refers to being ashen, usually because of mourning and sadness. In any case, the ancient Judeans would have looked more like today's Middle Eastern peoples—that is to say, darker than most whites and lighter than most blacks.[3]

Interestingly, DNA studies of those claiming to be descendants of Aaron have indicated a common genetic history for many of them (they often have the last name "Cohen," which means "priest" in Hebrew), while DNA evidence for those tracing their ancestry more broadly to the tribe of Levi (often having Levi as their last name as well) is substantial but not nearly as strong.[4] Other Jews claim that they can trace their descent back to David, also citing genetic evidence.[5] (For the alleged connection between Native Americans and Israel, see #27.)

As for the meaning of the Hebrew word for Jew (*y'hudah*), some have cited Genesis 49:8, "Judah [*y'hudah*], your brothers will praise you [*yoduka*]," where the name Judah is connected to the verb *praise*. Based on this connection, it is often stated that *Jew* is derived from the root "to praise" (*y-d-h*), or, more directly, "Judah means someone who praises God." This, however, is somewhat exaggerated, and there is no reason to think that the Jewish people in biblical days thought of themselves as "praisers." Rather, Genesis 49:8 simply reflects a play on words, very common in the Hebrew Bible, and similar to saying, "His name is Frank because he is very frank," although the name Frank is unrelated to the adjective *frank*. It is possible that *y'hudah* does, in fact, come from the root *y-d-h*, "to confess" or "to praise," but again, that does not mean that this identification would be prominent in the minds of the people.

27

What are the Ten Lost Tribes of Israel?

The concept of the Ten Lost Tribes is partly mythical and partly truthful. It is partly mythical since, as Rabbi Joseph Telushkin writes, "We lack precise information on the Ten Tribe's fate," and therefore:

A large body of legends has grown up speculating on what became of them. As a rule, any nation that has acted sympathetically to the Jews (for example, England after it issued the Balfour Declaration), or practiced any ritual that corresponds to some ritual in the Torah (as do some American Indian tribes), has been rumored to be descended from the Ten Lost Tribes. . . . In the darkest period of the Middle Ages, when almost all Jews lived under Christian or Muslim oppression, tales spread of a mighty kingdom beyond the legendary Sabatyon, inhabited by the Ten Tribes, which would someday come and rescue its suffering brothers.[6]

This concept is partly truthful in that a large percentage of the inhabitants of the ten northern tribes of Israel went into exile and were scattered among the nations more than 2,700 years ago, and the identity of many of them has been completely lost. Let us retrace the relevant biblical accounts and then separate the myths from the reality.

Because of King David's sin with Bathsheba, the prophet Nathan declared to him, "The sword will never depart from your house" (2 Samuel 12:10). This, in a sense, was the beginning of the downfall of the united kingdom of Israel and Judah, and when King Solomon, David's son, fell into gross idolatry, the Lord declared to Jeroboam, "See, I am going to tear the kingdom out of Solomon's hand and give you ten tribes. But for the sake of my servant David and the city of Jerusalem, which I have chosen out of all the tribes of Israel, he will have one tribe" (1 Kings 11:31–32). After Solomon died, the kingdom did split, being divided between the ten northern tribes, called the kingdom of Israel, and the two southern tribes, Judah and Benjamin, called the kingdom of Judah. (The capital of Israel was Samaria; the capital of Judah was Jerusalem.)

In 721 B.C., the Assyrians decimated the ten northern tribes because of their sin, as described in 2 Kings 17:20, 23: "Therefore the Lord rejected all the people of Israel; he afflicted them and gave them into the hands of plunderers, until he thrust them from his presence. . . . So the people of Israel were taken from their homeland into exile in Assyria, and they are still there." (This verse was written more than 2,500 years ago, so "they are still there" referred to that period of time.)

What happened to the tribes of the kingdom of Israel? (1) Some of the people remained in Samaria and became known as the Samaritans. They consider themselves to be true Israelites, but other Jews, especially in ancient times, have considered them to be half breeds (see #28). (2) Some of the people may have made their way to Judah and became incorporated into the larger "Jewish" population (see especially 2 Chronicles 34:3–9, which indicates that a remnant of the ten northern tribes remained intact after the Assyrian exile). This is reflected in New Testament references that speak of "the twelve tribes of Israel" (see Acts 26:7; James 1:1), indicating that this was the conscious understanding of the Jews in New Testament times, namely that they represented the twelve tribes of Israel and not just Judah, Benjamin and Levi. Note also that the twelve tribes of Israel remain part of God's future plans (see Matthew 19:28; Luke 22:30). (3) Some of the people became completely assimilated into the nations, where they were scattered and have become lost to history (but not to myth!). (4) Some may have actually retained their Israelite-Jewish origins, retaining their ancient traditions and continuing to preserve a conscious identification as Israelites or Jews. Among these would possibly be groups such as the Ethiopian Jews.

Now, despite many myths and wild theories (including the "Two House Theory"; see #54), it appears that many Israelites who were scattered among the nations were, in fact, completely lost to history. It was part of God's judgment on the nation, and from everything we can tell, for these Israelites, it was final. There is simply no truth to the claims of groups such as the "British Israelites," who believe that "the Lost Ten Tribes of the Northern House of Israel's descendants are to be found in the Anglo-Saxon-Celtic and kindred peoples of today,"[7] nor is there any support for the Mormon claim that the Native Americans are descended from the ancient Israelites—despite the fact that no less a Semitic scholar than C. H. Gordon (1908–2001) pointed to possible links between the Israelites (or, more precisely, Judeans) and Native Americans, claiming that there was evidence for ancient Hebrew inscriptions in America.[8] DNA evidence (among other things) is against such an identification, and, not surprisingly, the recent book by former Mormon bishop Simon G. Southerton, a molecular geneticist from Australia, entitled *Losing a Lost Tribe: Native Americans, DNA, and the Mormon Church*,[9] has generated a fierce backlash from Mormon apologists, so damning are its conclusions to Mormonism.[10]

On the other hand, there are different groups around the world that have retained biblical Jewish commands such as circumcision and Sabbath observance—but not later, rabbinic traditions—and who trace their ancestry to the biblical tribes of Israel. While there is some dispute as to the authenticity of their claims—e.g., some traditions claim that the Ethiopian Jews are descendants of the biblical tribe of Dan while other traditions claim that they are the descendants of the alleged union of Solomon and the queen of Sheba—the State of Israel today embraces these different groups, either as people who converted to Judaism at different times in history and now need to get fully integrated, or as legitimate descendants of the ancient tribes of Israel.

Related to this was a report on World Net Daily, November 23, 2006: "'Lost tribe of Israel' returns home. Group from India 'descended from Joseph' arrives in Jewish state."[11] One of the main organizations involved with helping groups such as this return to Israel is called Shavei Israel (Shavei.org; the name means "those who return to Israel"; the organization was originally called Amishav). The website states, "Comprised of a team of academics, educators and rabbinical figures, Shavei Israel reaches out to 'lost Jews' and assists them in coming to terms with their heritage and identity in a spirit of tolerance and understanding."[12] This is a serious endeavor!

The head of Shavei Israel, Michael Freund, said, "I truly believe this is a miracle of immense historical and even biblical significance. Just as the prophets foretold so long ago, the lost tribes of Israel are being brought back from the exile."[13]

All told, there are about eight thousand such Indian Jews, called the Bnei Menashe, based on their belief that they have descended from the tribe of Manasseh (*Menashe* in Hebrew), and the great majority of them are still in India. But are they really true Israelites? There has obviously been some degree of intermarriage (the same can be said about Ethiopian Jews and other groups), but that can be said for other Jews (and Israelites) throughout history, albeit not on such a large scale.

Interestingly, there are ultra-Orthodox rabbis in Israel who have strongly disputed the claims of these different groups, one reason being that these groups are familiar with certain biblical commandments but have no knowledge of the traditions of the Oral Law. Yet according to rabbinic Judaism, God gave Moses both the Written and Oral Laws, and if groups such as the Bnei Menashe were truly Jewish, they would have known the traditions of the Oral Law (see #3). Others, however, point to groups such as this as proof positive that no Oral Law was given to Moses and that the traditions of the rabbis postdated the biblical period. (I concur with the latter position, namely, that God did not give Moses an authoritative Oral Law, but I do not have an expert opinion on the "original Israelite" claims of these various groups.)

All this being said, the general consensus of the Israeli population is that these groups should be warmly welcomed back into their midst, and they support government operations such as the famous Operation Solomon, which brought thousands of Ethiopian Jews back to the land in 1991 in an extraordinary, well-planned effort in the midst of very unstable conditions in Ethiopia. Moreover, when the traditional rabbis insisted that these Ethiopian Jews had to undergo certain elements of Jewish conversion, the public sentiment was with the Ethiopians and against the traditional rabbis (although such antitraditional sentiments are typical in Israel today). Similar requirements were made of the Bnei Menashe, namely, that they also formally converted to Judaism. Their history is quite touching:

> According to Bnei Menashe oral tradition, the tribe was exiled from Israel and pushed to the east, eventually settling in the border regions of China and India, where most remain today. Most kept customs similar to Jewish tradition, including observing Shabbat, keeping the laws of Kosher, practicing circumcision on the eighth day of a baby boy's life and observing Talmudic family purity.
>
> In the 1950s, several thousand Bnei Menashe say they set out on foot to Israel but were quickly halted by Indian authorities. Undeterred, many began practicing Orthodox Judaism and pledged to make it to Israel. They now attend community centers established by Shavei Israel to teach the Bnei Menashe Jewish tradition and modern Hebrew.
>
> Arbi Khiangte, one of the Bnei Menashe who arrived here Tuesday, said, "The Holy One, Blessed be He, commanded us to live there. It is a mitzva (positive good deed), and it is one that my ancestors have been waiting for so long to fulfill."[14]

Are there other Israelite groups yet to be discovered? Only God knows.[15]

28
Are the Samaritans really Jews?

It is a misnomer to refer to the Samaritans as Jews, since the Samaritans understand themselves to be direct descendants of the northern kingdom of Israel—which had as its capital the city of Samaria—rather than descendants of the southern kingdom of Judah, from which most Jews trace their origin (see #26). So, at best, the Samaritans, who live primarily in communities near Mount Gerizim and in Holon (near Tel Aviv), numbering less than seven hundred today (even that number is due to increased intermarriage in recent years), should be considered Israelites rather than Jews.

But are they truly Israelites? The Samaritans see themselves as the true remnant of Israel, the faithful keepers of the Torah, still practicing animal sacrifices and circumcision, still celebrating the biblical holy days, but rejecting the later traditions of the Jewish rabbis. They follow only the Torah and their religious traditions, not recognizing the authority of the rest of the Scriptures, and they continue to worship on Mount Gerizim. The spiritual leader of the people is the Samaritan high priest.[16]

According to their official website, *"The Samaritans are the descendants of the ancient northern kingdom of Israel. This remnant [sic] are the heirs of the Ten Lost Tribes that still bear the flag of the ancient sanctuaries of Israel."*[17] They also claim that as of the fourth century A.D., they numbered one million people, but through persecution and opposition, their numbers had dwindled to about 150 by the turn of the twentieth century.[18]

The Samaritans have their own unique form of the Hebrew script (different from the style that was adopted by the Jewish communities after the Babylonian exile), their own Hebrew liturgical traditions (including a unique pronunciation of ancient Hebrew) and their own distinct manuscripts of the Torah, which vary slightly from the Masoretic textual tradition (see #6).

Why, then, is their legitimacy as true Israelites questioned? And why did the Talmudic rabbis view them at best as converts? Let us look at the account in 2 Kings 17, describing what happened when the northern kingdom of Israel was decimated by the Assyrians because of Israelite idolatry:

> So the people of Israel were taken from their homeland into exile in Assyria, and they are still there.
>
> The king of Assyria brought people from Babylon, Cuthah, Avva, Hamath and Sepharvaim and settled them in the towns of Samaria to replace the Israelites. They took over Samaria and lived in its towns. When they first lived there, they did not worship the LORD; so he sent lions among them and they killed some of the

people. It was reported to the king of Assyria: "The people you deported and resettled in the towns of Samaria do not know what the god of that country requires. He has sent lions among them, which are killing them off, because the people do not know what he requires."

Then the king of Assyria gave this order: "Have one of the priests you took captive from Samaria go back to live there and teach the people what the god of the land requires." So one of the priests who had been exiled from Samaria came to live in Bethel and taught them how to worship the LORD.

verses 23–28

If this text, which is not recognized as sacred by the Samaritans, describes their origins, then they are simply very ancient converts to the Israelite faith, but they are not part of the original ten tribes of the northern kingdom (see #27; for mass conversions, see Esther 8:17). Even in this light, however, some Talmudic rabbis questioned the legitimacy of the conversion of the Samaritans—assuming again that this text describes their origins—since, it was claimed, their conversion came about under coercion (lions!) rather than out of love for the truth. And despite the fact that there are some Talmudic traditions that praise the Torah observance of the Samaritans (called *Kuthim*) and are accepting toward them, for the most part, they were considered to be second-class citizens or, worse still, half breeds.[19] Over the centuries, the fact that the Samaritans did not accept many of the rabbinic traditions was an affront to the rabbinic community, since the rabbis claimed to have traditions that went straight back to Moses on Mount Sinai (see #3), yet the Samaritans claimed a more ancient pedigree than the rabbis and did not confirm the concept of an Oral Law going back to Moses.

Jewish animosity toward the Samaritans is reflected in the comment made in John 4:9, namely, that "Jews do not associate with Samaritans." John's gospel also reflects the controversy over sacred locations of worship: Is it Jerusalem, as the Jews say, or is it Gerizim, as the Samaritans say? New Testament commentator Merrill C. Tenney explains:

> The Samaritans founded their claim on the historic fact that when Moses instructed the people concerning the entrance into the Promised Land, he commanded that they set up an altar on Mount Ebal and that the tribes should be divided, half on Ebal and half on Gerizim. As the Levites read the Law, the people responded antiphonally. Those on Gerizim pronounced the blessings of God and those on Ebal, the curses of God on sin (Deuteronomy 27:1–28:68). The Jews held that since Solomon had been commissioned to build the temple in Jerusalem, the center of worship would be located there.[20]

To this day, Mount Gerizim is considered sacred by the Samaritans, and they claim that Jewish Torah scrolls have been edited so as to downplay the importance of Gerizim and put undue emphasis on Jerusalem.

Are the Samaritans, then, true Israelites, a living remnant of the Ten Lost Tribes? Or are they ancient converts, dating back more than 2,700 years? Either way, they should be recognized as people who believe in the God of Israel and whose traditions are indeed quite ancient, people who have been preserved, perhaps miraculously, through the centuries. Interestingly, Yeshua Himself seemed to place the Samaritans in their own unique class, speaking of the Gentiles, the Samaritans and the house of Israel in Matthew 10:5–6, an understanding that seems to be reflected in Acts as well (note 8:4–18).

29
Who are the Karaites?

The Karaites are Jews who accept the authority of the Hebrew Bible but reject the authority of the rabbinic traditions. (The

Karaites are not believers in Jesus and so have that in common with rabbinic Jews.) Their name is derived from the Hebrew root *k-r-'* (or *q-r-'*), "to read," related most directly to the noun *mikra'* (or *miqra'*), "Scripture." Thus, the Karaites see themselves as the ultimate "people of the Book." What are the origins of this Jewish group, a group that numbers less than fifteen thousand people today?

An official Karaite website boldly states:

> Karaism is the original Judaism which has existed throughout history under various names including Righteous, Sadducees, Boethusians, Ananites and Karaites, all of whom obeyed the Torah with no additions.[21]

What exactly does this mean? Their website spells things out in greater detail:

> Karaism has been around since God gave his laws to the Jewish people. At first those who followed YHWH's laws were merely called "Righteous" and it was only in the 9th century CE that they came to be called Karaites. The question of why God's followers are today called Karaites is really a question of the origin of the other sects. At first there was no reason to label the righteous as a separate sect because there was only the one sect which consisted of the whole Jewish people. Throughout history a variety of sects appeared and it was only to distinguish the righteous from these other groups which caused them in different periods to take on such names as Sadducees, Boethusians, Ananites, and Karaites.[22]

So then, just as traditional Jews today claim to be the true bearers of the Torah, the Karaites make a similar boast. They argue that: (1) in Old Testament times, those called "righteous" were identical to those later called Karaites, since the righteous in biblical times adhered to the written Torah without the rabbinic traditions, just as the Karaites do; (2) once Pharisaic Judaism began to develop more than two thousand years ago, the Pharisees ostracized other groups like the Sadducees and Boethusians (a sect apparently closely related to the Sadducees), since these groups rejected the Pharisaic traditions. According to the Karaites, it was groups like the Sadducees and Boethusians that were authentic and true to the Torah, while it was the Pharisees, whose traditions developed into rabbinic Judaism, who were the inauthentic ones; (3) beginning in the eighth or ninth century A.D., the true followers of Torah were identified as Ananites (i.e., followers of Anan ben David; for more on him, see immediately below) and then as Karaites, the latter name sticking to this day. Thus the Karaites trace themselves back 3,500 years to Moses and the Torah.

Is there any truth to this claim? On the one hand, it is similar to the Islamic claim that all past true worshipers—including Abraham, Moses and Jesus—were actually Muslims. That is to say, the Karaites are projecting their own beliefs back onto the Bible, just as Muslims do (with the very marked distinction that the Quran rewrites and distorts the Tanakh and New Testament whereas the Karaites hold tenaciously to the veracity of the Tanakh). On the other hand, the Karaites are correct in rejecting the antiquity of Pharisaic Judaism, meaning, they are correct in stating that the rabbinic traditions do not go back to Moses in an authoritative, unbroken chain.

From a historical standpoint, however, the Karaites are wrong in claiming that there has been an unbroken chain of Karaite Jews. Rather, rabbinic Judaism largely held the day among the Jewish people for a number of centuries, with relatively few dissenting voices, until it was challenged by Anan ben David and others beginning in the eighth to ninth centuries A.D. Anan proclaimed himself the exilarch of Babylonian Jewry—this was a leading, governing position—and led other antirabbinic Jews into a different expression of Judaism, one that was subsequently developed into Karaism by more practically minded, yet antirabbinic Jews. (According to the *Jewish Encyclopedia*, Anan's legislation "was better fitted for the world-renouncing recluse than for the free citizen of the world."[23])

This growing antirabbinic movement—specifically, in its initial Ananite phase—was the subject of strong polemical attacks by Rabbi Saadiah Gaon, the leading tenth-century voice in Babylon (A.D. 892–942), and his writings helped turn the tide against the antirabbinic Jews. The Karaite attack on rabbinic Judaism was fierce as well, as reflected in a famous antirabbinic polemic by the tenth-century Karaite leader Salmon ben Yeruham, part of which contrasted the spirit of the Mishnah (see #3) with the spirit of the Bible:

> I have discovered in my heart another argument,
>   A handsome one, and majestic enough
> To be placed as a crown for the Karaites,
>   To be their ornament, pride, and glory.
>
> I have looked again into the six divisions of the Mishnah,
>   And behold, they represent the words of modern men.
> There are no majestic signs and miracles in them,
>   And they lack the formula: "And the Lord spoke unto
>   Moses and unto Aaron."
>
> I therefore put them aside, and I said, There is no true
> Law in them,
>   For the Law is set forth in a different manner,
> In a majestic display of prophets, of signs, and of miracles;
>   Yet all this majestic beauty we do not see in the whole
>   Mishnah.[24]

So then, according to the Karaites, the rabbinic writings were the words of men, in sharp contrast with the Scriptures, which were the Word of God.

Some scholars have estimated that, at its heyday, roughly one thousand years ago, Karaite Jews made up as much as 10 percent of the world's Jewish population, presenting a real threat to rabbinic Judaism, which had limited or no authority over them in some of the Muslim lands in which both Karaite Jews and rabbinic Jews lived. During this golden age of Karaism, a number of fine commentaries were written on parts of the Tanakh—indeed, the greatest of the Karaites were excellent Hebrew scholars and thoroughly immersed in the biblical text—but only a tiny portion of these writings has been preserved. Other important legal material was developed by the Karaite authors, although, again, almost none of it has been preserved. Ironically, a book entitled *Hizzuk Emunah* (meaning "Faith Strengthened"), which religious Jews often cite as the most effective, anti-Christian work ever written, was penned by a sixteenth-century Karaite, Isaac Troki! Subsequent editions of this book incorporate quotes from the Talmud and other rabbinic sources—sources that Troki himself would have repudiated—making it appear more "orthodox." So, a major polemical work used by rabbinic Jews for centuries was actually written by a Karaite.

On the flip side, it is ironic that the Karaites developed traditions and law codes of their own, some of which were in harmony with rabbinic traditions, which would seem to support the rabbinic claim that, without their oral traditions, it is impossible to observe the Torah (see #3). The Karaites, however, claimed that their traditions were subject to the Scriptures and were derived by proper scriptural interpretation.[25]

In any case, over the course of the centuries, Karaite numbers dwindled dramatically, squeezed out by the overwhelming numbers of rabbinic Judaism, and thus a popular online entry states: "At one time Karaites were a significant portion of the Jewish population. However today there are left an estimated 2,000 Karaites in the USA, about 100 families in Istanbul, and about 12,000 in Israel, most of them living near the town of Ramleh."[26]

Earlier in this book, we explained why traditional Jewish men wear white fringes on their clothes, why they put black boxes, called phylacteries or *tefillin*, on their heads and left arms when they pray and why they wear side curls (see #18, #19 and #20). In contrast, Karaite Jews wear blue fringes, do not use phylacteries and do not wear side curls. The Karaite explanations for their practices, in contrast with rabbinic Judaism, provide excellent example of contemporary Karaite biblical interpretation. For the question of the fringes, see http://www.karaite-korner.org/tzitzit.shtml; for the question of phylacteries, see http://www.karaite-korner.org/tefillin.shtml; for the question of shaving and wearing side curls, see http://www.karaite-korner.org/shaving.shtml.

30
Why have Jewish people been so hated and persecuted through the centuries?

I devoted much of my book *Our Hands Are Stained with Blood* to the subject of anti-Semitism, and on several occasions I have delivered lectures on the question of *why* anti-Semitism exists. Out of all the hatreds in the world, anti-Semitism is unique.

At the invitation of Christian campus groups, I spoke on this topic at both Yale and Columbia universities, two of America's most prestigious centers of learning, each time fielding questions from the listeners for better than an hour. My challenge was simple: "I have a supernatural, biblical explanation for the phenomenon of anti-Semitism, one which even includes the devil himself"—not the most popular theory on a university campus! "Do any of you have a better answer?"

After each lecture, I listened carefully to proposal after proposal, and despite the educational background of many of those in the audience, which included students and graduates of these universities, not one proposal could fully explain the "why" of anti-Semitism. In fact, the best theory that anyone offered was that, perhaps, anti-Semitism was due to aliens! (For more on "alien anti-Semitism," stay tuned. I'm actually going to address that shortly.) What then makes anti-Semitism such a unique hatred?

First, it is *the longest hatred* of all time, dating back at least 2,300 years (and even longer if the book of Esther is included). As expressed by the Catholic scholar Edward Flannery, "Antisemitism is the longest and deepest hatred of human history. . . . What other hatred has endured some twenty-three centuries and survived a genocide of 6,000,000 of its victims in its twenty-third century of existence only to find itself still intact and rich in potential for many years of life?"[27] Today, anti-Semitism is at its highest levels since immediately before the Holocaust, equaling, in fact, those pre-Holocaust levels. How can this be?

These words, penned 25 centuries ago, still ring true in the hearts of many anti-Semites today: "There is a certain people dispersed and scattered among the peoples . . . whose customs are different from those of all other people and who do not obey [international] laws; it is not in [our] best interest to tolerate them" (Esther 3:8, with slight modifications made to make this more contemporary). Why has this hatred and fear of the Jews persisted for so long?

Consider this attack on the Jewish people made in Ezra's day, also roughly 2,500 years ago:

> The king should know that the Jews who came up to us from you have gone to Jerusalem and are rebuilding that rebellious and wicked city. They are restoring the walls and repairing the founda- tions. Furthermore, the king should know that if this city is built and its walls are restored, no more taxes, tribute or duty will be paid, and the royal revenues will suffer. Now since we are under obligation to the palace and it is not proper for us to see the king dishonored, we are sending this message to inform the king, so that a search may be made in the archives of your predecessors.

In these records you will find that this city is a rebellious city, troublesome to kings and provinces, a place of rebellion from ancient times. That is why this city was destroyed.

Ezra 4:12–15

To this day, Jerusalem remains the center of international controversy, the only capital city not recognized by the rest of the nations. Why Jerusalem? Why the Jews?

Second, anti-Semitism is *the most widespread hatred* of all time. It can be traced from the Greco-Roman world to Christianity (yes, Christianity, including vicious comments from some of the Church's greatest leaders);[28] from Islam to Fascism to Communism (intense anti-Semitism links Muslim terrorists, Adolf Hitler and Joseph Stalin!); from White Supremacists to Black Supremacists (yes, *both* groups bash the Jews); from university campuses to the world press; from the philosopher Voltaire to the historian Arnold Toynbee; from the composer Richard Wagner to the car designer Henry Ford; from Japan to Russia to Iran. Why the Jews?

A few years ago, a very bizarre group made a big media splash when they claimed to have produced the world's first human clone. The group, called the Raelians, is a UFO religion, led by its founder Rael, who claims to have been enlightened by aliens. (This is the literal claim: "On the 13th of December 1973, French journalist Rael was contacted by a visitor from another planet, and asked to establish an Embassy to welcome these people back to Earth.")[29] After hearing the cloning report, which was universally dismissed by scientists as a cheap publicity stunt, I went to the Raelian website, purely out of curiosity. (As of this writing, the site was available in more than 25 languages.)[30] To my utter amazement, the featured message from Rael was laced with anti-Jewish sentiments, including the charge that "Israel is engaged in State terrorism" and the claim that "a small handful of the millions of American Jews are holding the rest of the 250 million Americans

130

hostage."[31] Even the Raelians were polluted by an anti-Semitic stream! Why this widespread hatred of the Jews?

Third, anti-Semitism is *the most vicious hatred* of all time, and both the incredible violence and the depth of animosity against the Jews defy rational explanation. The enormity and depravity of the Holocaust alone is testimony to the viciousness of this hatred, and yet the Holocaust is simply the worst of countless acts of Jew hatred over the centuries. This horrific crime included several nations and led to the cooperative and systematic execution of 6 million Jews, including 1.5 million babies and children. So depraved were the Nazis (and other Jew killers) that Jewish infants were sometimes thrown into burning pits alive in order to save a bullet, leading to the oft-quoted dictum of Rabbi Irving Greenberg: "Moreover, summon up the principle that no statement should be made [about the Holocaust] that could not be made in the presence of the burning children."[32] Nothing more needs to be said.

Fourth, anti-Semitism is *the most irrational hatred* of all time. The absurdity of the anti-Semitic libels simply defies rational explanation. When the Black Plague decimated Europe, Jews were accused of starting the plague by poisoning the wells with a mixture made of spiders, lizards and the hearts of Christians mixed together with the sacred elements of the Lord's Supper. Outraged mobs slaughtered thousands of Jews as a result of this pernicious rumor. When the Catholic Church declared in 1215 that the elements of Communion literally became the body and blood of Jesus, Jews were accused of stealing and torturing Communion wafers, leading to whole Jewish communities being burned at the stake. In the Muslim world today, it is still believed that every year, Jews kidnap and torture a priest (or other victim), using his blood to make Passover matzah (unleavened bread). The Muslim world also takes seriously the Protocols of the Elders of Zion, a notorious forged document from the nineteenth century that claims to report the secret plans of a hidden group of Jewish leaders who are poised to take over the entire world—ultimately bringing it into subjection to the Hindu god Vishnu! (To quote from the Protocols: "Our kingdom will be an apologia of the divinity Vishnu, in whom is found its personification.") Jews have also been blamed for the spreading of AIDS as well as for orchestrating the terrorist attacks of September 11, 2001. (Several Muslim cabdrivers in New York City explained this to me with real conviction, not realizing that I was a Jew.) Jews have even been accused of controlling the Catholic Church!

Article Seventeen of the Hamas Charter states: "Zionist organizations under various names and shapes, such as Freemasons, Rotary Clubs, espionage groups and others are all nothing more than cells of subversion and saboteurs. These organizations have ample resources that enable them to play their role in societies for the purpose of achieving the Zionist targets and to deepen the concepts that would serve the enemy."[33] Even the Masons are controlled by the Jews!

So irrational are the lies told about the Jews that even an utter rationalist like Sigmund Freud had to say, "With regard to anti-Semitism, I don't really want to search for explanations; I feel a strong inclination to surrender my affects in this matter and find myself confirmed in my wholly nonscientific belief that mankind on the average and taken by and large are a wretched lot."[34]

What, then, are some of the explanations offered to explain the phenomenon of anti-Semitism?

1. "It all traces back to Christianity," meaning that the charge that the Jews killed Jesus (see #45), thus making them guilty of deicide (killing God), has so permeated Western history and culture that "Christian" anti-Semitism provides a link between all manifestations of anti-Semitism. But this theory is seriously flawed. How do we explain *pre-Christian* anti-Semitism? And does Christian anti-Semitism

adequately explain Islamic anti-Semitism? And what of Christian philo-Semitism, a direct result of the testimony of the very New Testament that allegedly produced worldwide anti-Semitism?

2. "It is because there always has to be a scapegoat," meaning that someone always has to be blamed for bad things that happen in the world. But this begs the question rather than answers it. Why are *the Jews* always being blamed? As George Orwell remarked, "However true the 'scapegoat' theory may be in general terms, it does not explain why the Jews rather than some other minority group are picked on, nor does it make clear what they are a scapegoat for."[35]

3. "It is because of the Jewish religion, which makes the Jewish people different," and so people attack what they don't understand. The problem with this view is that secular Jews have often been singled out for persecution. In keeping with this, it has often been said that at the time of the Holocaust, most German Jews were more German than Jewish. Not only so, but the Nazis slaughtered Jews who were even "one-quarter" Jewish—meaning only one grandparent was Jewish—also murdering Jews who had converted to Christianity. There is also worldwide animosity toward the modern State of Israel, despite the fact that the nation is far more secular than it is religious. And why haven't Muslims been universally hated for being different?

4. "It is because the Jewish people are especially bad" (this was actually stated to me by a Pakistani cabdriver with whom I discussed the question of anti-Semitism)—but this theory hardly needs refutation, since Jews are often some of the most moral and ethical people in the world, and, to be sure, there are plenty of rotten Gentiles! So, to put it mildly, Jews certainly don't have a monopoly on being bad.

5. "It is because the Jews always have all the money"—which, in fact, is not a theory but rather another anti-Semitic libel. In any case, through the centuries, Jews have often been the poorest people in their societies, often because of oppressive laws passed against them. But they were hated and persecuted nonetheless.

6. "It is because of Jewish guilt, leading to divine judgment"—a harsh-sounding charge, but with some truth to it, since the Torah clearly states that national obedience would be blessed while national disobedience would be cursed (see Leviticus 26; Deuteronomy 28). But the hatred has been too intense, too vile, too destructive to be explained by this alone, and even within the Tanakh itself, God often expressed His displeasure with the nations whom He used to judge His people, stating clearly that they had gone too far (see Isaiah 10:5–19; more broadly, see Zechariah 1:14–15).

Clearly, all of these theories fall short in one way or another, failing to explain the intense, irrational and long-lived nature of anti-Semitism and failing to connect all the dots. What, then, is the explanation for anti-Semitism in the world? It is simply this: God has singled out the Jewish people as His instrument for world redemption, He has promised that they will always remain on the earth as a distinct people—despite their sins and failures—and the devil himself has marked them out for destruction. Ultimately, it is through the Jewish people that the knowledge of the one true God has come to the world, through the Jewish people that the Messiah has come, and through the Jewish people that the message of the Messiah went to the nations. And it is the Jewish people in Jerusalem who will ultimately welcome the Messiah back to earth to set up His Kingdom (see Matthew 23:37–39). That's why the devil hates them so!

As I wrote in *Our Hands Are Stained with Blood*:

Why does Satan so passionately despise the Jews? For one thing, it is a reflection of his hatred for God. The Jews are God's chosen people! By hurting them he seeks to hurt the Lord and take revenge for his own sentence of death. His effort to annihilate the Jews is also an attempt to discredit the Lord, since He has sworn in His Word that they will never be destroyed. If Israel ceases to exist as a distinct people, then God did not, or could not, keep His promise. That would mean that He was either powerless or that He lied!

But there is another reason the devil despises the Jews: The salvation of Israel means the return of Jesus, the resurrection of the righteous, the revival of the Church and the restoration of the earth. The fulfillment of the Jews' destiny will seal the devil's doom. Yes, "the God of peace will soon crush Satan under your feet" (Rom. 16:20) . . . and he is beginning to squirm! The time to favor Israel is upon us and Satan is quaking with fear. The countdown has begun.[36]

Understanding, then, that anti-Semitism is ultimately a spiritual phenomenon rather than a cultural, ethnic or even religious phenomenon, we can also understand that anti-Semitism has to do with *God* and His purposes rather than with the *Jewish people* themselves. That is to say, it is not because the Jews are better or worse than anyone else; it is because God chose the descendants of Abraham, Isaac and Jacob to bring redemption to the world, the Messiah Himself being a Jew. In that light, it will be a bad day for anti-Semites when they realize that the all-powerful King coming in flaming fire is a glorified Jew.[37]

31
Do contemporary Jews want to rebuild the Temple?

Jewish sentiments about the rebuilding of the Temple can be divided into three categories: (1) those who don't think about the question at all (representing the vast majority of contemporary Jews); (2) those who pray for it daily and long for its rebuilding in the Messianic age (representing the vast majority of religious Jews); and (3) those who are actively working toward its rebuilding (representing a very small but increasingly well-known group). Among those who are praying and longing for the rebuilding of the Temple are religious Jews who militantly oppose both the modern State of Israel and, even more so, the rebuilding of the Temple by anyone other than the Messiah. We'll talk about this last group in a moment.

Since 90 percent of Jews worldwide today are not Orthodox, it is not surprising that the rebuilding of the Temple is not a major issue to most of them. Why would it be? They are not particularly religious people—in other words, their Judaism is roughly equivalent to the faith commitment of a nominal Christian—and whatever sense of solidarity they feel with the nation of Israel is unrelated to the concept of a Temple. They may believe in the importance of having a Jewish homeland and they may even find it to be a moving experience to go to Israel and pray at the Wailing Wall, but that is a far cry from thinking about a rebuilt Temple in Jerusalem. That's almost like going back to Bible days again! Or to put this another way, since most Jews worldwide are thinking more about this world than about the Messianic era and the world to come, why would they be thinking about rebuilding an ancient Temple that we haven't had for almost two thousand years? Reform Jews (see #1) don't even pray for the rebuilding of the Temple in their prayer books, and they make up better than one-third of America's Jews.

In contrast with this, traditional Jews pray three times a day for the rebuilding of the Temple, and some pious Jews through the centuries have risen from bed at midnight to mourn over the destruction of the second Temple in A.D. 70. Restoration of the Temple is part and parcel of a larger act of divine restoration and favor for God's people.

The central prayer in the daily prayer service is called the *Amidah* (literally, "standing," because Jews must recite this prayer while standing), repeated three times a day. It is also called the *Shemoneh Esreh*, which means "eighteen," because there were originally eighteen major petitions and benedictions in this prayer (the final number came to nineteen). A number of these relate to the coming of the Messiah, the redemption of the people of Israel and the rebuilding of the Temple, all closely related concepts.[38]

All this, however, is a matter for prayer rather than human effort, other than the effort of religious Jews to observe the Torah and thereby hope to hasten the redemption. The idea of actually trying to rebuild the Temple, however, is quite foreign to religious Jewish thinking, just as the idea of Christians trying to set up the Messiah's throne in Jerusalem would be totally foreign to traditional Christian thinking.

There is a very small minority of ultra-Orthodox Jews, called *Neturei Karta* (Aramaic for "keepers of the city"), who not only oppose the idea of anyone other than the Messiah rebuilding the Temple, but who virulently oppose even the existence of the State of Israel today. Since they believe that only the Messiah can regather the exiles and reestablish the nation of Israel, in their eyes, the very existence of modern Israel actually stands in the way of redemption (in contrast, the great majority of religious Jews see modern Israel as a sign of the beginning of redemption). Not only so, but Neturei Karta Jews believe that modern Israel is not only the product of human effort, but it is the product of *atheistic*, *sinful* human effort, also provoking worldwide hatred of the Jewish people.[39]

Some of these ultra-Orthodox Jews actually live in Israel, while others live in America and Europe. They represent a tiny minority of the Jewish people and are despised by the larger Jewish population. Adding to their infamy was their participation in Iran's December 2006, Holocaust denial conference, praising the radical

Muslim government of Iran and saying that they felt at home there.[40] Even ultra-Orthodox Jewish sects like the Satmar Hasidim, who themselves oppose the modern State of Israel (see #2), roundly condemned the actions of these Neturei Karta leaders.

In total contrast with this stands the Temple Mount Faithful, led by Gershon Salomon.[41] Their long-term objectives are: (1) liberating the Temple Mount from Arab (Islamic) occupation; (2) consecrating the Temple Mount to the Name of G-d so that it can become the moral and spiritual center of Israel, of the Jewish people and of the entire world; (3) rebuilding the third Temple; (4) providing a biblical point of assembly in order that all Israel may fulfill the commandment to assemble three times annually at the times of G-d's festivals and at the place where G-d established His name forever; (5) making biblical Jerusalem the real, undivided capital of the State of Israel; (6) rejecting false "peace talks" that will result in the dividing of Israel and the breaking of G-d's covenant; and (7) supporting the settlements in Jerusalem, Judea, Samaria and the Golan Heights as they are holy.[42]

So, these Jews, some of whom are religious, feel the responsibility to help speed redemption by taking concrete action, and in this they have the enthusiastic backing of some evangelical Christians.[43] In conjunction with this Temple Mount movement, some religious Jews of priestly or Levitical lineage are actually preparing for priestly service, studying the relevant texts, while replicas of the Temple items and priestly garments have been made, awaiting the rebuilding of the Temple. Parallel to this, although unrelated officially, is the search for the red heifer, since, according to Numbers 19, only the ashes of a red heifer can be used in purification rites, and without these ashes, the Jewish people have existed in a state of ritual impurity for more than 1,900 years. Reports of the birth of a baby red cow, without blemish, cause great excitement in some Jewish and Christian circles, but to date, none of the animals has ended up meeting the requirements.

So, will there be a third Temple before Messiah returns? Verses such as 2 Thessalonians 2:1–4 and Matthew 24:15–31 (with a still-future application) suggest this, but the subject remains a topic of lively debate among students of the Word.

32
Has there been a continuous presence of Jews in the land of Israel for the last two thousand years?

Rather than provide a dry, century-by-century survey filled with statistics that are readily obtained elsewhere,[44] it is best to answer this question concisely: With rare exception, there has been a continuous presence of Jews in the land of Israel for the last two thousand years. And when we speak of the nation as a whole, dating back to the time of Moses, there has been a virtually unbroken Jewish-Israelite presence in the land for almost 3,400 years, and this despite much suffering and forced dispersion through the centuries.[45] As noted in Mitchell Bard's excellent compendium *Myths and Facts: A Guide to the Israeli-Arab Conflict*,[46] now available online as well (see http://www.jewishvirtuallibrary.org/jsource/myths/mftoc.html):

> A common misperception is that all the Jews were forced into the Diaspora by the Romans after the destruction of the Second Temple in Jerusalem in the year 70 C.E. and then, 1,800 years later, suddenly returned to Palestine demanding their country back. In reality, the Jewish people have maintained ties to their historic homeland for more than 3,700 years. . . .
>
> Even after the destruction of the Second Temple in Jerusalem and the beginning of the exile, Jewish life in the Land of Israel continued and often flourished. Large communities were reestablished in Jerusalem and Tiberias by the 9th century. In the 11th century, Jewish communities grew in Rafah, Gaza, Ashkelon, Jaffa and Caesarea.

The Crusaders massacred many Jews during the 12th century, but the community rebounded in the next two centuries as large numbers of rabbis and Jewish pilgrims immigrated to Jerusalem and the Galilee. Prominent rabbis established communities in Safed, Jerusalem and elsewhere during the next 300 years. By the early 19th century—years before the birth of the modern Zionist movement—more than 10,000 Jews lived throughout what is today Israel. The 78 years of nation-building, beginning in 1870, culminated in the reestablishment of the Jewish State.[47]

Of course, during the last fifteen hundred years, Arabs and Turks and others have lived in Israel, which was dubbed Palestine by the Romans in the second century A.D. (see #34). But at no time was Palestine considered an independent Arab nation (see again #34), and throughout the millennia, only one group claimed this land as its ancestral homeland: the Jews! That is why Jews face Jerusalem when they pray, wherever they are in the world—in contrast with Muslims, who face Mecca, meaning that those living in parts of the Middle East pray with their *backs* to Jerusalem—and that is why the Jewish Passover Seder every year includes the words "Next year in Jerusalem!" That has been the hope and passion of religious Jews through the ages, and for that reason, there has been a virtually continuous presence of Jewish people in Israel despite the collapse of a national state for almost 1,900 years. Living in the post-Holocaust era, a national Jewish slogan has been "Never again!"—meaning, there can never be and will never be another Holocaust for our people—and it is understood that a national homeland is the only way to ensure this.

33
Should all Jews move back to Israel?

The basis for this question seems to be twofold. First, if Israel is the Jewish homeland and if exile is a negative state associated with divine judgment, then shouldn't all Jews go back to their homeland now that it has been reestablished? Second, if anti-Semitism is spreading and even nations like America could one day turn against their Jewish populations, just as European nations did during the Holocaust, isn't it wise for Jews to make the move back to Israel? Books like Tom Hess's *Let My People Go: The Struggle of the American Jew to Come Home to Israel,* first published in the 1980s, emphasized both of these points, predicting that things *will* get bad for Jews outside of Israel, including Jews in America. In fact, while some of Hess's warnings for American Jews have not yet materialized, some of his warnings about Jews in the former Soviet Union seemed quite relevant shortly after the Russian edition of his book was released, and they appear increasingly relevant in that part of the world today.

So then, do the Scriptures clearly call all Jews worldwide to return to the Land, and are there pragmatic reasons for all Jews to be in Israel?

For Jewish followers of Jesus, their responsibility is to study the Word of God, seek His face and live wherever the Lord calls them to live as part of their Great Commission and Kingdom responsibility—be it in America, Russia, Israel or anywhere else. There is simply nothing in the Scriptures that clearly states otherwise, especially if the individual has a sense of calling to be serving in a particular place. Where does the New Testament hint at anything other than this? And aren't Jewish believers called to be a light to the nations?

What about Jewish people who are not born again and, in that sense, are not in touch with their Kingdom destiny and calling? Does God want all of them back in Israel? Again, I do not see that the Scriptures address this clearly in terms of Jews living in the Diaspora today.

What, then, of the two questions asked at the outset of this section, namely, shouldn't Jews worldwide return from exile to

Israel? And, isn't it clear that the safest place for Jews worldwide is in Israel?

To me, the key to both of these questions is timing. It is true that the Word speaks of a complete return of all Jewish people to the land of Israel, a matter of unfinished divine business and unrealized prophetic promises dating back to the Babylonian exile. Through several prophetic voices, God promised a glorious regathering of His people, a regathering not just from Babylon, but from all the nations to which they had been scattered (see Jeremiah 16:14–15). To this day, those promises have not yet been fulfilled—including the promise in Isaiah 11 that the Lord would bring His people back to the Land a second time—the first time being after the Babylonian exile.

With that in mind, we can see a remaining application for verses such as this well-known passage from Isaiah:

> Do not be afraid, for I am with you;
>   I will bring your children from the east
>   and gather you from the west.
> I will say to the north, "Give them up!"
>   and to the south, "Do not hold them back."
> Bring my sons from afar
>   and my daughters from the ends of the earth—
> everyone who is called by my name,
>   whom I created for my glory,
>   whom I formed and made.
>
> 43:5–7

But note carefully: There is a big difference between "You will return," and "Return!"; between "I will bring you home," and "Go home!" The former speaks of something that will happen one day; the latter gives a command—and I do not believe that God is commanding all of the Jewish people to return to Israel today, although that day may yet come—perhaps even *after* the

Messiah's return, at which time verses such as Isaiah 11:16 could be *literally* fulfilled.

Do I believe that God is calling more and more of His ancient people back to Israel today, both believers and nonbelievers? Absolutely! And I believe this will only increase in the years to come. In fact, within a matter of decades, the Jewish population *within* Israel could be greater than the Jewish population *outside* of Israel. But this is something God is doing, and therefore we can encourage *aliyah* (returning to Israel) but we cannot legislate or mandate it.

Are there signs of anti-Semitism rising to dangerous levels worldwide? Without a doubt (see #30). And is it possible that, one day, it could be dangerous for Jews to live in America? It is certainly possible, although, thankfully, America does not have a history of national anti-Semitism. Should that day come, however, we have good reason to expect that God will send clear and definite warnings to His people, letting us know that now is the time to get back to the Land.

We do well to pray regularly for the Lord to fulfill His eternal purposes for His ancient, covenant people, since, in a very real sense, the destiny of the nations is intimately tied to their destiny (see Romans 11:11–15), especially as it pertains to the Jewish people living in Israel at the end of the age (see Zechariah 12–14).

34
Are the Palestinians descendants of the ancient Canaanites?

This is a politically charged question, but there is not a shred of truth to the claim that the Palestinian people are descendants of the ancient Canaanites, and if not for anti-Israel propaganda, it is hard to imagine that such a ridiculous claim would ever have been made.

To begin with, historically speaking, *there is no such thing as a Palestinian people*. It is true that there have been Arabs living in the land of Palestine for centuries (Israel was called Palestine by the Romans in the second century A.D.). And it is true that some of these families have lived in Palestine without interruption for many generations. But at no time before 1967 did these Arabs ever identify themselves as "Palestinians," nor did they seek to achieve any kind of statehood there. There was no Palestinian nationalism and no attempt to develop the territory as a homeland for these Arabs, and in 1936, when the Palestine Orchestra was formed, it was a *Jewish* orchestra! In the oft-quoted words of the late Arab historian and Princeton University professor Phillip K. Hitti, "There is no such thing as 'Palestine' in history."[48] (He was speaking in terms of Arabic, Palestinian history.)

In the early 1990s, I was invited to attend a fund-raising event for the Jerusalem Foundation that featured a discussion between former Secretary of State Henry Kissinger and John Hopkins University professor Fouad Ajami, a respected Lebanese scholar, mediated by Dan Rather. When the time for questions came, I asked Professor Ajami if there was such a thing as a Palestinian people. He answered quite candidly, saying that there was not. When I pressed him as to why the media does not tell us that, he said that the media never would.

Where, then, did this concept of the Palestinian people come from? There is no question that today there are several million people who identify themselves as Palestinians, and they are eager to have a homeland. There is also no question that these people have suffered great hardship in recent years and that some of their families lived in the land of Israel prior to 1948. Nonetheless, the *concept* of a Palestinian people is a recent invention, postdating the year 1967. As expressed by former terrorist Walid Shoebat, "Why is it that on June 4th 1967 I was a Jordanian and overnight I became a Palestinian?"[49] Moreover, the *reality* of a displaced Palestinian people is more of an internal Arab issue than a Jewish one.

Mitchell Bard explains:[50]

> Prior to partition, Palestinian Arabs did not view themselves as having a separate identity. When the First Congress of Muslim-Christian Associations met in Jerusalem in February 1919 to choose Palestinian representatives for the Paris Peace Conference, the following resolution was adopted:
>
> We consider Palestine as part of Arab Syria, as it has never been separated from it at any time. We are connected with it by national, religious, linguistic, natural, economic and geographical bonds.[51]
>
> In 1937, a local Arab leader, Auni Bey Abdul-Hadi, told the Peel Commission, which ultimately suggested the partition of Palestine: "There is no such country [as Palestine]! 'Palestine' is a term the Zionists invented! There is no Palestine in the Bible. Our country was for centuries part of Syria."[52]

Arieh L. Avneri pointed out that the estimated population of Muslims, Christians and Jews in Palestine grew from 205,000 in 1554 to just 275,000 in the year 1800. Where was the cry of "Palestine is our homeland" among the worldwide Arab population? It simply did not exist. At what point in time, then, did the Arab population in Palestine begin to rise dramatically? It was when Jews began to return to the land in larger numbers, especially after 1880, at which time the bulk of the more than 400,000 Arabs living in Palestine were themselves relatively recent immigrants.[53] Moving ahead to the mid-twentieth century, Michael Comay points out that in 1948, just before the British withdrawal from Palestine began, 9 percent of the land was owned by Jews, 3 percent by Arab national citizens living in the Land, "17 percent was abandoned Arab land and the remaining 71 percent was Crown or State Land vested in the Mandatory [British] Government and subsequently in the State of Israel."[54]

Note also that the population of the so-called West Bank (actually, Judea and Samaria) and Gaza was only 450,000 in 1967. Today it is approaching 3.5 million, and many of these Palestinians have moved into the region in the last forty years. Add to this the fact that from the late nineteenth century into the mid-twentieth century, a large percentage of Arabs living in Palestine were themselves recent émigrés who moved there when the Jews began to develop the land, which had been swamp-infested and largely neglected for centuries. In this context, Mark Twain's description of Palestine in his day has been quoted many times. It is, he writes, "a desolate country whose soil is rich enough, but is given over wholly to weeds—a silent mournful expanse. . . . A desolation is here that not even imagination can grace with the pomp of life and action. . . . We never saw a human being on the whole route. . . . There was hardly a tree or a shrub anywhere. Even the olive and the cactus, those fast friends of a worthless soil, had almost deserted the country."[55] It is a well-known fact that many Jewish settlers in the twentieth century died of malaria while draining the swamps and developing the land. So, the idea of a numerous and ancient Palestinian people living in the land for multiplied centuries is simply a myth.[56]

What about the 650,000 Arabs who were displaced from Palestine when the Jews were given their statehood?[57] In reality, Israel accepted the United Nations' proposed partitioning of the land into a Jewish and Arab state, but the Arab nations did not, declaring war. Still, the Israelis distributed literature to their Arab neighbors within Israel, telling them they were not their enemies and urging them to stay. They were told, however, by their Arab comrades that "a cannon cannot distinguish between a Jew and an Arab," meaning, they could be innocent casualties of the war at the hands of their own people, and they were urged to leave the Land until the war was over and the Jews were wiped out, at which time they could return to their homeland. But the Jews were not wiped out.

Why then didn't the surrounding Arab nations absorb these displaced peoples, just as Israel absorbed more than 800,000 Jews displaced from Arab lands during the war? In fact, the Jewish state, 640 times *smaller* than the Arab world and only one-fiftieth of its population, successfully absorbed most of its Jewish refugees. Why haven't the Arab nations absorbed the Palestinians?[58] Sadly, it is because their homelessness served as a weapon to be used against Israel, and it has proved a massively effective weapon in the decades since. To this day, displaced Palestinians have been expelled from other Arab nations—including Saudi Arabia and Kuwait after the 1991 Gulf War and, as of January 2007, Jordan and Syria have refused to take in 735 Arabs displaced by the war in Iraq and now living in refugee camps—because they have Palestinian pedigree.[59]

One more element needs to be factored in. In the words of King Hussein of Jordan in 1981, "The truth is that Jordan is Palestine and Palestine is Jordan." Put another way—and I am not putting these words into the late king's mouth—the Palestinians already have a homeland, and it is called Jordan. Indeed, more than half of Jordan's population considers itself Palestinian.

I am fully aware that news reports present a terribly skewed picture of all this, and I don't discount the genuine suffering experienced by many Arabs when the nation of Israel was rebirthed.[60] But facts are facts, and it is no secret that the so-called West Bank (part of the so-called Occupied Territories) and Gaza were under the control of Jordan and Egypt from 1948 to 1967. Yet neither country made any effort to form a Palestinian state for the refugees, and neither country ever spoke of these areas as "Palestine." Yet today, Israel is accused of uprooting the Palestinian people from their ancestral homeland. This charge is patently untrue.

As to the claim of Canaanite descent, no national or ethnic group can trace itself back to the ancient Canaanites, since these nations were either wiped out or became totally assimilated into the surrounding nations millennia ago. The same can be said about the ancient Philistines, who were not even of Semitic stock. In fact, "the Philistines were not Arabs nor even Semites, they were most closely related to the Greeks originating from Asia Minor and Greek localities. They did not speak Arabic. They had no connection, ethnic, linguistic or historical with Arabia or Arabs."[61] They ceased to exist as a distinguishable people more than two thousand years ago, and when the Romans decided to call the land of Israel "Palestine," they did *not* do so because the Philistines owned or controlled or dominated the country. (Actually, these seafaring peoples only lived in the southwest portion of Israel before being completely assimilated.)

As for the name "Palestine,"

> The name "Falastin" that Arabs today use for "Palestine" is not an Arabic name. It is the Arab pronunciation of the Roman "Palaestina." Quoting Golda Meir:
> "The British chose to call the land they mandated Palestine, and the Arabs picked it up as their nation's supposed ancient name, though they couldn't even pronounce it correctly and turned it into Falastin, a fictional entity."[62]

As for the Arabs who have lived in the land of Israel through the centuries, their origins as Arabic—not Canaanite!—peoples are well attested.

Having said this, and despite the anti-Israel slant that is so prevalent in the media, a slant that tends to demonize the Israelis, especially in the world press outside of America, those who identify themselves as Palestinians today are deserving of compassion, and should their leaders abandon all efforts to destroy the modern State of Israel, the vast majority of Israelis would gladly live side by side with them in peace. In truth, however, it seems clear from the Scriptures (see especially Zechariah 12–14; 1 Thessalonians 5:1–3; many also apply Ezekiel 38–39 to a future scenario) that there will be no lasting, true peace between Israel and their Arab neighbors before Yeshua returns, and He alone remains the only hope of the region.

35

In the Bible, is the fig tree a prophetic symbol for Israel?

For many years, prophecy teachers commonly stated that there was an excellent possibility that Jesus would return before 1988, based on the Lord's words in Matthew 24:32–34:

> Now learn this lesson from the fig tree: As soon as its twigs get tender and its leaves come out, you know that summer is near. Even so, when you see all these things, you know that it is near, right at the door. I tell you the truth, this generation will certainly not pass away until all these things have happened.

The logic was simple: The fig tree represented Israel, the fig tree beginning to blossom referred to the rebirth of the State of Israel in 1948, and "this generation" referred to the generation that would see these things happen. Since it was understood that a biblical generation represented forty years, it is obvious to see why many prophecy teachers expected the Lord to return before 1988.

Needless to say, this interpretation was wrong, since we are now in the 21st century and Jesus still has not returned. But this was not just a matter of bad prophetic timing; it was also a matter of bad prophetic interpretation. Specifically, we must ask: Does the fig tree really represent Israel? Is that what is taught by the Scriptures?

I am fully aware, of course, that this seems like an odd question. After all, doesn't everyone know that the fig tree serves as a prophetic type of Israel? Isn't this a "given" in prophetic interpretation? Actually, this is one of those concepts that is constantly taught and repeated and taught again, but very few people take the time to examine the biblical witness. If the fig tree represents Israel, shouldn't the Bible tell us so?

In the Scriptures, Israel is often likened to a vine, as in Jeremiah 2:21 ("I had planted you like a choice vine"); Psalm 80:8 ("You brought a vine out of Egypt; you drove out the nations and planted it"); and Isaiah 5:1 ("My loved one had a vineyard on a fertile hillside"), which is why Jesus referred to Himself as the true Vine in John 15:1. And in Romans 11:17–24, Israel is likened to an olive tree. But is the fig tree also an image of Israel in the Word of God?

The term *fig tree* occurs about thirty times in the Scriptures, almost equally divided between the Old Testament and the New Testament. In some contexts, the image of sitting under one's fig tree refers to dwelling in safety and prosperity, as in 1 Kings 4:25 (see also 2 Kings 18:31; Isaiah 36:16; Micah 4:4; Zechariah 3:10). In other contexts, the fig tree is listed among other plants and trees, often because its fruit (or the loss of its fruit) was especially conspicuous (see Isaiah 34:4; Hosea 9:10; Joel 1:12; 2:22; Habakkuk 3:17; Haggai 2:19; see also Song of Solomon 2:13; for the fig tree in a parable, but not representing Israel, see Judges 9:10–11; for a general teaching about tending one's fig tree, see Proverbs 27:18).

At this point you might be wondering, *Okay. You've listed all the verses in the Old Testament where the fig tree does not specifically refer to Israel. What about the verses where it does?*

Well, I just listed all the verses in the Hebrew Bible where the term is found. That's it! On what basis, then, can we state that, when Jesus made reference to the fig tree in Matthew 24, He was clearly referring to Israel? How do we know that?

Actually, the notion that the fig tree is Israel has caused some interpreters to claim that God is through with Israel, based on the Lord's cursing of the fig tree in Matthew 21:19 (see also Mark 11:20–21), when He pronounced the words, "May you never bear fruit again!" So, if the fig tree represented national Israel, was Jesus cursing His people forever? Perish the thought! This wrong interpretation has also been adduced by some teachers based on Luke 13:6–9, the parable of the fig tree that did not bear fruit and was about to be cut down. Of course, this parable clearly applied to the impending judgment on Israel, but *not* because the fig tree had special significance. Instead, it was simply used to illustrate a point, just as, in other parables, other plants, trees or objects of nature are used.

How then should we interpret Jesus' teaching in Matthew 24 (found also in Mark 13:28)? The parallel passage in Luke 21:29–30 holds the key: "He told them this parable: 'Look at the fig tree and all the trees. When they sprout leaves, you can see for yourselves and know that summer is near." In other words, the fig tree is simply one of a number of trees, but, just as in the Old Testament, it is used because of the conspicuous nature of its leaves and fruit.

As explained by Walter W. Wessel in his commentary on Mark, "In [Israel] most trees are evergreen, but the fig tree is an exception. In the fall it loses its leaves; and when in the spring the sap rises in its branches and the tree begins to leaf out, summer cannot be far off."[63] So, Jesus is simply saying, "Here is a lesson for you: When you see the fig tree sprouting its leaves, you know that summer is near. In the same way, when you see these prophetic signs come to pass, you know My coming is near." That's it!

As paraphrased in *The Message*, "He told them a story. 'Look at a fig tree. Any tree for that matter. When the leaves begin to show, one look tells you that summer is right around the corner. The same here—when you see these things happen, you know God's kingdom is about here'" (Luke 21:29–31). Or, as explained by New Testament scholar Craig Keener, "The signs Jesus lists show that the end is imminent, just as a fig tree's leaves show what season it is. (In winter the fig tree appeared more bare than other trees.)"[64]

What, then, is the meaning of the oft-discussed phrase "This generation will certainly not pass away until all these things have happened"? At the risk of bursting some bubbles, the most plausible interpretation is this: The generation that sees these specific signs unfold, as outlined in Matthew 24 (beginning especially in verse 15), is the generation that will see the Lord return.

Of course, there are many prophetic strands to unravel in Matthew 24 (and its parallels in Mark 13 and Luke 21), and there is absolutely no question that the reestablishment of Israel in 1948 is of tremendous prophetic and biblical significance, not to mention the importance of Jerusalem coming back into Jewish control in 1967. And there is no question that, as we get closer to the end of the age, we must keep our attention focused on Israel and the Jewish people. But it is high time to abandon the dogmatic, unquestioning interpretation that the fig tree is Israel, lest we continue to get our times and seasons wrong.

Part 3

Rabbi Yeshua and the Jewish Background to the New Testament

36

Was Jesus really a rabbi?

The answer is, "Yes, no, and it depends on what you mean by 'rabbi.'" Sound confusing? Actually, it is fairly simple.

We know from the gospels that Jesus was sometimes called "Rabbi" by His followers (the term literally means, "My teacher, my master"), just as John the Immerser (John the Baptist) was called "rabbi" by his followers (for the latter, see John 3:26). So, in that sense we can answer in the affirmative and say yes, Jesus really was a rabbi, and quite a rabbi at that—a rabbi who opened blind eyes (see Mark 10:51; John 9:2), raised the dead (see John 11:8), walked on water (see John 6:25) and had power over nature (see Mark 11:21; He is also addressed as rabbi in Matthew 26:25, 49; Mark 9:5; 14:45; John 1:38, 49; 3:2; 4:31).

This underscores both the Jewishness of our Savior and the Jewish roots of our faith, especially when we remember that:

- He was called rabbi, not reverend;
- He went to synagogue, not to church;
- He celebrated Passover, not Easter; and
- He knew all about the story of His miraculous birth but never heard of Christmas.

In one sense of the word, then, it is right to say that Jesus was a rabbi. On the other hand, official rabbinic ordination (called s'mikha) had not yet been established in Jesus' day and so, there was no way to become a rabbi in any formal sense of the word. The term *rabbi* was an informal title of honor and esteem used in Jewish circles, reflecting the way in which a disciple would address his teacher, rather than signifying a formal title associated with public ordination. In that sense of the word, there were no rabbis in Yeshua's day.

And this leads to the last part of our answer—"It depends on what you mean by 'rabbi'"—since there is quite a difference between what "rabbi" meant in the early first century and what it means today. Judaism has come a long way in the last two thousand years, developing thousands of traditions and producing hundreds of sacred books, most of which would have been unknown in Jesus' day (see #3 and #7). More importantly, Judaism as a religion does not recognize Yeshua as Messiah and Lord.

A rabbi today, especially in traditional Jewish circles, is primarily a scholar, expected to give himself to study and to be responsible for teaching and for making judgments in Jewish law, along with being—at least on some level—an inspirational leader by example and even a shepherd of his flock. Although Jesus fulfilled some of these roles, He does not fit the mold of a traditional Jewish rabbi, nor would He endorse some of the man-made traditions of Judaism that, in His words, make the Word of God void (see Mark 7:8–9).

It would therefore be misleading to think of Jesus as being a rabbi in the traditional Jewish sense of the word. But I hasten to add that it would be wrong to think of Him as a member of the Christian clergy! We do well, then, to put Yeshua in a special class of His own, never forgetting that from a historical perspective, He was more of a "rabbi" than a "reverend," and it was out of Jewish soil that the roots of our faith grew (see #37, #42 and #43).

37

Did Jesus follow the Oral Law?

As we explained earlier (see #3), traditional Jews believe that when God gave Moses the written Torah on Mount Sinai, He also gave him an oral Torah, consisting of explanations to the written commandments. This unwritten Torah was then allegedly passed on in a virtually unbroken chain right up to the time of Yeshua, after which time it gradually began to be put in written form.

In reality, the idea of an unbroken Oral Law going back to Moses is a religious myth. However, there is no question that various traditions did develop among the Jewish people in the Old Testament period. And in the centuries immediately preceding the New Testament period, the Pharisees began to develop a body of tradition that ultimately became the foundation of traditional Judaism. It is these Pharisaic traditions that are specifically mentioned in the gospels, referred to as "the traditions of the elders" (see Matthew 15:2; Mark 7:3). Did Jesus adhere to these traditions?

On the one hand, it is clear that, at times, He differed with some of the traditions, to the point of saying to the Pharisees, "You have let go of the commands of God and are holding on to the traditions of men. . . . You have a fine way of setting aside the commands of God in order to observe your own traditions!" (Mark 7:8–9). It is against this backdrop that many of the conflicts between Jesus and the religious leaders can be explained (see Mark 2:23–3:6; John 5:1–18; 9:1–41), and He reserved some of His most scathing comments for hypocritical religious leaders, pointing specifically to some of their traditions (see Matthew 23:1–4, 16–22).

On the other hand, Jesus accepted, affirmed or practiced some of these traditions (see Mark 6:41; 8:6; 14:22–23, 26, all of which reflect traditional Jewish practices of the day; see also Matthew 23:23–24, where Jesus says that the Pharisees *should* have continued their scrupulous practice of tithing as long as they first emphasized "justice, mercy and faithfulness"). The synagogue itself was a traditional institution—it is not mentioned in the Hebrew Scriptures—and there are numerous accounts in the gospels of Yeshua attending synagogue services.

Putting this evidence together, we can see that Jesus was a Jew of His time, living within many of the traditions that existed, actively embracing some of the traditions that He was at home with while strongly rejecting those traditions that violated the spirit and intent of God's Word and God's heart.[1]

So what about Matthew 23:2–3? There Yeshua tells the crowds and His disciples that, because "the teachers of the law and the Pharisees sit in Moses' seat," the people are to obey the teachers of the law and "do everything they tell you." However, their example was not to be followed, which Jesus makes clear in the very next verse: "But do not do what they do, for they do not practice what they preach. They tie up heavy loads and put them on men's shoulders, but they themselves are not willing to lift a finger to move them" (verses 3–4). Does this mean that the Lord was instructing His followers to submit to the Pharisaic traditions? Or, more radically, does this mean that followers of Jesus today should submit to the rulings of traditional Jewish rabbis?

Based on the fact that Jesus rebuked some of these very leaders for replacing divine truth with their man-made traditions (see again Mark 7:8–9), and based on the different system that He set in motion—founded on different spiritual principles (see Matthew 12:1–14, which follows Matthew 11:28–30; see also #46)—it is inconceivable that He mandated that all of His followers should submit unconditionally to the teachings of the Pharisees and teachers of the Law. Elsewhere in the gospels, Jesus warned His disciples about the "yeast of the Pharisees and Sadducees," namely, "the teaching of the Pharisees and Sadducees" (Matthew 16:6, 12), and throughout Matthew 23, Yeshua has nothing but searing rebuke for the hypocrisy of some of these leaders. He was hardly ordering His followers to submit to everything they taught! Not only so, but it is clear that the disciples in the book of Acts did not feel the need to submit to all the rulings of the religious leadership, stating clearly that, when push came to shove, "We must obey God rather than men!" (Acts 5:29).

What, then, was Yeshua saying in Matthew 23:2–3? There are several plausible explanations:

1. *He was using biting sarcasm or irony.* According to this view, which is espoused by Professor D. A. Carson, the Lord was saying, "Yes, you have the name and the prestige and you call out to God—but it is all a show! So, everyone, be sure to listen to everything these men say—right!—but do not follow their example." Based on this interpretation, which would be in harmony with the larger critique of the Pharisees in the gospels as well as the rest of this chapter, Jesus was *not* stating that His disciples should submit to their teaching, using biting, prophetic sarcasm to make His point.

2. *The Lord was making a temporary concession.* According to this view, Jesus was saying, "For now, these men sit in the seat of authority, so you have to submit to their rulings. But soon enough they will be displaced." Support for this is found in Matthew 21, which culminates with a parable that concludes, "I tell you that the kingdom of God will be taken away from you and given to a people who will produce its fruit" (verse 43). Significantly, verse 45 states, "When the chief priests and the Pharisees heard Jesus' parables, they knew he was talking about them." Their authority over the people was soon to be displaced, given instead to the new generation of leaders being raised up by Yeshua, a picture in harmony with the situation in Acts. Matthew 22 reinforces the Lord's critique of the religious leaders, and it is these chapters, Matthew 21–22, that lead directly into chapter 23.

3. *Jesus was saying that the religious leaders should be followed to the extent they adhered to the teachings of Moses.* This is the view of Professor Donald Hagner, who argued that what Yeshua meant was that His disciples (and the Jewish people in general, by extension) should submit to the teaching of the Pharisees *insofar as* they accurately represent Moses. This is certainly logical, since it would be unthinkable for anyone to be granted carte blanche religious and civil authority in *whatever they said.*

4. *Jesus was making reference to the precedent set in Exodus 18:13–18, where Moses appointed leaders to adjudicate disputes between the people.* According to this view, Yeshua is simply saying, "To the extent that the Pharisees and scribes function as judges in the society, submit to whatever they say [cf. Deuteronomy 17:8–13]—but by no means follow their example or submit to their broader teaching."[2]

5. *There was an original Hebrew text, different from our current Greek Matthew, which preserved a different reading of the text.* Although there is scholarly dispute about the existence of an original Hebrew Matthew (see #40), and although no ancient manuscript of this Hebrew text has ever been discovered, some scholars believe that a medieval copy of Matthew in Hebrew preserves some of the original wording. In Matthew 23:2–3, there is a variant in the Hebrew text, and contemporary Karaite teacher Nehemiah Gordon has argued that this reflects Yeshua's original words: As translated by Gordon, the Hebrew text states: "The Pharisees and sages sit upon the seat of Moses. Therefore all that he [meaning, Moses] says to you, diligently do, but according to their reforms [*takkanot*] and their precedents [*ma'asim*, literally, "deeds"] do not do, because they talk but they do not do."[3] In other words, to the extent the religious leaders tell you to follow Moses, do that, but don't listen to the rest

of what they have to say, and don't follow their example.[4] This is similar to some of the other views presented, but it is based on a different textual reading.

While there is more scholarly support for some of these positions than others, each of them effectively refutes the very erroneous notion that, for all time, Jesus was commanding His Jewish followers to submit to Pharisaic-Orthodox-traditional Judaism. To the contrary, it was His *halakha* (i.e., legal principles and rulings) that was to be followed (see also #46), and with the dawning of the new covenant through Yeshua's death and resurrection (see Jeremiah 31:31–34; Luke 22:14–21; Hebrews 8:1–13), we have been given a new heart and a new spirit (see Ezekiel 36:26–27) by which we now live in the newness of the Spirit (see Romans 7:1–6; 8:1–4).[5]

38

What is the original Hebrew name for Jesus? And is it true that the name Jesus (Greek *Iēsous*) is really a pagan corruption of the name Zeus?

The original Hebrew-Aramaic name of Jesus is *yeshu'a*, which is short for *yehōshu'a* (Joshua), just as Mike is short for Michael. The name *yeshu'a* occurs 27 times in the Hebrew Scriptures, primarily referring to the high priest after the Babylonian exile, called both *yehōshu'a* (see Zechariah 3:3) and, more frequently, *yeshu'a* (see Ezra 3:2).[6] So, Yeshua's name was not unusual; in fact, as many as five different men had that name in the Old Testament.

Interestingly, this high priest, Yehoshua/Yeshua, was singled out in the book of Zechariah as being a symbol of the "man called the Branch" (see Zechariah 3:8; 6:9–15)—which was a distinct Messianic title (see Jeremiah 23:5). Even more significantly, in a symbolic ceremony, this *priest* was put on a throne and crowned, with the words:

> Tell him this is what the LORD Almighty says: "Here is the man whose name is the Branch, and he will branch out from his place and build the temple of the LORD. It is he who will build the temple of the LORD, and he will be clothed with majesty and will sit and rule on his throne. And he will be a priest on his throne. And there will be harmony between the two [meaning the kingship and the priesthood]."
>
> Zechariah 6:12–13

It is altogether fitting, then, that the Branch Himself should bear the same name as this high priest who symbolically prefigured the Messiah's royal priesthood, especially when the meaning of Yehoshua/Yeshua is "Yahweh is salvation" (see Matthew 1:21).

So, the answer to the first question is quite simple: The original Hebrew/Aramaic name for Jesus is *yeshuʻa*.

Why then do some people refer to Jesus as Yahshua? There is absolutely *no* support for this pronunciation—none at all—and I say this as someone holding a Ph.D. in Semitic languages. My educated guess is that some zealous but linguistically ignorant people thought that Yahweh's name must have been a more overt part of our Savior's name, hence YAHshua rather than Yeshua— but again, there is no support of any kind for this theory. The Hebrew Bible has *yeshuʻa*; when the Septuagint authors rendered this name in Greek, they rendered it as Ιησους (*Iēsous*, with no hint of *yah* at the beginning of the name); and the same can be said of the Peshitta translators (see #41) when they rendered Yeshua's name into Syriac (part of the Aramaic language family).[7] All this is consistent and clear: The original form of the name Jesus is *yeshuʻa*, and there is no such name as *yahshuʻa*.[8]

What about the alleged connection between the name Jesus (Greek *Iēsous*) and Zeus? This is one of the more bizarre claims that has ever been made, but it has received some circulation in recent years (the Internet is an amazing tool of misinformation), and there are some believers who feel that it is not only preferable to use the original Hebrew/Aramaic name, Yeshua, but that it is *wrong* to use the name Jesus. Because of this, we will briefly examine this claim and expose the fallacies that underlie it.

According to the late A. B. Traina in his *Holy Name Bible*, "The name of the Son, Yahshua, has been substituted by Jesus, Iesus, and Ea-Zeus (Healing Zeus)."[9] In this one short sentence, two complete myths are stated as fact: First, there is no such name as Yahshua (as we have just explained), and second, there is no connection of any kind between the Greek name *Iēsous* (or the English name Jesus) and the name Zeus. Absolutely none! You might as well argue that Tiger Woods is the name of a tiger-infested jungle in India as try to connect the name Jesus to the pagan god Zeus. It is that absurd, based on serious linguistic ignorance.

According to the Institute for Scripture Research,

Consider Iesous, rendered as 'Jesus' in English versions up to now. For example the authoritative Greek-English Lexicon of Liddell and Scott, under Iaso: The Greek goddess of healing reveals that the name Iaso is Ieso in the Ionic dialect of the Greeks, Iesous being the contracted genitive form! In David Kravitz' Dictionary of Greek and Roman Mythology we find a similar form, namely Iasus. There were four different Greek deities with the name Iasus, one of them being the Son of Rhea.[10]

Does this sound impressive? It is actually complete nonsense, as far as any connection with the name *Iēsous*/Jesus is concerned, and the citation from the authoritative lexicon of Liddell and Scott has *nothing* to do with the name *Iēsous* either. Of course, the author of this comment might be sincere, not intentionally trying to mislead, but the argument is absolutely worthless from

162

an etymological standpoint. (Etymology refers to the linguistic origins of words.)

Here is another, equally ridiculous statement:

> Basically, to keep it simple, "Jesus" is a very poor Roman translation from Latin, that was also poorly translated from the Greek, which IN NO WAY resembles His Hebrew name, "Yahushua." [Did you catch that? The correct name is now Yahushua!] Whew! Get all that? Moreover, according to the ENCYCLOPEDIA BRITAN-NICA, the name Ieusus (Jesus) is a combination of 2 mythical deities, IEU and SUS (ZEUS, a Greek god). In Gnostic and Greek mythologies they are actually one and the same pagan deity. So, it appears the name "Jesus" has some documented pagan origins. That's not good! In fairness, some Messianic believers disagree and state that there is no definitive evidence to connect "Jesus" to "Zeus." However, I disagree with them.[11]

Let me respond to these statements (which have as much support as the latest Elvis sightings): (1) We know where the name *Iēsous* came from: the Jewish Septuagint! In other words, this was not some later, pagan corruption of the Savior's name; rather, it was the natural Greek way of rendering the Hebrew/Aramaic name Yeshua at least two centuries before His birth, and it is the form of the name found in *more than five thousand Greek manuscripts of the New Testament.* This is saying something! The name *Iēsous* is also found in Greek writings outside the New Testament and dating to that same general time frame. (2) The Greek forms with *iaso* are completely unrelated to the name *Iēsous*. The word *iaso* has an *alpha* for its second letter, reflecting its derivation from the verb *iaomai*, "to heal"; the name *Iēsous* has an *ēta* for its second letter, showing that it is completely unrelated to the root for healing in Greek. (3) As noted on a website devoted to refuting the bizarre claims of the Sacred Name Movement, citation from the Liddell-Scott lexicon is also erroneous:

For Iaso, the genitive, as given by [Institute for Scripture Research], in Greek letters is Iasous. For Jesus, the genitive in Greek letters is Iesou. The impression the Institute desires to leave with us and certainly with avid Sacred Name converts who read their Bible and its notes is that the words are the same. However, the words are not at all the same. They are like the English words bell and ball.... One is not derived from the other. The Greek words Iasous and Ihsou to some may look alike and they, too, sound a bit alike. There ends their similarity. One is in no case derived from the other. The people at Institute for Scripture Research know this. Add to this the fact that Liddell and Scott's Lexicon, at least the one on my bookshelf, makes no mention of Iaso being Ieso in the Iconic dialect. Perhaps someone misread it.[12]

(4) Although it is claimed that the *Encyclopedia Britannica* says that "the name Ieusus (Jesus) is a combination of 2 mythical deities, IEU and SUS (ZEUS, a Greek god)" it actually says no such thing. This is a complete fabrication, intentional or not.

In short, "Jesus is as much related to Zeus as Moses is to mice."[13] Unfortunately, some popular teachers continue to espouse the Jesus-Zeus connection, and many believers follow the pseudo-scholarship in these fringe, "new revelation" teachings. Not only are these teachings and practices filled with error, but they do not profit in the least. So, to every English-speaking believer I say: Do not be ashamed to use the name JESUS! That is the proper way to say His name in English—just as Michael is the correct English way to say the Hebrew name *mi-kha-el* and Moses is the correct English way to say the Hebrew name *mo-sheh*.[14] Pray in Jesus' name, worship in Jesus' name and witness in Jesus' name. And for those who want to relate to our Messiah's Jewishness, then refer to Him by His original name, Yeshua—not Yahshua and not Yahushua—remembering that the power of the name is not in its pronunciation but in the *Person* to whom it refers, our Lord and Redeemer and King.

All this is really quite straightforward and without scholarly dispute. There are, however, two interesting developments related to the Savior's name. First, in the Koran, Yeshua is incorrectly referred to as 'isa, which should most probably be traced to the Hebrew name Esau, rather than the expected form *yesu'a*. This is apparently due to the fact that when Mohammed heard the Gospel story from Arabic-speaking Jews, he did not realize that they disparagingly referred to Yeshua as Esau, thinking instead that this was His real name.[15] Second, in the Talmud and rabbinic writings (and in Israel, among the general population until this day), Yeshua is referred to as *yeshu*, without the final *a*. It is true that some linguists argue that the final vowel dropped out of pronunciation almost two thousand years ago, and so there is nothing derogatory meant by this pronunciation. Indeed, when a secular Israeli person refers to Jesus as *yeshu*, he or she means nothing by it at all. That is simply the way they learned His name. But when a religious Jew says *yeshu*—especially an ultra-Orthodox Jew—he means something very negative by it, the Hebrew letters *y-sh-w* being used as an acronym for the words *yimakh sh'mo w'zikro*, meaning, "May His name and memory be obliterated!"

None of this should surprise us, since it is written that "repentance and forgiveness of sins will be preached *in his name* to all nations, beginning at Jerusalem" (Luke 24:47, emphasis added), and "Salvation is found in no one else, for there is *no other name* under heaven given to men by which we must be saved" (Acts 4:12) and "God exalted him to the highest place and gave him *the name that is above every name*, that at the name of Jesus [Yeshua] every knee should bow, in heaven and on earth and under the earth, and every tongue confess that Jesus Christ [Yeshua the Messiah] is Lord, to the glory of God the Father" (Philippians 2:9–11, emphasis added).

Neither the Koran nor the rabbinic traditions nor modern false teachings can diminish its power in the least.

39
What language did Jesus and the apostles speak?

While it is possible that Jesus and some of His apostles knew and used Greek (at least on certain occasions), it is clear that their primary language of communication was Aramaic and, quite possibly, Hebrew as well. Here is the key evidence.

The New Testament records several unmistakable instances of Aramaic usage. Most notable is Mark 5:41, where Jesus raises Jairus' daughter from the dead with the command, *Talitha koum[i]* ("Little girl, get up!"). Interestingly, if Peter spoke in Aramaic when he raised Tabitha from the dead, he would have used almost the exact same phrase: *Tabitha koum[i]* (see Acts 9:40).[16] Other examples of Aramaic on the lips of Yeshua include His words on the cross from Psalm 22:1, quoted in Matthew 27:46, "*Eloi, Eloi, lama sabachthani?*"[17] Acts 1:19 also provides a good example of Aramaic usage, since it speaks of the field in Jerusalem purchased by Judas Iscariot, and states that the people "called that field in their language Akeldama, that is, Field of Blood." This name, Akeldama, reflects the Aramaic words *haqal dama'*, "field of blood," and is definitely not a Hebrew construction.

Despite the attempts of some "Hebrew only" authors to downplay or eliminate these examples, they clearly point to Aramaic usage by Jesus and His followers.[18] Given the first-century Galilean background of the Lord and His disciples, Aramaic usage would make perfect sense and would be in keeping with the prevailing scholarly consensus.[19]

There are many other Aramaic names and terms in the New Testament (such as *Abba* and *Golgotha*), but they do not "prove" that Aramaic was commonly used any more than Native American place names on Long Island, New York, such as Copiague and Setauket and Nesconset "prove" that Long Islanders speak American

Indian dialects. There is, however, one key Aramaic phrase preserved in the Greek New Testament indicating its importance to the early believers. It is the word *Maranatha*, which is Aramaic, not Greek, and which most likely means, "Our Lord, come!" (see 1 Corinthians 16:22; it could also be translated, "Our Lord has come," or, "O Lord, come!"). The fact that Paul could use this expression in a letter to Greek speakers (who would *not* have known Aramaic) points to the widespread usage of Aramaic among the early Judean and Galilean disciples.

The New Testament points to at least some of the apostles speaking Greek. New Testament scholar Richard Bauckham notes that "Peter was surely able to speak Greek," adding, "In light of Peter's early life in the dominantly Gentile context of Bethsaida, Markus Bockmuehl speaks of 'a very strong likelihood that Peter grew up fully bilingual in a Jewish minority setting.'"[20] Bauckham also notes, "On the other hand, it is worth noting that Philip, also from Bethsaida, and Peter's brother Andrew, rather than Peter himself, are regarded as the disciples most proficient in Greek in John 12:21–22,"[21] where it is recorded, beginning in John 12:20, that some Greek-speaking Jews wanted to see Jesus: "They came to Philip, who was from Bethsaida in Galilee, with a request" (verse 21), indicating that he was known to them or referred to them as a Greek speaker. Many scholars also believe that Peter preached in Greek in Acts 2, which would have been the most widely understood language by the Jews from many different countries.[22]

Acts 6 also provides possible evidence that, side by side with Aramaic-speaking (or Hebrew-speaking) widows, there were Greek-speaking widows, all part of the same believing community in Jerusalem. It is possible, however, that Acts 6:1 refers to Hellenized Jews rather than Greek-speaking Jews, although it is likely that these Hellenized Jews spoke Greek. Another perspective is brought by New Testament commentator Craig Keener:

"Some scholars think that the 'Hellenists' (NRSV) here are simply Greek-speaking Palestinian Jews, but most Jews in Palestine were bilingual, and Greek was probably the first language for most Jerusalemites. The more likely proposal is that this text refers to Diaspora Jews who have settled in Jerusalem, as opposed to natives of Jewish Palestine."[23] This observation, however, only underscores the widespread usage of Greek in the land of Israel in the days of Jesus.

There is also evidence for the use of Hebrew by Jesus and His disciples. At the turn of the twentieth century, many non-Jewish scholars thought that Hebrew had basically become a dead language at least one or two centuries B.C.—a dead language, that is, as far as being a *spoken language*, because no one argued that Hebrew was not still used as a written, holy language during this time. Archaeological discoveries in the last century, however, raised serious questions about this assumption—obviously, we have no *recordings* of speeches or conversations from the first century A.D., but certain archaeological findings can point to common language usage in a given society—while many Jewish scholars had recognized that Hebrew had not entirely died out as a spoken language two thousand years ago.

As stated by the editors of a recent volume seeking to shed light on the words of Jesus,

> Jesus certainly knew and spoke Aramaic when needed, but many scholars now believe that he did his teaching in Hebrew. The rabbis of Jesus' day and for hundreds of years after him delivered their parables, legal rulings, prayers and sermons entirely in Hebrew. In fact, there are several thousand parables and prayers recorded in rabbinic literature, and virtually all are in Hebrew. This Hebrew was not the dialect of the Scriptures, but a newer, living language called Middle or Mishnaic Hebrew. If Jesus functioned within Jewish society, he most likely delivered his teachings in Hebrew as well. Evidence for this comes from

the fact that many Semitic idioms found in Jesus' stories and teachings translate well into Mishnaic Hebrew, but don't make sense in Aramaic at all.[24]

In terms of the last sentence, there are Aramaic scholars who claim that the *opposite* is true, and that many Semitic idioms found in Jesus' stories and teachings translate well into Aramaic, but don't make sense in Hebrew (see #41). The rest of the paragraph, however, raises some excellent points, suggesting—but still not proving—that when Jesus dialogued and debated with the religious leaders in Jerusalem, He may have done so primarily in Hebrew (or, as reflected in the later Talmudic literature, in both Hebrew and Aramaic). This would also suggest that when the New Testament speaks of the "Hebrew language" (*hebraidi dialekto*) it actually *means* Hebrew and not Aramaic, as many translators and commentators have believed (see Acts 21:40; 22:2, referring to Paul's speech; 26:14, referring to Yeshua addressing him on the road to Damascus; contrast the NRSV, which has "Hebrew" in the text, with the NIV, which has "Aramaic" in the text and "Hebrew" in the marginal notes). The question, however, is not so simple, as I pointed out in a somewhat technical article published in 1993, and "Hebrew" can simply mean "the language spoken by the Jewish people,"[25] meaning Aramaic rather than Hebrew. Other scholars have questioned whether a large Jewish audience in Jerusalem could have been expected to understand Paul preaching in Hebrew rather than Aramaic, while others, as noted above, have suggested that Peter must have preached in Greek in Acts 2, since that language would have been more widely understood than even Aramaic by the visiting Jews.

There are, however, some internal indications within the New Testament text that could point to Hebrew usage (although others claim that the indications point to Aramaic usage; see #40 and #41), and so some level of Hebrew usage cannot be ruled out, although those who argue that the key to rightly understanding the New Testament is reconstructing the alleged Hebrew original are certainly mistaken (see again, #40).

So, what language did Jesus and the apostles speak? As a whole, primarily Aramaic, at least in everyday use; in teaching settings, possibly Hebrew and in other cases Greek (although this is not to say that the Lord and the apostles were all able to speak three languages).

40
Was the New Testament originally written in Hebrew?

There is absolutely no evidence that the New Testament was originally written in Hebrew, despite many extravagant claims to the contrary. In fact, while there are more than five thousand ancient manuscripts containing all or part of the New Testament in Greek, there are no ancient manuscripts with even a single line from the New Testament written in Hebrew.

Nonetheless, claims such as the following are not uncommon these days: "We have created a Messianic, Sacred Name translation of the Scriptures which, for the first time ever, uses the Hebrew and Aramaic rather than Greek manuscripts for its 'New Testament.'"[26] Unfortunately, there are no such manuscripts—not one single, ancient Hebrew manuscript for any part of the New Testament. Yet the "translator" still states, "This Version is the first Messianic Version with a 'New Testament' translated from ancient Hebrew and Aramaic manuscripts rather than from Greek."[27] Not so! There are no extant, ancient Hebrew manuscripts of the New Testament. (For the claim that the New Testament was written in Aramaic, see #41.)

Yet time and again, claims are made—often to the captivated fascination of many Christian readers—that the only way to rightly understand the New Testament is to translate it back into the "original Hebrew." One popular book, *Understanding the Difficult Words of Jesus*, contains a mixture of good scholarship and dangerous, careless claims. It goes so far as to say that "one can keep reading the Bible until the day he dies, and the Bible will not tell him the meaning of these difficult Hebrew passages [in the New Testament]. They can be understood only when translated back into Hebrew."[28] Indeed, "had the Church been provided with a proper Hebraic understanding of the words of Jesus, most theological controversies would never have arisen in the first place."[29] Yet to reiterate, there are no ancient Hebrew manuscripts of the New Testament—not one!—in contrast with multiplied thousands of Greek manuscripts.

Many readers fail to realize that if such extravagant, baseless claims are true, then we have no inspired New Testament text— not even a reasonably well-preserved copy. All we have is a poorly translated, even hopelessly garbled collection of secondhand books that are nothing better than a rough approximation to God's Word. Amazingly, the authors of *Understanding the Difficult Words of Jesus* make statements that would support this ridiculous notion: "The [Greek] Gospels are rife with mistranslations"; indeed, some passages "have been misinterpreted to such an extent that they are potentially damaging to us spiritually.... Many Gospel expressions are not just poor Greek, but actually meaningless Greek."[30] Such statements would be *completely* rejected by the world's leading New Testament Greek scholars, men and women who are not covering up some kind of anti-Hebrew conspiracy.[31]

What makes matters worse is that some teachers are so convinced that the New Testament was written in Hebrew that they are determined to "translate" the Greek New Testament passages back into "the original Hebrew" (an "original," I remind you, that exists without a single manuscript to support it). To call this presumptuous is an understatement. As I noted in a previous article:

Almost 100 years ago, the Jewish Semitic scholar D. S. Margoliouth attempted to translate the Greek text of Ecclesiasticus (Ben Sira) back into Hebrew. He knew for a fact from the prologue to Ben Sira that it had been translated into Greek directly from a Hebrew original, and he had at his disposal not only the Greek text, but Syriac and Latin translations as well. Yet when sizable portions of a Hebrew Ben Sira were discovered in the Cairo Geniza [a depository of ancient documents hidden in a synagogue in Egypt], it was found that he *did not correctly translate even one single verse!*

Back-translation (called *"Rückübersetzung"* in German) is extremely touchy business, even when we are dealing with sources that are only *one step* removed from the original. But to postulate that accurate *Rückübersetzung* can be carried out from sources *four* or *five* steps removed from the alleged original is almost unthinkable.[32] And it is entirely out of the question to suggest that wholesale *reconstruction*—not just retranslation—of an alleged original text . . . can be carried out from such a distance. Such an effort can only be viewed as *pure conjecture.* To reconstruct the original Hebrew or Aramaic text of even the Lord's Prayer—based on the extant witness of Matthew and Luke—is fraught with difficulty.[33] To attempt to reconstruct the *entire* (alleged) *original Hebrew Gospel*—without access to even the supposed primary Greek sources—is nothing more than a counsel of despair.[34]

Despite all this, believers are often fascinated with claims of "the original meaning of the text," as if the plain, clear sense of the Scripture is not enough, as if there always must be some kind of mystical, deeper meaning, or as if we will become spiritually enriched if we can discover that Jesus actually did not mean what our Bibles say He meant. Really, the opposite is more often true: It is the passages in the Word that we *do* understand that are most troubling. As Dan Harman has said, "So long as Jesus was misunderstood, He was followed by the crowd. When they came to really understand Him, they crucified Him." For the most part, His words are all too clear! To quote Mark Twain, "It ain't those parts of the Bible that I can't understand that bother me, it is the parts that I do understand."

"But," you say, "I've heard that Matthew's gospel was originally written in Hebrew and that there is even a medieval copy of this Hebrew gospel. I've also heard that there are clear examples of Yeshua's teachings that can only be understood when we recover the Hebrew background of His words."

Actually, some of what you've heard is true. One early church leader stated that "Matthew put together the oracles [of the Lord] in the Hebrew language, and each one interpreted them as best he could" (Papias, quoted by Eusebius in his *Ecclesiastical History*, 3:39). This view was followed by Irenaeus, who wrote: "Matthew also issued a written gospel among the Hebrews in their own dialect while Peter and Paul were preaching at Rome and laying the foundations of the church" (*Adv. Haer.* 3.1.1). Similarly, Origen is quoted by Eusebius to have written that Matthew "was published for believers of Jewish origin, and was composed in Hebrew letters/language" (*Ecclesiastical History*, 6:25). Some of the church leaders even claimed to have seen this Hebrew Matthew.[35]

But the matter is not so clear, since: (1) the top Matthew scholars in the world are largely in agreement that the Greek Matthew we have was *not* a translation from Hebrew or any other language; (2) other church leaders claimed that Matthew wrote his gospel in Aramaic; and (3) it is possible that the expression "the Hebrew language" in the Papias quote could mean Aramaic (see above, #39; less likely is the suggestion that it simply means, "composed in Greek but in a Semitic style").

I personally think there was a Hebrew Matthew, used for some time by some of the early Jewish believers, but it might well have been a collection of the Lord's sayings in Hebrew, rather than the Matthew we know today, which remains the only Matthew that was cited and referenced by any church leaders from the second century on. That is to say, when these leaders, who were Greek- or

Latin-speaking Gentiles, quote Matthew's gospel, they virtually always quoted the Matthew that we have in Greek. So, even if there was a Hebrew Matthew, the Matthew that was universally used by most all of the ancient believers was written in Greek, and those who knew of the Hebrew Matthew never stated that it was different than the Greek Matthew. That was not an issue, and it did not dawn on them that they needed to "recover" this original text.

As for the medieval Hebrew Matthew manuscript—actually, manuscripts—this Hebrew Matthew appears *not* to be a distant copy of the alleged original document but rather a translation from Greek into Hebrew, although some scholars have argued that it contains some verses or expressions that point back to an original Hebrew Matthew.[36]

What about expressions in the gospels that can only be properly understood when their original Semitic background is uncovered? There is certainly something to this, and we know that Jesus did His teaching in Aramaic and Hebrew. But again, this does not mean that the gospels (or other parts of the New Testament) were originally *written in Hebrew*. Perhaps Yeshua's sayings in Hebrew were preserved in a collection compiled by Matthew. Perhaps there was even an original Hebrew Matthew, very close to our Greek Matthew. But this much is sure: God's desire was for His Word to be disseminated to the widest possible audience, and in order to do this, the New Testament was written in Greek.

This stands in distinct contrast to the Koran, which is only recognized as the Word of God by Muslims in Arabic. That's why some translations of the Koran are entitled *The Meaning of the Koran*, since it is only a *translation* of the holy book of Islam, not the book itself. Not so with the Bible, God's Word for all humanity. When you pick up your English Bible, you are reading the Word of God—translated, yes, and not a perfect representation of every nuance of the original Hebrew and Greek, but the Word of God nonetheless. This is in keeping with the spirit of the New Testament: Even though Yeshua Himself taught in Aramaic and Hebrew, His words were passed on to us in Greek translation so that the multitudes could hear the message of salvation.

Now, it is certainly quite profitable for scholars to look at the Greek gospels and ask, "How would this have been spoken in Hebrew or Aramaic? Is there further insight that can be gained into the Lord's words if we seek to reconstruct the original sayings?" But we must always bear in mind that: (1) the Greek New Testament is what God has preserved for us, and all the evidence that we have indicates that it was His choice to transmit the New Covenant Scriptures to us in Greek. Therefore, any "reconstruction" of the alleged original Hebrew or Aramaic that significantly alters the meaning of the Greek text—without any actual manuscript evidence to back up the claim—is to be seriously questioned if not rejected outright. Otherwise, the sky is the limit in "reconstructing" what Jesus originally said; and (2) in many cases, the Greek New Testament follows the established usage of the Septuagint, the Jewish translation of the Hebrew Bible into Greek in the centuries before Jesus. Related to this is the fact that the style of Greek used in much of the New Testament is quite "Jewish." That is to say, almost all of the authors of the New Testament were Jews, and when they wrote in Greek, they wrote in a decidedly Semitic style. This means that we are not dealing with a massive cultural and linguistic jump, similar, say, to translating a technical book on computer programming into a primitive tribal dialect.

It is also important to remember that today's top New Testament scholars are thoroughly versed in the subject of the Jewish background to the New Testament, including the question of Hebrew or Aramaic expressions that may underlie our current Greek text. In other words, there is not some secret knowledge floating around, known only to a few "Hebrew background" teachers, or, worse still, known to Christian scholars but suppressed in some sort of terrible conspiracy, as with the *Da Vinci Code* nonsense.

That being said, to recover the Jewish background to the New Testament is of great importance (see #42 and #43); to rightly place Yeshua in His first-century Jewish context is highly valuable; and to ask what His words might have been in the original Aramaic or Hebrew that He spoke is a noble enterprise. But we must accept the fact that God preserved the Tanakh for us in Hebrew (with a little Aramaic as well) but He preserved the New Testament in Greek, reflecting the fact that the New Testament was first and foremost a Book for the entire world, not for the Jewish people only, and writing it and disseminating it in Greek was the best way to get the Good News out to the largest number of people.[37]

41
Was the New Testament originally written in Aramaic?

This question is closely related to the preceding question, but with one very important difference. While there are no ancient Hebrew manuscripts of the New Testament, there are, in fact, ancient manuscripts of an *Aramaic* New Testament. But virtually all biblical scholars recognize that this Aramaic New Testament, called the *Peshitta*, is a *translation* from the Greek New Testament text rather than a copy of an alleged original Aramaic New Testament. Specifically, the Peshitta is written in Syriac, a major branch of Aramaic, and it covers the entire Bible, the Tanakh as well as the New Testament. It is generally dated between the second and fifth centuries A.D., and it is recognized as an important ancient *version*, like the Septuagint (translating the Tanakh into Greek) or the Vulgate (translating the entire Bible into Latin).

The name *Peshitta* is Syriac for "simple, plain," just as *Vulgate* means "common." (Similar to this is the name given to the Greek used by the New Testament writers: It was *koine* Greek, or common Greek, the language used by the majority of the society.)[38] Some scholars believe that the Peshitta version of the Old Testament was composed by Jews while the New Testament portion was composed by Christians, but others argue that the whole translation was composed by Christians. In either case, virtually all scholars accept that the Peshitta of the New Testament is a *translation* of those books rather than the original text of the New Testament books.

As a translation, however, the Peshitta is still very important for several reasons: (1) It is an ancient translation of the New Testament, predating some of the Greek manuscripts we have, and it provides a witness to the original wording of the New Testament. (2) Because it is written in Syriac, a major branch of Aramaic, a sister language to Hebrew,[39] and because Jesus spoke Aramaic (and, probably, Hebrew), it has a unique closeness to the Lord's original words, despite being a translation from the Greek. (In other words, Jesus spoke in Aramaic but the gospels translated His words into Greek. The Peshitta, then, would have translated these Greek words into Syriac, which, as a branch of Aramaic, would not have been radically different from the dialect of Aramaic Jesus would have spoken.) (3) Similarly, it has the potential of uncovering Semitic nuances in the Greek text. (As pointed out in #40, the Greek New Testament is filled with "Semitisms," meaning Hebraic and Aramaic ways of thinking expressed in Greek.)

There are a few scholars, however, who believe that the Peshitta is *not* a translation of the Greek New Testament but rather reflects the original text of the New Testament—in other words, the New Testament (at least part of it) was written in Aramaic. In keeping with this, they also believe that the Greek New Testament (at least part of it) is *not* the original text but rather a *translation* of the original Aramaic text. They have, therefore, turned things completely around, arguing that the translation (Aramaic) is the original and the original (Greek) is the translation.

The Peshitta.org website makes these claims regarding the history of the Peshitta:

> The Peshitta is the official Bible of the Church of the East. The name Peshitta in Aramaic means "Straight," in other words, the original and pure New Testament. [As noted previously, most scholars understand the name Peshitta to mean "simple" rather than "straight."] The Peshitta is the only authentic and pure text which contains the books in the New Testament that were written in Aramaic, the Language of Mshikha (the Messiah) and His Disciples.
>
> In reference to the originality of the Peshitta, the words of His Holiness Mar Eshai Shimun, Catholicos Patriarch of the Church of the East, are summarized as follows:
>
> "With reference to . . . the originality of the Peshitta text, as the Patriarch and Head of the Holy Apostolic and Catholic Church of the East, we wish to state, that the Church of the East received the scriptures from the hands of the blessed Apostles themselves in the Aramaic original, the language spoken by our Lord Jesus Christ Himself, and that the Peshitta is the text of the Church of the East which has come down from the Biblical times without any change or revision."
>
> Mar Eshai Shimun
by Grace, Catholicos Patriarch of the East
April 5, 1957[40]

This view was popularized by the late George Lamsa, a native speaker of modern Aramaic, which is a distant dialect to the first-century Aramaic Yeshua spoke, or even the later Syriac dialect used by the Peshitta translators.[41] Nonetheless, from Lamsa's perspective, the Syriac of the Peshitta was very close to his native tongue, and he produced a translation of the Peshitta into English (both Old and New Testaments), along with other books explaining what he believed were Aramaic idioms in the Peshitta that were misunderstood by the translators of the Greek New Testament.[42] (To repeat: The idea that the Greek New Testament was a translation from the Aramaic was Lamsa's view, not the view of almost all biblical scholars.) In recent years, Lamsa's views have gained a more popular following, with a number of books and websites devoted to further authenticating his claims. As explained on the AramaicNT.org site, "Was the New Testament originally written in Greek? The texts themselves seem to exhibit phenomena that point towards an Aramaic original, including mistranslations, polysemy, poetry, wordplay, and puns."[43]

So then, just as proponents of the "original Hebrew New Testament" theory argue that the New Testament Greek texts often make sense *only* when translated back into the (alleged) original Hebrew, so also proponents of the "original Aramaic New Testament" theory argue that the New Testament Greek texts often make sense *only* when translated back into the (alleged) original Aramaic! This alone should raise concerns about the accuracy of these claims (which, in fact, cancel each other out), instead reminding us that: (1) trying to translate any text back into another is tricky business (as pointed out in #40); and (2) New Testament Greek is often very Semitic (again, as pointed out in #40), and therefore different Semitic scholars speculate as to what Hebrew or Aramaic concepts may be represented in these Semitic expressions.

It is therefore not surprising that a number of scholars in past generations and even today have argued that the gospels were originally composed in Aramaic—after all, that would have been the native tongue of Yeshua and the apostles (see #39)—even though these scholars have understood that the Peshitta was a translation rather than an original text. That means that they worked with the Greek texts and tried to recover what the "original" Aramaic text was. Notable among these scholars were Charles Cutler Torrey (1922) and Frank Zimmerman (1979); similar efforts have been made by Gustaf Dalman (1929–30), Matthew Black (1967) and Gunter Schwartz (1989), among others, although not all of them have claimed that the gospels themselves were written in Aramaic.[44] All of them, however were seeking to recover the original words of Jesus, which they believed were Aramaic rather than Hebrew. Backers of the "Peshitta original" theory today are Andrew Gabriel Roth and Paul Younan, among others.[45]

These views, however, represent a tiny minority of scholars, since the Peshitta is almost universally recognized as a translation rather than an original text, and the scholars who have attempted to reconstruct an alleged Aramaic original are simply involved in educated guesswork, at best, with little agreement between them.[46] Moreover, when these scholars come up with what they feel is a new understanding of the Greek—that is to say, the Greek allegedly misunderstood the Aramaic original—the new, proposed Aramaic text does not agree with the Peshitta. So once again, we have nothing but speculation, and once again, we go back to the fact that the only original manuscripts we have today are in Greek rather than Aramaic.

As for the work of Aramaic teachers like Lamsa who are fluent in modern Aramaic, it is possible that they will spot idioms and insights that other readers will miss, but it is important to remember that Aramaic has changed dramatically over the last two thousand years, and that idioms and customs have changed as well, despite the continuity of customs and traditions in the Middle East over the centuries. So, there may be some insights that can be gleaned from Lamsa's work and the work of others following in his footsteps, but all extravagant claims of a corrupt Greek text and an original Aramaic text are to be rejected.

42

What are some examples of the Jewish background to the New Testament?

Since the New Testament was primarily written by Jews (all but probably Luke were Jewish) who would have been used to communicating in Aramaic or Hebrew, since the message of the New Testament centers on the life, death and resurrection of the Jewish Messiah, since much of the New Testament describes events that took place in the land of Israel and since the contents of the New Testament can only be understood fully in light of the Hebrew Scriptures, it is only natural that there are numerous, richly attested aspects of the Jewish background to the New Testament. Here are some examples.

Historical and religious background to specific verses. Most believers are familiar with the Lord's words in John 7:37–38: "If anyone is thirsty, let him come to me and drink. Whoever believes in me, as the Scripture has said, streams of living water will flow from within him." John 7:37 provides the background: "On the last and greatest day of the Feast, Jesus stood and said in a loud voice." But what is the significance of this? The Torah laws mention nothing that would explain why Jesus spoke these words on this particular day, but first-century Jewish traditions provide the background:

7:37 The "last day" of the Feast of Tabernacles (7:2) probably refers to the eighth day. For at least the first seven days of the feast, priests marched in procession from the Pool of Siloam to the Temple and poured out water at the base of the altar. Pilgrims to the feast watched this ritual, which Jews throughout the Roman world thus knew; it was even commemorated on souvenir jars they could take home with them.

7:38 The public reading of Scripture at this feast included the one passage in the Prophets that emphasized this feast, Zechariah 14, which was interpreted in conjunction with Ezekiel 47. Together these texts taught that rivers of living water would flow forth from the Temple (in Jewish teaching, at the very center of the earth, from the foundation stone of the Temple), bringing life to all the earth. The water-drawing ceremony (7:37) (originally meant to secure rain) pointed toward this hope.

7:39 Most of Judaism did not believe that the Spirit was prophetically active in their own time but expected the full outpouring of the Spirit in the Messianic age or the world to come. Water usually symbolized Torah (law) or wisdom in Jewish texts, but John follows Old Testament precedent in using it for the Spirit (see Isaiah 44:3; Ezekiel 36:24–27; Joel 2:28).[47]

Now look at Yeshua's words again. What an extraordinary statement He was making!

Names, words and terms. When you hear the words "Jesus Christ, son of Mary," you naturally think of something very "Christian" (and probably even Gentile). But when you hear the words "Yeshua the Messiah, son of Miriam," something very different comes to mind, something quite Jewish. But Jesus *was* Jewish, not Christian (see #36), and His mother's name was Miriam, not Mary. As simple as this is, just referring to Jesus as Yeshua—even on occasion—and referring to His mother as Miriam immediately serves to remind us that our Savior and His family were all Jews.

In my book *Revolution in the Church*, I included a Jewish roots chapter entitled "Have You Read the Epistle of Jacob Lately?" You might ask, "Which epistle is that? Is that one of those ancient documents that was discovered recently, like the gospel of Judas?" Not at all. As I explain:

Let's look at the opening verse of this epistle as rendered in a traditional English version: "James, a servant of God and of the Lord Jesus Christ, to the twelve tribes scattered among the nations: Greetings" (James 1:1, NIV). You might take this as saying, "This is the Christian leader James writing to Christians scattered around the world, figuratively referred to as the twelve tribes."

But what if we rendered the Greek literally, also rendering other names in a way that reflects their Hebrew/Aramaic background? It would sound like this: "Jacob, a servant of God and of the Lord Yeshua Messiah, to the twelve tribes scattered among the nations: Shalom." Now what comes to mind? You respond, "This is a letter from a Jewish believer in the Messiah to Jewish believers scattered around the world." Correct! And notice that one key word: *Jewish.* The New Testament is a Jewish book![48]

Yes, James in the original Greek is actually Jacob, as reflected in almost every translation into every other language.[49] Only in English is it James, a later form that came about when the Latin *Iacobus,* the equivalent of Greek *Iakobus,* was corrupted into *Iacomus,* which then made its way into English as James. Shall we turn, then, to the Letter of Jacob? What a difference a name can make!

Just think: Saying Abraham, Isaac and James almost sounds like mixing Judaism and Christianity; saying Abraham, Isaac and Jacob makes a world of difference. Well, two of Yeshua's disciples were named Jacob, and one of His blood brothers, the author of this letter, was also named Jacob.

How about turning now to the Letter of Judah (better known as Jude)? In this case, it is not a matter of a corrupt linguistic form, as in James rather than Jacob. It is simply remembering that the man called Jude in English would have been known to his colleagues as Judah. The Letters of Jacob and Judah. It is sounding like an entirely different Bible—a very Jewish one! Certainly, that was the world in which Yeshua and His disciples lived:

These are the names of the twelve emissaries:
First, Shim'on, called Kefa, and Andrew his brother,
Ya'akov Ben-Zavdai and Yochanan his brother,
Philip and Bar-Talmai,
T'oma and Mattityahu the tax-collector,
Ya'akov Bar-Halfai and Taddai,

Shim'on the Zealot, and Y'hudah from K'riot, who betrayed him.

Matthew 10:2–4, JNT

Yes, the disciples, too, were Jews, not Christians, and when they came to be called "Christians" (see Acts 11:26) it simply meant those who followed this *Christos* figure, a name with little meaning to the Greek-speaking world. (It would be like calling Billy Graham's followers "Grahamites," and in a derogatory way at that; see 1 Peter 4:12–16.)

Now let us take a look at a specific verse in Jacob, namely, Jacob 2:2, where the Greek word *synagogēs* is used:

The Greek word *synagoges*, meaning "assembly, meeting place, synagogue," occurs 56 times in the Greek New Testament, being found most frequently in the Gospels and Acts (53 times). Obviously, when you hear the word "synagogue," you think, "Jewish."

In the Gospels, Jesus frequently attended the local synagogues, where He generally found Himself in conflict with the Jewish leadership. This, of course, makes sense to us, since Jesus had not yet died on the cross and founded "Christianity," so it was OK for him to attend synagogue, right? In Acts, Paul, a converted Jew (correct?), went into the synagogues to preach Christianity to the unconverted Jews, which also makes sense, since he wanted to reach his own people with the good news about the Messiah. And how is *synagoges* translated each of these 53 times in the Gospels and Acts? Synagogue, of course.

The word also occurs twice in the book of Revelation, namely, in Revelation 2:9 and 3:9, speaking of those who claim to be Jews and are not, but are a *synagoges* of Satan. And once more, translators render the word with "synagogue"—this time, a Jewish synagogue of Satan (quite naturally, since the context is negative!). So, 55 out of 56 times, *synagoges* is translated "synagogue," indicating that there's not much dispute about the meaning of the word.

There's just one time in our English Bibles that *synagoges* is *not* translated "synagogue"—James 2:2! "Suppose a man comes into your *meeting* . . ." (NIV). Or, in the King James Version, "For if there come unto your *assembly*. . . ." What a revelation! Since this is a "Christian" context rather than a "Jewish" context, *synagoges* cannot possibly mean "synagogue." Rather, it has to mean "meeting" or "assembly," since Christians don't meet in synagogues. This, of course, is confirmed by 5:14, where those who are sick are enjoined to call for "the elders of *the church*."

There's only one problem with this line of reasoning: This is the epistle of Jacob, not James, and it was written to *Jewish Christians*, not Gentile Christians. That's why David Stern in his *Jewish New Testament* rightly renders this, "Suppose a man comes into your synagogue . . . ," while Kenneth Wuest's *Expanded Translation* reads, "For if there comes into your synagogue [the meeting place of Christian-Jews]. . . ." As New Testament scholar Craig Keener commented, the word translated " 'Assembly' (KJV, NASB, NRSV) or 'meeting' (NIV, GNB) is literally 'synagogue,' either because James wants the whole Jewish community to embrace his example, or because the Jewish-Christian congregations (cf. 5:14) also considered themselves messianic synagogues." It is the latter explanation that is most likely.

How novel this sounds to most Christian ears: a Jewish epistle written to Jewish believers who met in Messianic synagogues! But that is clearly what the text indicates, although it is not the way most Christian teachers have interpreted the text.[50]

Hebrew or Aramaic Usage. Although I have emphasized that God preserved the New Testament for us in Greek rather than in Hebrew or Aramaic (see #40 and #41), we know that Jesus taught in Aramaic or Hebrew, and therefore we should expect Hebrew or Aramaic concepts or expressions to underlie the Greek text at many points. A frequently cited example of this is found in Matthew 6:22–23, which the NIV translates:

The eye is the lamp of the body. If your eyes are good, your whole body will be full of light. But if your eyes are bad, your whole body will be full of darkness. If then the light within you is darkness, how great is that darkness!

This is rendered quite differently in David Stern's *Jewish New Testament*:

"The eye is the lamp of the body." So if you have a "good eye" [that is, if you are generous] your whole body will be full of light; but if you have an "evil eye" [if you are stingy] your whole body will be full of darkness. If, then, the light in you is darkness, how great is that darkness!

What is the basis for Stern's bracketed comments? Matthew commentator Donald Hagner explains:

These difficult verses can only be understood correctly by noting the context in which they stand, i.e., the pericopes [sections] on either side, both of which refer to concern with wealth. The *haplous* eye and the *ponēros* eye are not to be understood physically as a healthy and a diseased eye.... The eye is referred to metaphorically in this passage. The *ponēros* eye is the "evil eye" of Near Eastern cultures—an eye that enviously covets what belongs to another, a greedy or avaricious eye.... For the Jewish use of the expression in this sense, see *m. 'Abot* 2:12, 15; 5:16, 22.... Other references to an evil eye in this sense are found in Matthew 20:15 and Mark 7:22 (cf. Sir 14:8–10; Tob 4:7). The *haplous* eye, given the symmetrical structure of the passage, is probably the opposite of the evil eye, namely, a generous eye, as in the cognate adverb *haplōs*, "generously," in Jas 1:5 (cf. Rom 12:8; 2 Cor 8:2; 9:11, 13)—an eye that is not attached to wealth but is ready to part with it.[51]

To be sure, Hagner notes that not all scholars agree with this, based on other Greek evidence, and, as I pointed out in a previous article, the question of " 'single/sound/good eye' = 'generous' and 'not sound/evil eye' = 'stingy' (see Matthew 6:22–23) . . . has been the subject of lively discussion for decades, and it can be readily adduced from Septuagintal usage (cf. Proverbs 22:9) or even from the Greek New Testament itself (cf. Romans 12:8; 2 Corinthians 8:2; 9:11, 13; James 1:5; and Matthew 20:15) without any recourse to rabbinic literature." In other words, just reading the Septuagint and New Testament carefully, the same conclusions could be reached about the Greek words in Matthew 6:23 meaning "generous" and "stingy" rather than "good" and "bad." However, recognizing the Jewish usage of "evil eye" = "stingy" helps to confirm this interpretation, which makes excellent sense in the context of Matthew 6.

These, then, are just a few examples of the Jewish background of the New Testament. For many more examples, see David Stern's *Jewish New Testament Commentary*, although not all scholars would accept all of Stern's interpretations; see also Samuel Tobias Lachs, *A Rabbinic Commentary on the New Testament: The Gospels of Matthew, Mark and Luke* (Lachs is not a believer in Jesus); more broadly, see Craig Keener's *The IVP Bible Background Commentary: New Testament*. Other, more specific studies are listed in the bibliographical supplement to my study *Our Hands Are Stained with Blood*.

43
What does it mean to "restore the Jewish roots" of the Christian faith?

I have often said that God did not send His Son into the world as a Jewish rabbi to establish a lovely new Gentile religion called Christianity. Rather, Jesus came into the world to fulfill what was written in Moses and the Prophets, to bring to realization the promises made to Abraham, Isaac and Jacob, and to establish a new and better covenant with the house of Israel and the house of

Judah. In light of this, it is common for Jewish believers in Jesus to state clearly that they have not converted to Christianity—since that implies something alien and Gentile to Jewish people—and to say instead that they have found the Jewish Messiah. And for many Jewish believers, recognizing Yeshua as Messiah has caused them to deepen their personal sense of Jewishness and strengthen their commitment to the people of Israel worldwide.

Many Gentile Christians have also recognized that being joined together with Jesus meant that they were now uniquely connected to the Jewish people, which makes perfect sense. After all, if Jesus had been a good Russian who taught in Russian and was a child of Russian culture, and if all of His first followers had been Russian, and if the Russians were the chosen people and Jesus came first for His own Russian people, sending them to *share* the Good News with the rest of the world, wouldn't all of us feel a special solidarity with the Russians?

What, then, does it mean to restore the Jewish roots of the Christian faith? Here are some initial foundations for understanding. (1) It means that Gentile believers understand Paul's words in Romans 11:18, specifically, his warning that, "You do not support the root, but the root supports you." So, rather than the Church replacing Israel—an unbiblical and, in Jewish history, dangerous doctrine—Israel has expanded its borders to the nations. In this context, it should be emphasized that the Lord made His new covenant with the *house of Israel and the house of Judah* (see Jeremiah 31:31–34, quoted in Hebrews 8:8–12), not with the nations of the world, which means that Gentile believers are grafted into Israel's new covenant and thereby "share in the nourishing sap from the olive root" (Romans 11:17). (2) We understand that God's ideal was not for the Church to become a predominantly Gentile religion that severed its vital connection with its biblical Jewish foundations, changing the Sabbath to Sunday and separating Easter from Passover. (For the question of Sabbath

188

observance, see #49.) This also means that we understand that a Jew does not need to become Gentile to be a follower of Jesus. (3) We seek to grasp the spiritual and even cultural understanding that our Savior was a Jewish rabbi named Yeshua, recognizing that many of His teachings can only be fully understood against the historical and religious background of the day (see #42). (4) We take hold of the prophetic significance of the biblical calendar, beginning with Passover, which prophetically speaks of Yeshua's death, and ending with Tabernacles, which prophetically speaks of the final ingathering of the nations (see #51). (5) We recognize that Israel plays a special role in world redemption—and therefore the Good News of the Messiah is to the Jew first (see Romans 1:16). Therefore, we should pray regularly that Jerusalem will become the praise of all the earth (see Isaiah 62:6–7), and we should understand that Yeshua will not return to earth until His own people welcome Him back (see Matthew 23:37–39; see #58 and #59), and therefore Israel's salvation will mean life from the dead (see Romans 11:11–15).

There is much more, of course, that could be said, but these thoughts are meant to stimulate further study, prayer and action, all of which can be healthy, constructive and life-giving.

Unfortunately, there are many groups that have ended up on the fringes in their search for Jewish roots, and their teachings are confused at best and heretical at worst. Here are some of the characteristics of these fringe groups: (1) Torah gradually displaces Yeshua in terms of centrality, emphasis and devotion. In contrast with this, the Father has ordained that "in everything [Jesus] might have the supremacy. For God was pleased to have all his fullness dwell in him" (Colossians 1:18–19). The Torah finds its fulfillment in Yeshua, not the reverse (see Matthew 5:17–20; see also #46). (2) These fringe groups get caught up with externals and secondary things, such as never saying the name "Jesus"—as if it was the name of a false god or a curse word (see #38)—and major on the minors. (3) They teach that Gentile believers are *obligated* to observe the Torah, putting an *overemphasis* on Messiah's Jewish observance of the Torah as well. (For aspects of Torah observance that are right and aspects that are wrong, see #48 and #49.) (4) They have a disproportionate interest in "Jewish background" and emphasize Yeshua's Jewishness more than His Lordship, getting caught up in recovering the "original meaning" of His teachings as a rabbi far more than they get caught up with knowing and loving Him in His fullness. In keeping with this, they will spend more time studying rabbinic literature than the Word of God itself. (5) They begin to dress and act like traditional Jews (or even ancient Israelites), although they themselves are not Jewish, sometimes trying to find some connection to the people of Israel in their distant lineage. (Even for Messianic Jews, unless God has called them to reach out to traditional Jews and to live among them, in the spirit of 1 Corinthians 9:20–22, there is no good reason for them to dress and look like traditional Jews, since traditional lifestyles reflect rabbinic teaching more than Torah; see #18, #19 and #22.)

These practices are not in themselves heretical, but it is not uncommon for people on the fringes to take the plunge into heretical views, normally beginning with the denial of Yeshua's eternal deity and the outright rejection of God's tri-unity—in a private email to me, one teacher recently called the Trinity a "three-headed monster"!—and these heretical teachings lead to the rejection of the rest of the Body, all very perilous positions in terms of right connections with God's truth and God's people.

On the other hand, Church history has not always been that rosy—especially from a Jewish perspective—and many errors in theology and practice have crept in because of the Church's rejection of her Jewish roots. A very practical book on this subject is Ronald E. Diprose's *Israel and the Church: The Origins and Effects of Replacement Theology* (Carlisle, U.K.: Authentic Media,

2004; Dr. Diprose is a theological professor in Italy). The Church's ignorance of God's eternal purposes for Israel led to arrogance, which is always spiritually fatal (see Romans 11:25).

So then, it is detrimental for the Church to sever its Jewish roots and it is damaging for the Church to overemphasize its Jewish roots. The solution is a healthy recovery of those Jewish roots and foundations, with Yeshua remaining first and foremost in our devotion and proclamation.[52]

44

Was Paul really an educated Jew who knew the Hebrew language well?

To many Christians, this might seem like an odd question. After all, wasn't Paul a learned Jew, educated in Jerusalem at the feet of Rabban Gamaliel, the greatest Jewish teacher of his day (see Acts 22:3)? And didn't he debate for weeks on end in the synagogues (see Acts 18:4)? How could anyone question if Paul knew Hebrew?

On some level, this is a Jewish question more than a Christian question, but since Paul's credibility is always being challenged—it seems like, next to Jesus, Paul is at the top of the list for criticism and attack—it is worthwhile to take a moment to set the record straight.

Some argue against Paul's knowing Hebrew because, they say: (1) the references to Paul speaking in the "Hebrew language" in Acts actually mean Aramaic (see Acts 21:40; 22:2, and see #39 and #40); (2) Paul always quotes the Greek Septuagint when citing verses from the Hebrew Bible, which only makes sense if Paul couldn't read Hebrew; and (3) at times his citations seem to violate the meaning of the Hebrew, which again would point to his being unable to read the original. One Jewish scholar, followed recently by a Jewish journalist, has even argued that Paul was not even born Jewish but was rather a convert to Judaism—which would make him a bold-faced liar, too (see Philippians 3:4–6; Galatians 1:13–14).[53]

What, then, do some *Jewish* scholars say about Paul? Here are some statements from past generations.[54] First, I cite Joseph Klausner (1874–1958), who taught at the Hebrew University in Jerusalem. This was his verdict on Paul's Jewishness:

> It would be difficult to find more typically Talmudic expositions of Scripture than those in the Epistles of Paul.[55]
>
> Even at the end of his life, after he had had many sharp conflicts with the Jews . . . after all this, he called to his place of confinement first of all the Jews of Rome, and assured them that he had nothing 'whereof to accuse' his people ('my nation').[56]
>
> Truly, Paul was a Jew not only in his physical appearance, but he was also a typical Jew in his thinking and in his entire inner-life. For Saul-Paul was not only 'a Pharisee, a son of Pharisees,' but also one of those disciples of the Tannaim who were brought up on the exegesis of the Torah, and did not cease to cherish it to the end of their days.[57]
>
> Paul lived by Jewish law like a proper Jew; also, he knew the Old Testament in its Hebrew original and meditated much upon it. . . . Hence there are Semitisms and Hebraisms in the language of the Epistles, in spite of the richness of their Greek. If Paul was a 'Hebrew of the Hebrews' and 'a Pharisee, a son of Pharisees,' educated in Jerusalem and able to make speeches in Hebrew (or Aramaic), obviously he was not a 'Septuagint Jew' (Septuaginta-Jude) only, as various Christian scholars have been accustomed to picture him.[58]

Regarding Paul's allegedly deceptive missionary practices in which he said he acted "as a Jew to the Jews" (see 1 Corinthians 9:20–22), Professor David Daube, the respected author of *The New Testament and Rabbinic Judaism*, argues that Paul took over his missionary methods "from Jewish teaching on the subject:

the idea that you must adopt the customs and mood of the person you wish to win over, and the idea that, to be a successful maker of proselytes, you must become a servant of men and humble yourself."[59] Even here, Paul operated within a Jewish framework.

More recently, Professor Alan Segal wrote:

> Without knowing about first century Judaism, modern readers— even those committed by faith to reading him—are bound to misconstrue Paul's writing. . . . Paul is a trained Pharisee who became the apostle to the Gentiles.[60]

According to Talmudic and Aramaic scholar Daniel Boyarin:

> Paul has left us an extremely precious document for Jewish studies, the spiritual autobiography of a first-century Jew. . . . Moreover, if we take Paul at his word—and I see no a priori reason not to—he was a member of the Pharisaic wing of first-century Judaism.[61]

Rabbi Dr. Burton Visotzky, Appleman Chair of Midrash and Interreligious Studies, Jewish Theological Seminary, New York, wrote this in his endorsement of Professor Brad Young's *Paul the Jewish Theologian*: "The Pharisee Saul of Tarsus is arguably one of the most influential religious figures in the history of Western culture." Yes, the Pharisee Saul of Tarsus, not the deceiver Saul of Tarsus. Even the famous Rabbi Jacob Emden (1679–1776), a champion of Orthodox Judaism, said that "Paul was a scholar, an attendant of Rabban Gamaliel the Elder, well-versed in the laws of the Torah."[62]

Consider also the testimony of some of the world's leading New Testament scholars, a number of whom are thoroughly conversant with the best of early Jewish scholarship.

According to Dr. Peter J. Tomson:

As distinct from Philo, Paul had an openly avowed knowledge of Hebrew and of Pharisaic tradition. . . . Again, as opposed to Philo, Paul does not just draw on the Hebraist Jewish tradition of Midrash but proves an independent and creative master of the genre. . . . Although apparently descending from a prominent diaspora family who had acquired Roman citizenship, his mother tongue, quite probably, was not Tarsean Greek but the Hebrew and Aramaic of Jerusalem.[63]

According to John Dominic Crossan (a critical New Testament scholar) and Jonathan L. Reed (an archaeologist), "Paul was Jewish born and bred, understood Hebrew, was a Pharisee, and was proud of all that lineage. He identified himself as a Jew within Judaism."[64] (This assessment is all the more noteworthy given the skeptical presuppositions of the authors.)

The highly respected *Dictionary of Paul and His Letters* states:

Paul's use of Scripture, of midrashic techniques and of contemporary exegetical traditions in Romans 9:6–29 yielded a highly sophisticated composition. It cannot have been the product of an uneducated mind. If he was not trained by Gamaliel, then he was taught by some other Jewish master. In any case, it seems clear that Paul received a formal education in the Judaism of the time.

Today . . . NT scholarship finds more and more evidence for the Jewishness of Paul's life and thought. Indeed, this change is part of a general movement in Christian scholarship to rediscover the Jewish roots of Christianity. Concurrently, Jewish scholarship shows a growing interest in reclaiming the Jewishness of Jesus and Paul.[65]

Finally, I cite Professor Jarislov Pelikan, perhaps the world's foremost authority on church history. He writes that, in contrast with past scholarly views that often saw Paul as "the one chiefly responsible for the de-Judaization of the gospel and even for the transmutation of the person of Jesus from a rabbi in the Jewish sense to a divine being in the Greek sense," studies in the last few decades are seeing things much differently. Thus, "scholars have not only put the picture of Jesus back into the setting of first-century Judaism; they have also rediscovered the Jewishness of the New Testament, *and particularly of the apostle Paul,* and specifically of his Epistle to the Romans."[66] Yes, scholars are rediscovering the Jewishness of Paul![67]

The charge, then, that Paul didn't know Hebrew and, therefore, always cited the Septuagint would certainly be quite a surprise to the Jewish scholars cited above, most, if not all, of whom are fluent in Hebrew, Aramaic and Greek and can recognize the Hebraic fluency of Paul.

What indications, then, do we have that Paul knew Hebrew and was trained as a Pharisee, as he claimed? First, there is the testimony of the Jewish scholars cited above who recognized Paul as one of their own. Second, Paul did not always follow the Septuagint, despite the fact that he was writing to Gentiles who used the Septuagint exclusively and, for the most part, did not have access to any other translation. The most prominent example is found in his quotation of Habakkuk 2:4 (see Romans 1:17; Galatians 3:11), a foundational text for Paul, but one where he does not follow the Septuagint. Third, some Septuagint scholars have observed that, upon careful examination, in roughly half of the cases involved (approximately fifty out of one hundred), Paul does not follow the Septuagint exactly when he cites it, suggesting that he may have been involved in a revision of the text based on the Hebrew. Fourth, passages such as Romans 11:27–28, which some have cited as misquotations, actually point to a careful knowledge of the Hebrew text.[68]

There is every reason, then, to take Paul's testimony in Acts seriously, and for all those who have sought to plumb the depths of Paul's quotations from the Tanakh, it is clear that not only was he taught by the finest Jewish teachers of his day, he was taught by the Lord Himself.

45

Did the Jews really kill Jesus?

A good friend of mine who was a Conservative Jewish rabbi once said, "I could get into a boat and sail off in the ocean of Jewish blood that has been shed in Jesus' name." The ocean of Jewish blood shed in Jesus' name? Absolutely. Edward Flannery writes,

> The vast majority of Christians, even well educated, are all but totally ignorant of what happened to Jews in history and of the culpable involvement of the Church. . . . It is little exaggeration to state that those pages of history Jews have committed to memory are the very ones that have been torn from Christian (and secular) history books.[69]

What was it that provoked such "Christian" hostility toward the Jews? Above all, it was the belief that the Jews killed Jesus, leading to the charge of deicide (killing God!). Not surprisingly, some Jewish groups were up in arms before Mel Gibson's movie *The Passion of the Christ* came out in 2004, fearing similar attacks from "Christians" who watched the movie. That is how deeply this issue touches the Jewish people.[70]

Of course, even if the broad statement that "the Jews killed Jesus" was totally true, it would not justify Christian hatred or persecution of the Jewish people, and we can safely say that only hypocritical or counterfeit Christians could have been guilty of committing atrocities against the Jews for this reason. But did the Jews really kill Jesus? What does the New Testament say?

(1) The primary message of the New Testament is that God gave His Son for the salvation of the world, and therefore the death of Jesus was the explicit, foreordained will of God (see 1 Peter 1:18–20). True Christians, therefore, do not blame anyone for killing Jesus; rather, they thank God for sending His Son. This is

a central theme of the Scriptures: "For God so loved the world that he gave his one and only Son, that whoever believes in him shall not perish but have eternal life" (John 3:16). "But God demonstrates his own love for us in this: While we were still sinners, [Messiah] died for us" (Romans 5:8).

(2) Jesus Himself testified that no one took His life; He laid it down willingly.

> This is how we know what love is: Jesus [the Messiah] laid down his life for us.
>
> 1 John 3:16

> I am the good shepherd. The good shepherd lays down his life for the sheep. . . . The reason my Father loves me is that I lay down my life—only to take it up again. No one takes it from me, but I lay it down of my own accord. I have authority to lay it down and authority to take it up again. This command I received from my Father.
>
> John 10:11, 17–18

Who among us does not live with constant gratefulness to the Lord Jesus for laying down His life on our behalf? Who would ever think of blaming the Jews (or Romans or anyone) for killing Him? Yes, Jesus "loves us and has freed us from our sins by his blood" (Revelation 1:5), and for that we give thanks. That's why the words of Revelation 5:9 will be sung through the ages: "You are worthy to take the scroll and to open its seals, because you were slain, and with your blood you purchased men for God from every tribe and language and people and nation."

(3) Jesus died as the payment for our sins, and therefore it was our sins that nailed Him to the cross. As expressed in the classic words of Isaiah:

> Surely he took up our infirmities
>   and carried our sorrows,
> yet we considered him stricken by God,
>   smitten by him, and afflicted.
> But he was pierced for our transgressions,
>   he was crushed for our iniquities;
> the punishment that brought us peace was upon him,
>   and by his wounds we are healed.
> We all, like sheep, have gone astray,
>   each of us has turned to his own way;
> and the LORD has laid on him
>   the iniquity of us all.
>
> Isaiah 53:4–6

It has sometimes been said that a person has not truly repented until he realizes that it is his own sins that nailed Jesus to the cross. As expressed by John Newton, the former slave trader who went on to write the hymn "Amazing Grace":

> My conscience felt and owned its guilt,
>   And plunged me in despair;
> I saw my sins His blood had spilt
>   And helped to nail Him there.

I ask again: What man or woman with this understanding would think for a moment about blaming someone else for Yeshua's death?

(4) There is Jewish responsibility for rejecting the Messiah and giving Him over to the Romans to be executed, but when the Jewish people are confronted with this in the New Testament, the Jews are told either that they acted in ignorance, or that Jesus' death was ordained by God or that Jesus rose from the dead and that there is hope for redemption if they would repent. The message is even called "Good News"! (Note also that Jewish responsibility for the death of Jesus primarily fell on a limited number of

Jewish people as opposed to the nation as a whole.) Listen to the testimony of the Word:

> "Men of Israel, listen to this: Jesus of Nazareth . . . was handed over to you by God's set purpose and foreknowledge; and you, with the help of wicked men, put him to death by nailing him to the cross. . . . Therefore let all Israel be assured of this: God has made this Jesus, whom you crucified, both Lord and Christ." When the people heard this, they were cut to the heart and said to Peter and the other apostles, "Brothers, what shall we do?" Peter replied, "Repent and be baptized, every one of you, in the name of Jesus Christ for the forgiveness of your sins. And you will receive the gift of the Holy Spirit. The promise is for you and your children and for all who are far off—for all whom the Lord our God will call."
>
> Acts 2:22–23, 36–39; see also Acts 4:25–28

> The God of Abraham, Isaac and Jacob, the God of our fathers, has glorified his servant Jesus. You handed him over to be killed, and you disowned him before Pilate, though he had decided to let him go. You disowned the Holy and Righteous One and asked that a murderer be released to you. You killed the author of life, but God raised him from the dead. We are witnesses of this. . . . Now, brothers, I know that you acted in ignorance, as did your leaders.
>
> Acts 3:13–15, 17

> Brothers, children of Abraham, and you God-fearing Gentiles, it is to us that this message of salvation has been sent. The people of Jerusalem and their rulers did not recognize Jesus, yet in condemning him they fulfilled the words of the prophets that are read every Sabbath. Though they found no proper ground for a death sentence, they asked Pilate to have him executed. When they had carried out all that was written about him, they took him down from the tree and laid him in a tomb. But God raised

him from the dead, and for many days he was seen by those who had traveled with him from Galilee to Jerusalem. They are now his witnesses to our people.

We tell you the good news: What God promised our fathers he has fulfilled for us, their children, by raising up Jesus.

Acts 13:26–33

What a contrast between the historic "Christian" message, which condemned and hated Jews for killing Jesus, calling them "Christ killers" and often going on violent rampages against Jewish people after Easter services, and these New Testament messages, which recognize Jewish responsibility in giving Jesus over to the Romans to be crucified but which state that: (1) His death was the preordained will of God; (2) the leaders acted in ignorance; (3) Jesus rose from the dead; (4) the door of repentance and mercy is still open wide; (5) God wants to bless them, not curse them; and (6) the message is good news![71]

And note carefully that there is not a single time in the entire New Testament that the charge of deicide is ever raised, either explicitly or implicitly.

(5) The Romans made the legal decision and committed the physical act of crucifying the Son of God, but this only highlights the point I have been making, since no one would ever think of hating the Italians today because some of their ancestors crucified Jesus. Of course not!

With this in mind, we can see how utterly diabolical it has been to hate and persecute and blame Jews for the death of Jesus. Even the fact that the great majority of Jewish people have continued to reject Him as Messiah provides no justification for anti-Jewish sentiments, since the Word reminds us that we, too, were once ignorant and blind to God's love (see Titus 3:3–7; for Paul's own testimony, see 1 Timothy 1:12–13). Jesus also prayed for forgiveness for those who crucified Him (see Luke 23:34), and if Jewish people were guilty of His death, then they were included in His

200

prayer for forgiveness. Quite tragically, the "Church" has often been its own worst enemy, driving Jews away from Jesus rather than attracting them to Him.[72]

We can safely say, then, that to blame anyone for Jesus' death is to obscure the greatness of His self-sacrifice and to diminish the depth of His love, and if He died for any reason other than His willful atonement for our sins, we have no Gospel, no New Testament, no hope.

Part 4

Contemporary Christians, the Law of Moses and the State of Israel

46

Did Jesus abolish the Law?

Although many Christians think of God's Law (Torah, see #5) in negative terms, the fact is that if Jesus simply discarded the Torah, He could not be the Messiah. This would be like someone claiming to be Jesus in His second coming and yet announcing a new way of salvation in which faith in Jesus was no longer necessary and in which the cross was now powerless in its effect. Perish the thought! In the same way, it would be unthinkable for a God-fearing Jew in the first century to imagine that the Messiah would come and abolish God's holy Torah. As New Testament scholar John Nolland observes, "In Jewish terms any attempt to annul (Gk. *kataluein*) the Law could have been viewed only with horror. . . . The Law defined the identity of the Jewish people."[1]

In the Sermon on the Mount, the first full-length teaching of the Lord recorded by Matthew, Jesus Himself emphasized that His purpose was not to abolish the Torah:

> Do not think that I have come to abolish the Law or the Prophets; I have not come to abolish them but to fulfill them. I tell you the truth, until heaven and earth disappear, not the smallest letter, not the least stroke of a pen, will by any means disappear from the Law until everything is accomplished.
>
> Matthew 5:17–18; verses 19–20 are important as well[2]

"But," you ask, "didn't Jesus have lots of conflicts with the religious leaders over the Torah? And didn't He make lots of changes to the Law?"

I'll answer this by summarizing what Jesus did and taught in the gospels, adding some reflections based on the epistles as well. I recognize, of course, that many volumes have been written on this subject, but I'll try to highlight the main points.

(1) *Yeshua fulfilled the Torah and the Prophets.* Notice carefully that in Matthew 5:17–18 Yeshua did not say, "I have not come to abolish *the Law*" but rather, "I have not come to abolish *the Law or the Prophets*" (emphasis added), meaning the entire Tanakh. Notice also that He did not say, "I have not come to abolish them but to *reinforce* them." Rather, He said, "I have not come to abolish them but to *fulfill* them" (emphasis added). What does this mean? It means that the Hebrew Scriptures find their ultimate expression in Him.

As I wrote in volume 4 of my series on *Answering Jewish Objections to Jesus*:

> To begin with, the Torah laws dealing with sacrifice, atonement, ritual cleansing, priesthood, tabernacle/temple reach their goal in the Messiah, the ultimate and final sacrifice for sins—in keeping with the Rabbinic principle that "the death of the righteous atones" (see vol. 2, 3.15)—the great High Priest, and the living embodiment of the Shekhinah—that is, the manifest presence of God on earth (see vol. 2, 3.1–2). The Torah was pointing to him! That's why, when the Temple was destroyed and the sacrifices ceased and the priests could no longer fulfill many of the functions, the followers of Yeshua were not set back at all. He had already fulfilled this aspect of Torah and replaced the shadow with the substance (for this imagery, see Hebrews 8–10). . . .
>
> We also recognize that Yeshua is the fulfillment of the biblical calendar, as explained in volume 1, 2.1, with Passover pointing to his death as the Lamb of God, paving the way for a greater exodus, Firstfruits pointing to his resurrection, Shavuot (Pentecost)

corresponding to the outpouring of the Spirit, and then, still in the future, Trumpets (in Jewish tradition, Rosh HaShanah) pointing to his return, Yom Kippur to national atonement for Israel, and Sukkot (Tabernacles) to the final ingathering of the nations. Even the calendar ultimately points to Messiah, and all this is part of his fulfilling the Torah and Prophets.[3]

In addition to this, in the Sermon on the Mount, Jesus gives His own authoritative interpretation of Torah laws, taking the moral commands to a deeper level, thereby providing a template for the interpretation of other, similar Torah laws. (For a good example of this, see Matthew 19:16–26.) This, too, is part of His "fulfilling" the Torah.

(2) *Yeshua Himself transcended the Torah.* In His personal life, Jesus never violated anything *written* in the Torah. When He was accused of violating the Sabbath, the real conflict was with the wrong application of the Torah and with man-made traditions, not with an actual Torah command. On numerous occasions, He rejected the religious traditions that distorted the meaning and purpose of God's laws (see Mark 7). Having said this, it is also important to understand that He transcended the written Torah as the Son of God. No one else could have said, "My Father is always at his work to this very day, and I, too, am working" (see John 5:17; this was said to the religious leaders after He healed a man on the Sabbath).

In keeping with His transcendent nature, He also explained that the divorce command was not given as an ideal but rather as a concession (see Matthew 19:8: "Moses permitted you to divorce your wives because your hearts were hard. But it was not this way from the beginning"). In another act of transcendence, when a woman caught in adultery was brought to Jesus to be stoned, Jesus exposed the hypocrisy of her accusers rather than saying she should be stoned (see John 8:1–11), despite the Torah law that adulterers be stoned (see Leviticus 20:10; Deuteronomy 22:22–24).

(3) *Yeshua pointed to the true intent of the Torah.* When man-made traditions got in the way of the true purpose of the Sabbath, Jesus went out of His way to heal and work miracles on that very day, reminding the people that it was to be a day of liberation and rest (see Matthew 11:28–30, reading these verses as the introduction to the Sabbath accounts that follow in Matthew 12:1–14). In fact, the reason given for the Sabbath in Deuteronomy 5:12–15 is so that the Israelites will remember that God delivered them from Egypt and called them to Himself. So, when we come to Jesus, we find rest for our souls.

This, too, brought Him into conflict with some of the religious leaders, whom He accused of putting all kinds of extra burdens on God's people (see Matthew 23:1–4). It is important to remember, however, that His argument with them was over man-made traditions, not the Torah itself.

(4) *Yeshua gave us a new understanding of the purity laws.* Although some scholars, especially Messianic Jews, question whether Jesus actually abolished the dietary laws (see #50), it is clear that He brought a deeper understanding of defilement, explaining that "nothing outside a man can make him 'unclean' by going into him. Rather, it is what comes out of a man that makes him 'unclean'" (Mark 7:15). What we eat goes into our stomachs and is then processed out of our bodies, and therefore it does not affect our spiritual being and cannot make us truly "unclean" (see Mark 7:19). On the other hand, "from within, out of men's hearts, come evil thoughts, sexual immorality, theft, murder, adultery, greed, malice, deceit, lewdness, envy, slander, arrogance and folly. All these evils come from inside and make a man 'unclean'" (Mark 7:21–23; this entire account is paralleled in Matthew 15). Paul also spoke to this issue as well in several of his letters (see #50).

Because the Torah placed such a strong emphasis on ritual purity alongside moral purity, it was very easy for the Jewish people to think that eating forbidden food or eating food with unwashed hands (see Matthew 15:19) produced the same kind of defilement as did moral impurity. Jesus made it clear that *real* defilement was spiritual, not ritual, and the real issue was the condition of the heart.

(5) *Yeshua opened up the door for the Gentiles to receive God's full blessings without becoming Jews.* It is significant that both Matthew 15 and Mark 7 place the same two accounts back-to-back: Jesus' dispute with some religious leaders about eating food with unwashed hands and the Lord's journey to Tyre and Sidon, where He heals the Canaanite woman's daughter. What is so important about this? To quote again from volume 4 of my series:

> When Peter received a thrice-repeated vision in Acts 10 which ordered him to kill and eat all kinds of unclean animals, God was *not* telling him to change his dietary habits. Rather, it was a visionary lesson that Peter should no longer call *the Gentiles* unclean; instead, they would now be accepted as spiritual equals through the Messiah. In the same way here, Yeshua's teaching about "clean" and "unclean," about spiritual defilement coming from the inside and not the outside, about no food, in and of itself, being truly "unclean" (even if it carries that legal status), is now put into spiritual practice, as the Lord takes a long journey *into a Gentile region* and then reaches out in mercy to a needy "Canaanite." Was there nowhere else where Jesus could get alone for a little while?
>
> The object lesson is indisputable: Jesus was pointing to the fact that the Gentiles were no longer to be considered "unclean" if they put their trust in him. As articulated some years later by Paul, "As the Scripture says, 'Anyone who trusts in him will never be put to shame.' For there is no difference between Jew and Gentile—the same Lord is Lord of all and richly blesses all who call on him, for, 'Everyone who calls on the name of the Lord will be saved.'" (Romans 10:11–13, quoting Joel 2:32). So then, in terms of salvation, Jesus the Messiah broke down the walls of separation so that, in this respect, "there is no difference between Jew and Gentile."

This was revolutionary! (In fact, it still *is* revolutionary, an object of misunderstanding and spiritual stumbling for many Jews.)[4]

Several times in the gospels Jesus contrasted the great faith of Gentile believers with the unbelief of His own people, stating, "I say to you that many will come from the east and the west, and will take their places at the feast with Abraham, Isaac and Jacob in the kingdom of heaven. But the subjects of the kingdom will be thrown outside, into the darkness, where there will be weeping and gnashing of teeth" (Matthew 8:11–12).

The door has been opened wide to the Gentiles through the coming of the Messiah, and they can have right standing with God without having to become Jews.

(6) *Yeshua changed our relationship to the Torah.* Through the establishing of a new and better covenant, we stand in a new and better relationship with God (this is a theme throughout Hebrews, where the word *better* appears repeatedly). There is no more death penalty for nonobservance of the Sabbath (and a host of other sins) and no more condemnation of the Law (see Romans 8:1–2; see also #47). Through our identification with Jesus in His death and resurrection, we die to sin and rise in new life (see Romans 6:1–11), now being led by the indwelling Spirit to crucify the flesh and walk in newness of life (see Romans 8:3–4). We have been supernaturally empowered, and God's laws are now written on our hearts (see Jeremiah 31:31–34; Ezekiel 36:26–29; cf. Psalm 40:8).

In the words of the old poem,

> To run and work, the law commands
> Yet gives us neither feet nor hands.
> But better news the gospel brings;
> It bids us fly and gives us wings.

To be sure, there are grave consequences for willfully rejecting God's grace, more severe even than the consequences of rejecting the Law of Moses (see Hebrews 2:1–4; 10:26–31; 12:25–29), but for those who love the Lord and want to serve Him, they have nothing to fear (see John 10:27–29), being confident that He who began the good work in them will bring it to completion (see Philippians 1:6), an assurance beyond that of the righteous living under the Sinai covenant.

These, then, are just some of the key elements of how Jesus fulfilled the Law and Prophets, bringing the entire Tanakh to its full expression and inaugurating the Messianic kingdom, bringing about profound changes in our relationship to the Torah. We do well to follow that new and better way, one in which Jesus gives us rest (see Matthew 11:28–30).

As for the question of whether Jewish and Gentile believers are required to obey the Law, see #'s 48 through #51.

47
Did Paul abolish the Law?

Some prominent Jewish (and liberal Christian) scholars have pointed to Paul as the "founder of Christianity," arguing that Jesus was a good, Torah-keeping rabbi but that Paul was the one who deviated from the Jewish roots of the faith, abolished the Torah and started a new Gentile religion. Is there any truth to this claim?

On the one hand, there are a number of verses in his letters that seem to support the theory that he nullified the Torah, such as:

> For he [Jesus] himself is our peace, who has made the two one and has destroyed the barrier, the dividing wall of hostility, by abolishing in his flesh the law with its commandments and regulations. His purpose was to create in himself one new man out of the two, thus making peace, and in this one body to reconcile both of them to God through the cross, by which he put to death their hostility.
>
> Ephesians 2:14–16

Therefore no one will be declared righteous in his sight by observing the law; rather, through the law we become conscious
of sin.

Romans 3:20

Before this faith came, we were held prisoners by the law, locked
up until faith should be revealed. So the law was put in charge to
lead us to Christ that we might be justified by faith. Now that faith
has come, we are no longer under the supervision of the law.

Galatians 3:23–25

Neither circumcision nor uncircumcision means anything; what
counts is a new creation.

Galatians 6:15

See also Romans 2:28–29; 4:13–15; 6:14; 7:5–6, 8–9; 10:4;
1 Corinthians 7:19; 15:56–57; Galatians 2:15–16; 3:10–13; 5:4,
18. Verses such as these, especially as traditionally interpreted
by the Church, would seem to make clear that Paul did, in fact,
abolish the Law.

There are two major points that can be raised against this,
however. First, Paul had many positive, affirming things to say
about the Torah: "It is those who obey the law who will be declared
righteous" (Romans 2:13); "Circumcision has value if you observe
the law, but if you break the law, you have become as though you
had not been circumcised" (2:25); "Do we, then, nullify the law
by this faith? Not at all! Rather, we uphold the law" (3:31); "What
shall we say, then? Is the law sin? Certainly not! Indeed I would
not have known what sin was except through the law.... So then,
the law is holy, and the commandment is holy, righteous and
good.... We know that the law is spiritual; but I am unspiritual,
sold as a slave to sin" (7:7, 12, 14); "For what the law was powerless to do in that it was weakened by the sinful nature, God did
by sending his own Son in the likeness of sinful man to be a sin

211

offering. And so he condemned sin in sinful man, in order that the righteous requirements of the law might be fully met in us, who do not live according to the sinful nature but according to the Spirit" (8:3–4); see also Romans 10:4, as rendered in the *Jewish New Testament* (in contrast with the translation of this verse in most Christian translations).[5]

Second, according to the book of Acts, Paul himself lived in obedience to the Law. If the Torah was such a bad thing, and if he abolished it, why then in Acts 18 did he take on himself a Nazarite vow prescribed by the Torah—without any coercion or pressure to do so (see verse 18)? If Paul abolished the Law, why didn't he *agree* with the rumors that he was guilty of teaching "all the Jews who live among the Gentiles to turn away from Moses, telling them not to circumcise their children or live according to our customs" (21:21)? To the contrary, he went out of his way to demonstrate—in the words of Jacob (James) that "there is no truth in these reports about you, but that you yourself are living in obedience to the law" (verse 24; see also 22:3–5; 23:6–9; 26:4–7; 28:17; notice also the ready access that Paul had into the synagogues, indicating that he was recognized as a Jew; see Acts 13:13–15; 14:1; 16:4).

How, then, do we reconcile these two apparently contradictory Pauls, one who was pro-Torah and the other who was anti-Torah; one who lived by the Law and the other who said we were no longer under the Law?

When responding to the question, "Did Jesus abolish the Law?" I mentioned that multiple volumes have been written on this subject. Even more volumes—and countless articles—have been written on the subject of Paul and the Law, with very little consensus between the positions.[6] Nonetheless, I do believe that certain conclusions are unavoidable.[7]

(1) *Although Paul lived as a Torah-observant Jew (with the exception, perhaps, of breaking certain laws—such as dietary laws—in*

order to bring the Good News to the Gentiles), he taught clearly that we—meaning both Jewish and Gentile believers—are not under the law, which has at least three applications. First, we are not under the law's condemnation (see Romans 8:1–4); second, we are not under the law as a system of justification (see Romans 3:19–24); third, we are not under the law as a tutor to bring us to the Messiah (see Galatians 3:23–25).

(2) *For Paul, Jesus the Messiah was central, not Torah.* Were the two contradictory to him? Certainly not. But since Jesus *fulfilled* the Torah and Prophets, that means that everything was pointing to Him (see #46). Only someone totally centered on Yeshua and for whom Torah was secondary could write these words:

> If anyone else thinks he has reasons to put confidence in the flesh, I have more: circumcised on the eighth day, of the people of Israel, of the tribe of Benjamin, a Hebrew of Hebrews; in regard to the law, a Pharisee; as for zeal, persecuting the church; as for legalistic righteousness, faultless.
>
> But whatever was to my profit I now consider loss for the sake of [Messiah]. What is more, I consider everything a loss compared to the surpassing greatness of knowing [Messiah] Jesus my Lord, for whose sake I have lost all things. I consider them rubbish, that I may gain [Messiah] and be found in him, not having a righteousness of my own that comes from the law, but that which is through faith in [Messiah]—the righteousness that comes from God and is by faith. I want to know [Messiah] and the power of his resurrection and the fellowship of sharing in his sufferings, becoming like him in his death, and so, somehow, to attain to the resurrection from the dead.
>
> Philippians 3:4–11

In this light, Paul wrote that God will "bring all things in heaven and on earth together under one head, even [Messiah]"—not Torah (Ephesians 1:10). A simple, albeit lengthy, exercise will

213

confirm this: Read Paul's letters and take Jesus out. There is nothing left! Then, try taking out Torah: Jesus is still left!

(3) *Paul stood firmly against all forms of ethnic and spiritual exclusivity, and some scholars have seen this as the primary issue Paul had with the Law.* He therefore opposed any notion that Jews stood on a higher plane than Gentile believers (see Romans 2:25–27; 3:9; 10:11–13) or that, as Jews, they had some type of guaranteed and secure spiritual status (John the Immerser addressed this as well; see Matthew 3:7–10). There were certainly divine privileges given to the Jewish people (see Romans 3:1–3; 11:16), but not a higher spiritual status outside of faith in Jesus.

(4) *Paul emphasized the surpassing greatness of God's new covenant and the glory of life in the Spirit.* It is true that the first covenant was glorious, but it was not to be compared with the glory of the new covenant: "For what was glorious has no glory now in comparison with the surpassing glory. And if what was fading away came with glory, how much greater is the glory of that which lasts!" (2 Corinthians 3:10–11; all of 2 Corinthians 3 is relevant). The emphasis here and elsewhere is clearly on walking in newness of life by the power of the Spirit: "So I say, live by the Spirit, and you will not gratify the desires of the sinful nature. . . . But if you are led by the Spirit, you are not under law. . . . Those who belong to Christ Jesus have crucified the sinful nature with its passions and desires. Since we live by the Spirit, let us keep in step with the Spirit" (Galatians 5:16, 18, 24–25; see also Romans 8:1–14).

(5) *Paul understood that the new order had broken in and that we were already experiencing the life of the world to come while still in this world.* That, too, changed our relationship to the Torah. After all, when we leave this world and enter fully into our resurrected state, our relationship to God's commandments will, quite obviously, be very different. Paul stated that, already in this age, we are partaking of the life and order of the world to come (see

Ephesians 1:3; 2:6), and from that vantage point we are to deal with sin and the flesh (see Colossians 3:1–14).

There are some rabbinic traditions that state that there will be certain changes in the Torah in the world to come. For example, the only sacrifices in the world to come will be thanksgiving offerings, and even unclean animals will be considered clean in the world to come.[8] These concepts are not unrelated to some of Paul's teachings.

In conclusion, having laid out some of the main lines of Paul's teachings, I should note that some Messianic Jews would want to qualify these statements and make the case that all Messianic Jews are called to live in accordance with Torah as a covenantal responsibility (that is, as part of Jewish calling but having nothing to do with salvation, forgiveness of sins or righteousness). On the other hand we can state emphatically that Paul *never* required Gentile believers to observe the Torah, and he flatly rebuked them when they thought that circumcision or Torah observance was required or could deepen their spiritual standing in any way. Rather, in keeping with the principles set forth by Yeshua, he understood what really mattered and emphasized the righteousness that came by faith. His emphasis to Jewish believers in terms of what mattered most would doubtless be the same.

48
Should Christians keep the Law?

Believers today, without exception, are *not* under the binding authority of the Mosaic Law. This, however, is an overly simplistic answer, so, for the moment, let us make a distinction between Jewish and Gentile believers in Jesus, looking first at the question of Gentile Christians and the Law. Then let us ask this question in two different ways: (1) "*Must* Gentile Christians keep the Law?" If not, then, (2) "*Should* Gentile Christians keep any part of the

Law?" After answering these questions, we'll return to the issue of Jewish believers and Torah observance.

The answer to the first question, "*Must* Gentile Christians keep the Law?" is quite simple: Certainly not! Nowhere does the New Testament require Gentile believers to observe the Torah. To the contrary, when the Gentiles first started coming to faith in the book of Acts, some Jewish believers argued, "The Gentiles must be circumcised and required to obey the law of Moses" (Acts 15:5). After all, this was a Jewish message about a Jewish Messiah. Wasn't it necessary, then, for these Gentiles to live like practicing Jews? The emphatic answer from the apostolic community was summed up by Peter: "No! We believe it is through the grace of our Lord Jesus that we are saved, just as they are" (verse 11). Paul's letter to the Galatians addresses this issue quite forcefully, and he warns the believers there in no uncertain terms: "You who are trying to be justified by law have been alienated from Christ; you have fallen away from grace" (Galatians 5:4).

In other contexts, Paul made it clear that believers are not under the supervision of the Law (to bring them to the Messiah; see Galatians 3:23–25); that believers cannot gain righteousness through the Law (see Galatians 2:21); that believers do not receive the Spirit by observing the Law (see Galatians 3:1–5); that believers are not under the Law but rather under grace (see Romans 6:14); and that the circumcision that really counts is a spiritual, internal circumcision (see Philippians 3:2–3; Colossians 2:11–12; see also Romans 2:28–29; 1 Corinthians 7:19; Galatians 6:15). Although scholars have suggested different interpretations for verses such as these—and many more could be cited—the plain sense is quite compelling: Gentile believers are *not* required to obey the Mosaic law, and for a believer to put himself or herself under the Law is to go backward, not forward (see #47).

That leads us, then, to the second question: "*Should* Gentile Christians keep any part of the Law?" Let us take a look at Acts 15 again. Jacob (commonly known in English as James; see #42) stated things succinctly:

> It is my judgment, therefore, that we should not make it difficult for the Gentiles who are turning to God. Instead we should write to them, telling them to abstain from food polluted by idols, from sexual immorality, from the meat of strangled animals and from blood. For Moses has been preached in every city from the earliest times and is read in the synagogues on every Sabbath.
>
> verses 19–21

What does this mean? Some have interpreted Jacob's words to say, "Look. These Gentiles who are coming to faith already attend the synagogues—they are God-fearers who believe in the God of Israel—and they'll catch on to everything soon enough, since they hear the Torah read every week. So, we'll make it easy for them to start, and then they'll embrace the whole Torah in time."

Such an interpretation, however, goes against many verses in Paul's letters, some of which have been cited above (and see #47). It also goes against the overall context of Acts 15 where the consensus of Peter, Barnabas, Paul and Jacob was *not*, "Now that these Gentiles are saved, we need to be sure that they get fully integrated into a Torah-observant life one way or another." Not surprisingly, the interpretation that Jacob was stating that the Gentiles will quickly learn to follow the entire Torah is rarely found among biblical scholars, many of whom understand Jacob to be saying, "These new Gentile believers will have no trouble understanding the basic requirements we are making of them, since they've heard the Torah read many times in the synagogues and are familiar with such things."

So then, should Gentile Christians observe the moral law while recognizing that the civil law and the ceremonial law applied only to ancient Israel? The problem with this approach is that the Torah does not neatly divide itself into these categories—while useful, it is not self-evident in the Torah itself—and, more importantly, when Paul wrote to the Gentile congregations, he often made reference to the Law, but not in a binding way. So, when he called for morality and purity and holiness, he did not say, "Do what is written in the Law." Rather, he taught with a different emphasis: "It is God's will that you should be sanctified: that you should avoid sexual immorality. . . . For God did not call us to be impure, but to live a holy life. Therefore, he who rejects this instruction does not reject man but God, who gives you his Holy Spirit" (1 Thessalonians 4:3, 7–8).[9]

It is true that in Ephesians 6:1–3, he appealed to the Ten Commandments when teaching the children in Ephesus to obey their parents. Notice, however, that he first says, "for this is right" (Ephesians 6:1), rather than first quoting the Torah text, while in Colossians 3:20 he tells the children to obey their parents "for this pleases the Lord." Clearly, Paul did not teach the Gentile congregations to obey everything that was written in the Torah, although he could always point to the whole Tanakh as a source of spiritual authority and truth.

But aren't Gentile believers free to follow whatever biblical commandments they find edifying and helpful, whether those commandments are written in the Torah, the Prophets, the book of Proverbs or the New Testament? Absolutely, as long as: (1) they remember the principles articulated by Paul, cited above, understanding that they cannot increase their spiritual standing by keeping the Law; (2) they do not judge others based on keeping or not keeping certain commandments (see especially Romans 14:1–13; note also Colossians 2:16–19); and (3) they do not get caught up in the nonessentials. The whole thrust of the New Testament is that our life is found *in Him*—in Jesus, the Son of God. Those who find themselves getting caught up primarily in a Torah identity should spend time meditating on the first chapter of Ephesians, after which a devotional reading of Hebrews would prove useful.

(As for the question of Gentile Christians celebrating the Torah's holy days, see #51.)

Having said all this, there *are* certain Torah laws that are based on universal principles, laws by which God judged the Canaanites in antiquity (see also #25). These are found most prominently in Leviticus 18, where various sexual unions are forbidden, ranging from incest to bestiality to homosexuality.[10] It can safely be said, then, that if the Lord judged the pagans for certain sins, He certainly will not tolerate those sins among His redeemed people. Similarly, when God rebuked the pagan nations in Amos 1:1–2:5, He rebuked them for violation of His universal moral principles, such as covenant breaking and cruelty, before rebuking Israel more specifically for its violations of the Torah.

In any event, all believers should be encouraged to follow the moral precepts of the Torah—why shouldn't they?—although, most of these laws are articulated and repeated in the New Testament itself, so that someone living among a people group who had only the New Testament translated into their language would have sufficient understanding of God's moral, spiritual and purity requirements.

What about Jewish believers in particular? Must they continue to observe the Torah? Again, the answer is no in terms of "must." As emphasized in #46 and #47, the relationship of all believers to the Torah, Jew and Gentile alike, has changed dramatically with the coming of the Messiah, the instituting of the new covenant and the inbreaking of the new age. To reiterate: We are no longer under the condemnation of the Torah, no longer under the Torah as a schoolmaster to bring us to the Messiah and no longer under the Torah as a system of justification or righteousness. The glory of the Torah has faded in light of the glory of the Messiah, not because the Torah is bad but because the Messiah is better. As a New Testament scholar expressed to me, it is like a typewriter being replaced by a computer.

Should Jewish believers, then, observe the Torah? A good case can be made for this in terms of covenantal responsibility because of the divine election of Israel.[11] That is to say, many Messianic Jews feel called to live in an identifiable way as Jews to help preserve the identity of their people, in keeping with God's purposes and promises (see Jeremiah 31:35–37). In this way, they also provide an ongoing witness to their people, thereby disproving the notion that Jews who believe in Jesus always assimilate. Seventh-day Sabbath observance, dietary laws and following the biblical calendar are the most common ways in which this is lived out by many Jewish believers.

Still, it must be emphasized that this should only be done to the extent that: (1) God writes it on the individual's (or congregation's) heart; (2) it is done in light of New Covenant realities and life in the Spirit, as emphasized above; (3) Yeshua must always be kept central; (4) this is always done out of freedom and not out of bondage; (5) other Jewish believers who do not have this written on their hearts should not be judged; and (6) the rest of the Body should not be judged and that Jewish believers who feel this covenantal calling should not separate themselves from the rest of the Body of Christ.[12]

The testimony of Messianic Jewish liturgist Jeremiah Greenberg, written in the third person, states things well:

> After spending the next ten years in the Church, God gave him the "Messianic Vision," which to him is two-fold. First, if God said that in the End Times Jewish people would come to know the Messiah, then it makes sense that at least some of them would remain visibly, identifiably Jewish as believers, rather than assimilate into other cultures.
>
> Secondly, it is a very powerful witness to our Jewish friends and brethren when we remain identifiably Jewish as believers. Then they can see that we have not changed our religion, but like the Israelite believers in the first century, have received the Messianic fulfillment, Jesus, Yeshua, that is prophesied in Scripture.

To Jeremiah it is a calling. It is not something that everyone should be doing, but rather just those who believe that they are being led in this direction. On the other hand, the Church could still regain a little more respect for her Jewish roots, and recognize, for example, that the Jewish feasts are really BIBLICAL feasts, having spiritual significance for all believers, and pointing continually to the Messiah.

Since then, Jeremiah has remained rooted in the Messianic community, while seeing Jews and non-Jews as EQUALS in the body of Messiah.[13]

49

Should Christians observe the Sabbath on Saturday?

Having addressed the larger question of the relationship between Christians and the Law of Moses in general (see #48), we can now address the specific question of the Sabbath. Are followers of Jesus—speaking in particular of Gentile followers of the Lord—*required* to keep the Sabbath? And if so, should it be on Saturday, as originally given, or on Sunday, as it has been observed through much of church history? Is it more scriptural simply to set aside *any one day* as holy to the Lord, a day to rest from normal work? Or is this a completely wrong approach to the Sabbath question for a Christian, since in Jesus, every day is holy to the Lord and we have already entered into rest from our labors?

Here are some key points for consideration:

(1) *The seventh-day Sabbath was sanctified at Creation and, according to the prophetic Scriptures, it will be part of the future age.* Normally, when we think of the Sabbath, we think of the Ten Commandments, but in reality, the Sabbath was sanctified at Creation (see Genesis 2:2–3), although there is no command associated with it at that time, and the Creation account forms the basis for the command to observe the Sabbath in Exodus 20:11:

"For in six days the LORD made the heavens and the earth, the sea, and all that is in them, but he rested on the seventh day. Therefore the LORD blessed the Sabbath day and made it holy."

But these words in Exodus 20, spoken by the Lord at Mount Sinai, do not represent the first time that God spoke to Israel about the Sabbath. This took place in Exodus 16, before the Israelites arrived at Sinai, when God commanded His people not to gather manna on the seventh day (see verses 22–26).

So then, the Sabbath was established at Creation and then given to the Israelites before Sinai, then commanded again at Sinai, and, according to Isaiah, it appears that the Sabbath will continue in the world to come:

> "As the new heavens and the new earth that I make will endure before me," declares the LORD, "so will your name and descendants endure. From one New Moon to another and from one Sabbath to another, all mankind will come and bow down before me," says the LORD.
>
> Isaiah 66:22–23

In any case, it can be stated clearly that in the Hebrew Bible, the Sabbath precedes Mount Sinai and appears to continue into the millennial age.

(2) *The seventh-day Sabbath was given as a special sign between God and Israel.* According to Exodus 31:17, God said that the Sabbath was to be "a sign between me and the Israelites forever, for in six days the LORD made the heavens and the earth, and on the seventh day he abstained from work and rested." He reiterated this centuries later through the prophet Ezekiel: "I gave them my Sabbaths as a sign between us. . . . Keep my Sabbaths holy, that they may be a sign between us" (Ezekiel 20:12, 20).

God did not call any other nation to observe the Sabbath, although He did open the door for Gentiles to join themselves to His covenant with Israel in Isaiah 56:4–7, which is addressed to "the eunuchs who keep my Sabbaths." So, the door was open for the Gentiles to enter into Israel's covenant, but the specific covenantal, seventh-day Sabbath sign was given exclusively to the people of Israel.

(3) *In the New Testament, Gentile believers are never called or required to observe the seventh-day Sabbath, and they become full citizens along with Israel without having to observe the full requirements of the Law* (see also #53).

It is true that many of the first Gentile believers were actually "God-fearers" who heard the message of the Gospel in synagogues (see Acts 13:26; 17:4, 17), and they would have been familiar with the seventh-day Sabbath.[14] In fact, they would have heard Paul preaching on the Sabbath. Nonetheless, as seen earlier (#48), the verdict of Acts 15 was clear: Gentile believers were not required to observe all the Torah laws.

Of course, the other books of the New Testament contain many ethical and moral instructions for the Gentile believers (see Ephesians 4:17–6:9), but nowhere are they commanded or called to observe the Sabbath. (For the correct interpretation of Acts 15:21, see #48.) To the contrary, they are exhorted not to allow anyone to pass judgment on them based on their observance or nonobservance of the Sabbath and other holy days: "Therefore do not let anyone judge you by what you eat or drink, or with regard to a religious festival, a New Moon celebration or a Sabbath day. These are a shadow of the things that were to come; the reality, however, is found in Christ" (Colossians 2:16–17).

In a different setting, Paul addressed this in Romans as well:

One man considers one day more sacred than another; another man considers every day alike. Each one should be fully convinced in his own mind. He who regards one day as special, does so to the Lord. . . . For none of us lives to himself alone and none of us dies to himself alone. If we live, we live to the Lord; and if we die, we die to the Lord. So, whether we live or die, we belong to the Lord.

Romans 14:5–8

Despite many different interpretations to this passage,[15] the conclusion seems unavoidable: Gentile believers were not called or expected to observe one specific day as uniquely set apart and holy to the Lord, and we have no evidence from early Church history that Gentile believers observed the seventh-day Sabbath.

(4) *There is no biblical support for the view that after the resurrection of Jesus, the Sabbath was changed to Sunday.* There is some evidence that as early as the late first or early second century, believers gathered before or after work on Sundays to celebrate the Lord's resurrection, but this was not related to the concept of the Sabbath, and strong arguments can be made against the Sabbath being changed to Sunday within the New Testament itself.[16] It was not until the fourth century that the Church formally declared that the Sabbath had been moved to Sunday, with the question begging to be asked, "By what authority did you do this?"

(5) *On the other hand, since God never commanded Gentile believers to observe the seventh-day Sabbath—it is simply not stated in the New Testament—there is no reason why they cannot set Sunday aside as a special day of rest and worship for the Lord, thereby incorporating the principle of Sabbath into their lives.* To the extent that Christians feel led to set aside Sunday as their Sabbath, there is nothing wrong with doing so, as long as they realize that they cannot judge others who do not share this conviction (see especially Romans 14).

This also means, however, that there is no reason that Gentile Christians cannot observe the Sabbath as Saturday, but again, I caution: This should not be done in a legalistic or binding way, despite the strong arguments brought by Seventh-Day Adventists, and, regardless of one's views, all extreme, anti-Sunday rhetoric such as the following should be rejected:

> Now we have come to know that Sunday is the mark of the papacy (the beast), and that Satan will soon make it almost impossible for people to honor God's sacred seventh day of rest by using the USA to impose universal Sunday laws. We should begin to honor the Sabbath (training ourselves while times are easier) and share this truth with others to try to win as many souls as we can. . . . From the overwhelming weight of evidence, we can decisively conclude that the beast of Revelation 13 and 14 is the Roman Catholic Church, and that its mark (the mark of the beast) is Sunday observance. . . . The Creator seeks your worship on His holy Sabbath day, and Satan, seeking to be like the Creator, wants your worship on his Sunday. Which will you choose?[17]

Nonsensical statements like this should be treated as such.

(6) *The Sabbath should be set aside as a day of delight in the Lord.* This was clearly stated by the Lord in Isaiah 58:13–14, and Jesus also taught that "the Sabbath was made for man, not man for the Sabbath" (Mark 2:27). This means that however this day is observed, it should be done with joy and gladness, truly honoring the Lord and truly bringing liberation to others. In keeping with this, Jesus frequently healed the sick on the Sabbath.

(7) *Our ultimate rest is found in a Person, not a day, so Sabbath observance should be both spiritual and practical.* It is clear that God set up a system of weekly renewal in which we would rest from our daily labors and focus on Him. On a certain level, through the work of the Messiah, we have entered into a perpetual rest from our own labors (see Matthew 11:28–30; Romans 4:4–5; Hebrews 4:9–11). On another level, the demands and distractions of this life are ever upon us, so it is good to slow down and turn aside from these things every week, at the same time directing our attention to the Lord to find renewal in Him.

Some of these same principles apply to Jewish believers, but we must remember that the seventh-day Sabbath *was* given as a special sign to Israel, and in keeping with that, it is especially appropriate for Messianic Jews to observe the seventh-day Sabbath, also worshiping as congregations on that day as well. Nonetheless, as we have stressed, this is a matter of conviction and calling, and other Jewish believers may sense a different calling and responsibility in the Lord, part of their being all things to all men so as to save some (see 1 Corinthians 9:20–22) and part of their liberty in the Lord. In that respect, we must always remember that, with the coming of the Messiah into the world, our relationship to the Torah was radically changed as well (see #46 and #47), and that includes our relationship to the Sabbath.

50
Should Christians adhere to the dietary laws?

Christians are perfectly free to adhere to the dietary laws, be they Jewish or Gentile believers, but believers today, be they Jewish or Gentile, are not *required* to keep the dietary laws, and it is wrong for anyone to try to bring God's people into a sense of bondage to the dietary laws.

Some Christians choose to adhere to the dietary laws for health purposes, believing that hygiene was a major reason for the dietary laws in the first place. This is certainly a commendable practice, but there is some dispute as to whether health concerns were the primary divine motivation behind the dietary laws (see #12). Some Messianic Jews choose to adhere to the dietary laws in covenantal solidarity with the Jewish people, which is also commendable, as long as they do not force their convictions on others (see #48, #49 and #51).

It is also important for all those who choose to follow the dietary laws to remember a number of important New Testament principles, some of which are touched on in #46, point 4.

1. *Jesus taught plainly that nothing that we eat can make us spiritually unclean, since food doesn't go into our hearts but into our stomachs, from which it leaves our bodies.* So what we eat does not make us unclean. Rather,

   > What comes out of a man is what makes him "unclean." For from within, out of men's hearts, come evil thoughts, sexual immorality, theft, murder, adultery, greed, malice, deceit, lewdness, envy, slander, arrogance and folly. All these evils come from inside and make a man "unclean."
   >
   > Mark 7:20–23

2. *Nothing is unclean in and of itself.* As Paul expressed to the Romans, "I know and am persuaded in the Lord Jesus that nothing is unclean in itself, but it is unclean for anyone who thinks it unclean" (Romans 14:14, ESV). Therefore, we must be sensitive to the fact that one believer can freely eat all foods with a "clean" conscience before God, while another believer cannot.

3. *Food does not possess spiritual qualities.* To quote Paul again, "Food does not bring us near to God; we are no worse if we do not eat, and no better if we do" (1 Corinthians 8:8). Certainly, it is important that we are good stewards over our bodies, and in that context, what we eat is important. But eating chicken, in and of itself, doesn't produce greater spirituality, and eating lobster, in and of itself, does not produce greater carnality.

4. *The dietary laws were symbolic of the separation of the Gentiles from the Jews, a separation removed by the cross.* It is important, then, that dietary laws are not used to breed separation between believers or to feed into attitudes of supposed spiritual superiority. And it is important that individual convictions be honored and that those who choose to follow the dietary laws be free to do so. But it is equally

important that those who are not convicted to adhere to these laws not be judged. We do well to remember that Paul made the following statement in the context of dietary habits: "Who are you to judge someone else's servant? To his own master he stands or falls. And he will stand, for the Lord is able to make him stand" (Romans 14:4).

5. *Adherence to the dietary laws must take second place to evangelism and, at times, fellowship.* Although the exact import of Paul's words in 1 Corinthians 9:20–22 has been disputed, the overall message is quite clear: He became "all things to all men so that by all possible means [he] might save some" (1 Corinthians 9:22). If it is necessary to eat pork to reach someone with the Gospel, then we should eat pork, and if for the sake of preserving fellowship it is necessary to eat a ritually unclean bird, we should do it. Many missionaries can attest to this, especially among people who have been rejected by the general society. To refuse their food, even if they are believers, is to reject them as people and to tell them that their best is not good enough for you, and there is no scriptural justification for this. The New Testament principles just articulated add further weight to this practical truth.

51
Should Christians observe the biblical Jewish holidays?

It is increasingly common for Gentile Christians to celebrate the biblical Jewish holidays, and there are many commendable reasons for doing so. Here are a few:

1. *The biblical holy days are infused with spiritual and prophetic significance.* Passover corresponds to Yeshua's death (see

1 Corinthians 5:7–8), Firstfruits to His resurrection (see 1 Corinthians 15:20) and the Festival of Weeks (*Shavu'ot*, or Pentecost) corresponds to the giving of the Spirit (see Acts 2:1–4). Trumpets points to the Lord's return with the sound of the trumpet (see Matthew 24:31; 1 Corinthians 15:52; 1 Thessalonians 4:16; Revelation 11:15), the Day of Atonement (Yom Kippur) points to Israel's final cleansing (see Zechariah 13:1, which follows from Zechariah 12:10), and Tabernacles (*Sukkot*) points to the final ingathering of the nations (see Zechariah 14:16–19; see also Revelation 7:9 and Leviticus 23:40, for palm branches and Tabernacles).

2. *The biblical holy days have great historic significance.* Although the Messianic significance of the biblical holy days is certainly of greater significance to Christians than is the historical significance, the origin and meaning of these holy days in Israel's history is also important. So, if it is okay to celebrate Thanksgiving and July 4 in America and to remember the events connected with those days, how can it be wrong to remember Israel's deliverance from Egypt in the Passover? When connecting this season to the death and resurrection of Yeshua, it can be very powerful.

3. *Celebrating the biblical holy days is a good way to teach about God's acts of redemption.* Paul freely made reference to the holy days when writing to the Corinthians, making a spiritual application of Passover in 1 Corinthians 5:7–8 and possibly referencing Firstfruits directly in 1 Corinthians 15:20; notice also how Luke casually made reference to Yom Kippur (the Fast) in Acts 27:9, assuming his readers would understand. Yet many Christians today do not understand these references, being so divorced from the Jewish roots of the faith (see #42 and #43). Celebration of the holy days—or at the least, annual teaching about

229

them—is a good way to educate a whole congregation, from the young to the old.

4. *Celebrating the biblical holy days is a good way to recover the Jewish roots of the Christian faith.* It is absolutely clear that everything God does is summed up in His Son Jesus, that our Messiah and King is to have centrality in every way and that our fullness is found in Him rather than in celebrating holy days or observing special seasons. That being said, the Church has become so Gentilized (see #53), so detached from its biblical Jewish origins, that an appreciation for the biblical Jewish calendar—the calendar of Yeshua and the apostles—is certainly helpful. To give one example, think of the positive benefits of calling churches to fast and pray for the salvation of Jewish people worldwide on the Day of Atonement, a day when millions of Jews are fasting and asking God to forgive their sins. What's wrong with doing that?

It is also fair to ask where the Scriptures make reference to Christmas. I personally have no issue with believers celebrating Jesus' birth (even though this practice does not seem to go back to the apostolic church), and some of the most wonderful hymns ever written are often sung during the Christmas season, while the birth narratives in the gospels are recited and repeated afresh. And if Christians want to celebrate Jesus' birth on December 25—despite the fact that He was not born on that day—there is nothing in the Word that forbids that.[18] Certainly, the anti-Christmas rhetoric of some teachers is quite extreme, as illustrated by the comments of one eccentric author who states that a Christmas tree is "an evergreen phallic symbol."[19] On the other hand, why is it right to celebrate Christmas but wrong to celebrate Tabernacles? Which has biblical precedent?

Having said all this, it is important to emphasize that many believers do get caught up in unhealthy practices associated with the celebration of the feasts, and there are some direct warnings in the New Testament. In light of this, I will restate some points I have been making with regard to Christians and the Law: (1) Celebration of the biblical feasts is *not* a means for a Gentile believer to "become Jewish." Jews and Gentiles have equal standing in the Lord, and Jews are not called to become Gentiles nor are Gentiles called to become Jews (see #53). (2) Jesus must be central in everything we do. (I'm aware that I just stated this, but it *cannot* be overemphasized.) (3) Celebration of the feasts is *not* commanded in the New Testament and should not be practiced in a binding or legalistic way.[20]

This was addressed by Paul when expressing his concern about the Galatians: "You are observing special days and months and seasons and years! I fear for you, that somehow I have wasted my efforts on you" (Galatians 4:10–11).[21] What was the problem? While commentators point out different nuances of the text, it seems clear that the Galatians thought they were required to observe "special days and months and seasons and years," and, worse still, they thought that in doing so, they would increase their spiritual standing in the Lord. Neither of these is true!

Paul addressed a related phenomenon in Colossians 2:16–17: "Therefore do not let anyone judge you by what you eat or drink, or with regard to a religious festival, a New Moon celebration or a Sabbath day. These are a shadow of the things that were to come; the reality, however, is found in Christ." (See also #49.)

So, let everything we do as believers find its fullness in Yeshua, let no celebration or observance be done in a binding way, let no believers judge one another based on their observance or non-observance, let no one feel "unspiritual" if they get nothing out of the celebration of the feasts—and if the Lord puts it in your heart to do, then be blessed in the celebration of the feasts! (For specific thoughts for Messianic Jews, see #48.)

52

What is the difference between Passover and Easter?

In terms of world religions, most people would say that Passover is a Jewish holiday, celebrating the exodus from Egypt, while Easter is a Christian holiday, celebrating the resurrection of Jesus. In many ways, this is a faulty and superficial understanding.

First, in the New Testament period, there was no such thing as "Easter," despite the King James Version rendering of Acts 12:4: "And when he had apprehended him, he put *him* in prison, and delivered *him* to four quaternions of soldiers to keep him; intending after Easter to bring him forth to the people" (emphasis added). The Greek text reads *to pascha*, meaning "the Passover," as rendered correctly in virtually all other English versions, including the New King James.[22]

Second, the New Testament plainly associates the death of Jesus with the Passover, and Paul explicitly states in 1 Corinthians 5:7 that Messiah "our Passover lamb, has been sacrificed." (Note also John 1:29, where John refers to Jesus as "the Lamb of God, who takes away the sin of the world!") Paul also associates the Lord's resurrection with Firstfruits, which was also celebrated in conjunction with the Passover, possibly on a Sunday (see 1 Corinthians 15:20; Leviticus 23:4–14; see also #51). This means that to the extent the first believers commemorated Yeshua's resurrection at a specific time of the year—and it is not certain that this was widely done[23]—they did it in conjunction with the Passover celebration. Messiah died and rose, leading to an even greater exodus and a deeper call to remove the "leaven" from the midst of God's people (see 1 Corinthians 5:6–8; see again #51).

Dr. Mark Kinzer notes, however, that at the end of the second century "a controversy arose that manifested the desire of the

Gentile ekklesia to break free from all Jewish connection and influence." He continues:

> The point of disagreement was this: should the Gentile ekklesia [congregation, church] commemorate the death and resurrection of Yeshua on the fourteenth of Nisan, when the Jews celebrate the Passover? Those who said yes were called the Quartodecimans (from the Latin word for "fourteenth"). Their practice likely derived from the early Jewish ekklesia. The small communities of Jewish Yeshua-believers in the second century almost certainly maintained this custom. . . . The problem came from the fact that the Gentile ekklesia of the province of Asia (in Asia minor) was Quartodeciman and claimed that their practice was of apostolic origin.
>
> The Quartodeciman controversy observing was disturbing, since (if followed) it would obligate the entire ekklesia to order its liturgical calendar in accordance with the decisions of the Jewish community. In a matter of great practical import it expressed dependence upon and even solidarity with the wider Jewish world.[24]

The problem, then, was simple: Following the Jewish calendar was too Jewish for the increasingly Gentile church! The idea of a Sunday celebration of the resurrection was not the real issue, since that could have been done, theoretically, in conjunction with Firstfruits. The issue was having a major Christian (i.e., non-Jewish!) holy day determined by the Jewish calendar. That was simply unacceptable, leading to the final decision at the Nicene Council in A.D. 325. As Kinzer notes, "Constantine's language is almost embarrassingly direct."[25]

> It was declared to be particularly unworthy for this, the holiest of all festivals, to follow the custom [the calculation] of the Jews, who had soiled their hands with the most fearful of crimes, and whose minds were blinded. In rejecting their custom, we may

transmit to our descendants the legitimate mode of celebrating Easter, which we have observed from the time of the Saviour's Passion to the present day [according to the day of the week]. We ought not, therefore, to have anything in common with the Jews, for the Saviour has shown us another way; our worship follows a more legitimate and more convenient course (the order of the days of the week); and consequently, in unanimously adopting this mode, we desire, dearest brethren, to separate ourselves from the detestable company of the Jews, for it is truly shameful for us to hear them boast that without their direction we could not keep the feast . . . it would still be your duty not to tarnish your soul by communications with such wicked people [the Jews].[26]

Yes, such language is "almost embarrassingly direct," not to mention shamefully unchristian. How painfully ironic that the resurrection of Yeshua the Messiah had to be separated from anything Jewish! If ever there was a tragic severing of Jewish roots, this was it (see #42 and #43).

How, then, should Christians respond today? Jesus' death and resurrection should be celebrated in conjunction with the Passover, which means following the dates set by the Jewish community worldwide. The resurrection can still be celebrated on a Sunday, quite legitimately, but if church dating separates Easter from Passover, then the Passover dates should be followed. This is not only a biblical thing to do, it is also a way to repudiate the historic church's anti-Semitism, reconnecting with our true Jewish and biblical heritage.

As for the term *Easter*, the late F. F. Bruce explained that it was "a word used in the Germanic languages to denote the festival of the vernal equinox, and subsequently, with the coming of Christianity, to denote the anniversary of the resurrection of Christ (which in Gk. and Romance tongues is denoted by *pascha*, 'Passover', and its derivatives)."[27] Thus, while the word's origins were not specifically Christian, "Easter" was taken over by the Church with a completely different meaning, and it is that meaning that has been preserved in a positive sense until this day. Many Christians, however, prefer to speak of "Resurrection Sunday" as opposed to Easter, and this is certainly commendable, although the extreme attacks on the term *Easter* are completely unjustified, such as Michael Rood's claim that "Easter is the rehearsal of child sacrifice and fertility rites of pagan sun god worshipers"![28]

53

Are Gentile Christians spiritual Jews?

The New Testament clearly states that Jewish and Gentile believers have equal standing in the Lord, are equally loved by the Lord, are equally redeemed by the Lord and have equal access to all of His spiritual promises. As stated by Paul,

> For there is no difference between Jew and Gentile—the same Lord is Lord of all and richly blesses all who call on him, for, "Everyone who calls on the name of the Lord will be saved."
>
> Romans 10:12–13

> But now in Christ Jesus you who once were far away have been brought near through the blood of Christ. For he himself is our peace, who has made the two one and has destroyed the barrier, the dividing wall of hostility. . . . He came and preached peace to you who were far away and peace to those who were near. For through him we both have access to the Father by one Spirit. Consequently, you are no longer foreigners and aliens, but fellow citizens with God's people and members of God's household, built on the foundation of the apostles and prophets, with Christ Jesus himself as the chief cornerstone. In him the whole building is joined together and rises to become a holy temple in the Lord. And in him you too are being built together to become a dwelling in which God lives by his Spirit.
>
> Ephesians 2:13–14, 17–22

In Jesus, Jew and Gentile are one—that in itself is an extraordinary statement—but does that mean that Gentile Christians are spiritual Jews? Paul actually comes very close to saying that very thing: (1) he tells the Gentile believers in Philippi that "it is we who are the circumcision" (Philippians 3:3; the text does not refer to Jewish believers only); (2) he explains to the Gentile believers in Colossae that in Jesus "you were also circumcised" (Colossians 2:11); (3) he tells the Gentile believers in Rome that they were grafted into Israel's olive tree (see Romans 11:17–18); (4) he writes to the Gentile believers in Corinth about "our forefathers," with reference to Israel's forefathers (see 1 Corinthians 10:1); and (5) he tells the Gentile believers in Galatia that if they belong to Messiah, then they are Abraham's seed, and heirs according to the promise (see Galatians 3:29), having just stated that, "There is neither Jew nor Greek, slave nor free, male nor female, for you are all one in [Messiah] Jesus" (verse 28).

Yet Paul never explicitly calls Gentile believers spiritual Jews or spiritual Israel, and in the one place where he could have made himself perfectly clear about this, namely Romans 9–11, he actually says the opposite, writing to the Gentiles about Israel. Let us look at this section more carefully.

Romans 9–11 is Paul's major doctrinal statement on God's purposes for Israel, and he makes explicit reference to "Israel" or "Israelites" eleven times in these chapters (see 9:4, 6, 27, 31; 10:19, 21; 11:1, 2, 7, 25, 26), never speaking of "Israel" in Romans outside of chapters 9–11 (though elsewhere he speaks of "Jews"). Then, in Romans 11, he likens the Gentile believers to a "wild olive shoot" that has been grafted in among the "natural branches" (verses 17–21), making it clear that, having been grafted in "among the others" they "now share in the nourishing sap from the olive root" (verse 17).

Does this mean that these Gentile believers are spiritual Israelites? If so, this would have been an excellent time to say so! To the contrary, Paul continues to address these believers as Gentiles in this passage. In fact, this is one of the few times in the New Testament that believers are explicitly *addressed* as Gentiles.

Listen carefully to the apostle's words. After speaking *about* God's dealing with the Gentiles earlier in the book (both in judgment and in salvation; see Romans 1:5, 13, 16; 2:9–10, 14, 24; 3:9, 29; 9:24, 30; 10:12; 11:11–12), he then writes, "*I am talking to you Gentiles*. Inasmuch as I am the apostle to the Gentiles" (11:13, emphasis added). After this, he continues to speak *about* the Gentiles and their role in God's plan through the rest of his letter (see 11:25; 15:9–12, 16, 18, 27; 16:4), but in 11:13, immediately before stating that Gentile believers have been grafted into Israel's spiritual tree, he explicitly *calls them Gentiles*. They have not become spiritual Jews or spiritual Israelites. Rather, they have become joint heirs in the family of God, equally loved, equally called and equally saved. But they have *not* become spiritual Jews or spiritual Israelites.

Paul is quite clear on this: "Is God the God of Jews only? Is he not the God of Gentiles too? Yes, of Gentiles too, since there is only one God, who will justify the circumcised by faith and the uncircumcised through that same faith" (3:29–30). Yes, He is the God of the Gentiles and the Jews—but Jews who do not believe do not become Gentiles, and Gentiles who do believe do not become Jews.

Again Paul writes, "What then shall we say? That the Gentiles, who did not pursue righteousness, have obtained it, a righteousness that is by faith; but Israel, who pursued a law of righteousness, has not attained it" (9:30–31). So, there are Gentiles who have obtained righteousness through faith and there are Jews (or Israelites) who have not obtained it—but their identity as Gentiles or Jews is not affected by this. Only their standing with God is affected: "For there is no difference between Jew and Gentile—the same Lord is Lord of all and richly blesses all who call on him, for, 'Everyone who calls on the name of the Lord will be saved' " (10:12–13).

To repeat: If there was ever a time to tell Gentile believers that they were spiritual Israelites, Romans 9–11 was the passage, and yet Paul does the opposite here: He actually *addresses them as Gentiles.*

How then should we understand Paul's words in Romans 9:6–8? He writes:

> It is not as though God's word had failed. For not all who are descended from Israel are Israel. Nor because they are his descendants are they all Abraham's children. On the contrary, "It is through Isaac that your offspring will be reckoned." In other words, it is not the natural children who are God's children, but it is the children of the promise who are regarded as Abraham's offspring.

Is Paul teaching here that Gentiles are spiritual Israelites? Absolutely not, despite many careless interpretations of this passage that claim he is.

Why do I call these interpretations careless? It is because Paul is not addressing the issue of Gentile believers here at all. Rather, he is saying that there is an Israel within Israel, a true remnant within the larger nation, which has nothing whatsoever to do with those outside of the nation. Put another way, if I say that not everyone in the church is really the Church, I am not saying that Buddhists and Muslims are the Church. Of course not! Rather, I am saying that not everyone who calls himself a believer is really a believer. In the same way, Paul was stating that, in the fullest sense of the word, not all Israel is really Israel, after which he returns to the normal use of "Israel" for the rest of Romans. But to repeat: He was not saying that Gentile believers became Israel.

Rather, Paul's explicit statement was this: "This mystery is that through the gospel the Gentiles are heirs together with Israel, members together of one body, and sharers together in the promise in Christ Jesus" (Ephesians 3:6). This really says it all: Gentile believers do not become Israel, but redeemed Gentiles and redeemed Jews are "members together of one body, and sharers together in the promise in Christ Jesus."

What about Galatians 6:16? The NIV translates this with, "Peace and mercy to all who follow this rule, even to the Israel of God," but this is not the most natural translation of the end of this verse, which is better rendered "and to the Israel of God." The NIV translates the Greek word *kai* with "even," but in most other versions (see KJV, NKJV, NASB, ESV) it is translated with "and," which is its most common meaning.[29] So, Paul was not calling the Gentile believers in Galatia the Israel of God; instead, after his many strong warnings about wrongheaded Jewish teachers who were leading the Galatians astray, he ends his letter with a blessing on those Jewish believers who were in right relationship with the Lord, calling them "the Israel of God," the Israel within Israel that Paul spoke of in Romans 9:6–9.

What about Romans 2:28–29? Here Paul writes, "A man is not a Jew if he is *only* one outwardly, nor is circumcision *merely* outward and physical. No, a man is a Jew if he is one inwardly; and circumcision is circumcision of the heart, by the Spirit, not by the written code. Such a man's praise is not from men, but from God" (emphasis added). Notice the italicized words in the text: "only" and "merely." They do not appear in the original Greek but they do, in fact, convey Paul's point, which was this: *Between two Jews*, who is the real Jew, the one who is only circumcised outwardly or the one who is also circumcised inwardly? That is, in keeping with the other verses we have just studied (Romans 9:6–9 and Galatians 6:16), and while Paul can refer to Gentile believers as being "the circumcision" (as in Philippians 3:3, cited above), he never calls them Jews or Israelites.

Study this for yourself, looking up every reference to *Jew* or *Jews* or *Jewish* in the New Testament, along with every reference to *Israel* or *Israelite*. The totals are overwhelmingly clear: The words *Israel* or *Israelite(s)* occur a total of 77 times in the New Testament, and in every case but one (see Galatians 6:16), they refer explicitly to the literal people of Israel, while Galatians 6:16 in all probability has the same meaning as well. As for the words *Jew(s)* or *Jewish*, they occur more than 190 times total in the New Testament, and in almost every case, they clearly refer to ethnic Jews.[30]

Over the years, I have met godly Christians who told me with joy that they were spiritual Jews, and it was clear that their hearts were deeply joined to Israel and the Jewish people. I have nothing but appreciation for them, and I never try to correct them, understanding what they mean and what this means to them. But it is not accurate scripturally and, at times in church history, it has contributed to the dangerously wrong concept that the Church has replaced Israel (see #43). It also has contributed to the misguided notion that being Jewish somehow puts a person on a higher spiritual plane, leading some Christians to search for Jewish ancestry in their past to "confirm" their Jewishness. (For a related, erroneous teaching, see #54.) To end, then, where we started, we do well to remember Paul's words in Romans 10:12: "For there is no difference between Jew and Gentile—the same Lord is Lord of all and richly blesses all who call on him."

54
What is the "Two House Theory"?

This is a very recent teaching that, despite its real fringe status, is gaining a growing (but still very tiny) number of adherents. It is variously called the Ephraimite, Restoration of Israel, Two Covenant Israel, or Two House movement. According to this teaching, not only do Gentile Christians spiritually represent

Old Testament Ephraim, but they actually *are* Ephraim. In other words, all Gentile believers are actually descendants of biblical Ephraim, or, more precisely, descendants of the Ten Lost Tribes. Interestingly, this movement "has recently gained ground in some areas among ardent Christian Zionists"[31] who have obviously gone one big step too far in their identification with Israel.

A position paper written by Messianic Jewish leaders gives further details:

> The movement's proponents . . . argue that these dispersed "Israelites," or "Ephraimites," whose identities have remained undisclosed even to themselves until recent times, primarily settled in areas now recognized as largely populated by Anglo-Saxons. At times they argue that all Anglo-Saxons, and even all of humanity, are descended from these lost Ephraimites. At other times, that only born-again Christians can claim descent. In either case, Christians from Anglo-Saxon lands, such as Great Britain, Australia, Canada, and the United States, can feel assured that they are most likely direct blood descendants of the ancient people of Ephraim.
>
> It is now incumbent upon these members of "Ephraim," they argue, to "accept their birthright" and live as members of Israel. They urge Gentile Christians to keep the Torah in obedience to the Hebrew scriptures, to strive to re-educate Jews and other Christians about their new, "latter-day prophecy," and to work toward the repatriation of the land of Israel by their own number.[32]

What exactly does this mean? Let us say you are a Gentile who was raised in an atheistic home in America, but at the age of twenty you had a wonderful, born-again experience, joined a local church and were enjoying your walk with the Lord. You loved the Jewish people and prayed for Israel, feeling a special spiritual connection with God's ancient, covenant people, but that, of course, seemed quite natural. Then you heard this Two House teaching, and the light went on.

"Could it be that I'm actually a *real* Israelite? Could it be that, unbeknown to all of my family members for many generations, we are not really Gentiles but actually descendants of the Ten Lost Tribes? Now I understand! And if I'm an Israelite, then I'm responsible to observe the Torah—and I even have a birthright to the land of Israel!"

Does this sound bizarre? It certainly is. Yet the proponents of this teaching claim to have scriptural justification. Let us briefly examine some of their claims, recognizing that the Two House teachers would expand on each of these arguments and add many other arguments, all of which can be refuted by the careful study of Scripture.[33]

(1) *The promises to the patriarchs speak of their descendants being a multitude of (Gentile) nations, which means that the Israelites will become a multitude of "Gentile" nations—and the Jews are neither a multitude nor are they Gentiles.* Support for this is drawn from Genesis 48:19, where Jacob prophesies over the baby Ephraim that his "descendants will become a group of nations"; note that the Hebrew for "nation" here is *goy*, the word used for "Gentile" in parts of the Bible and in Jewish history until today. In refutation of this is the fact that *goy* in the Tanakh frequently refers to Israel and the Jewish people (see Deuteronomy 32:28, cf. 32:45; Joshua 10:12–13; Isaiah 1:4; 26:2; Jeremiah 31:36; Zephaniah 2:9). In fact, God promised Abram that He would make him a great *goy* in Genesis 12:2—obviously not meaning a great Gentile nation![34] To take this further, at the time of the patriarchs, there was no such thing as "Gentile," since there was no such thing as the nation of Israel or the Jewish people in any formal or distinct way. So, "the term 'Gentile' is anachronistic as [Two House teachers] employ it in this context."[35] Other verses erroneously cited in similar fashion include Genesis 17:5; 28:3; 35:11.

The Two House teachers also argue that the promises to the patriarchs about innumerable descendants (see Genesis 13:16) could not apply to the Jewish people, since their numbers today are approximately fourteen million. This must, therefore, apply to other Gentile nations who number in the hundreds of millions. Of course, simple logic would tell you that, if we can count the number of people on the earth today—roughly 6.5 billion— then they are *not* innumerable, which means that the promise to Abraham in Genesis 13:16 was meant as a figure of speech: From one man, millions and millions will spring up! Moses actually marveled at how God had made the people of Israel into a great multitude, using some of the very same language that was used in the promises to the patriarchs: "The LORD your God has increased your numbers so that today you are as many as the stars in the sky" (Deuteronomy 1:10; note also the language used in 2 Chronicles 1:9, and remember that in Old Testament times, the population of Israel was substantially less than the worldwide Jewish population today).

There is also a spiritual dimension to the promises to Abraham in which he becomes the father of all who believe in Jesus, both Jews and Gentiles, as Paul explains in Romans and Galatians (see Romans 4:9–17; Galatians 3:6–9, 26–29), but to apply this in a physical, lineal way, as if all believers were his blood descendants, is to negate completely Paul's message.

(2) *The term* Ephraim, *which is frequently used to describe the northern kingdom of Israel (i.e., the ten tribes) as a whole, is never used for Jews, and therefore the promises to Ephraim must be fulfilled through another people group.* Actually, while Ephraim primarily refers to the northern kingdom of Israel, it is often used in the context of the nation as a whole, decidedly not to the exclusion of the Jewish people. A simple, straightforward reading of Jeremiah 31 makes this clear (and remember: this chapter was written more than a century after the exile and dispersion of the ten northern tribes and the immediate context had to do with the Babylonian exile of Judah). More significantly, since Ephraim is often used

interchangeably with the names Israel and Jacob in the prophetic literature (again, Jeremiah 31 provides a good example of this), and if, as the Two House teachers claim, Ephraim/Israel is distinct from the Jewish people, then it would stand to follow that Israel or the house of Israel would not be used synonymously with the Jewish people. The opposite is actually true, in very decisive terms. In fact, the southern kingdom of Judah could actually be addressed as "all the clans of the house of Israel" (see Jeremiah 2:2, 4: "Go and proclaim in the hearing of Jerusalem"—that means the southern kingdom of Judah—"Hear the word of the LORD, O house of Jacob, all you clans of the house of Israel"). So, the Jewish people are being addressed in their capital city of Jerusalem, but they are addressed corporately as the "house of Jacob" and as "all you clans of the house of Israel."

If the Two House teachers were correct, then Jeremiah's audience should have stopped him and said, "What are you talking about? We are not all the clans of the house of Israel; we are just Judah. There are multitudes of other peoples, already scattered among the nations, that you should be addressing. They are the real house of Israel, the Ephraimites. We are just Jews." Hardly! Similar instances could be cited throughout the prophetic books. (Note again the first verse of Jeremiah 31, a chapter just referenced, above: "'At that time,' declares the LORD, 'I will be the God of all the clans of Israel, and they will be my people.'" The chapter then unfolds in the context of the exile of the Judeans. For other aspects to this discussion, along with the question of Jewish national identity, see #26 and #27.)

Carrying this over to the New Testament, we can see that Jesus referred to the *Jewish people* as "the lost sheep of Israel" (Matthew 10:6). In fact, He distinguished "the lost sheep of Israel" from the Gentiles! Had the Two House teachers been correct, He should have said, "Now, don't go to the Gentiles, who are actually the Ten Lost Tribes, but go instead to the Jews." Instead, He said, "Don't go

244

to the Gentiles but only go to the lost sheep of Israel" (see Matthew 10:5–6). These verses alone are a sufficient refutation of the Two House teaching. Notice also that Paul spoke of his Jewish people as "our twelve tribes... [who] earnestly serve God day and night" (Acts 26:7), while Jacob (James) addresses his letter, which was written to Jewish believers, "To the twelve tribes scattered among the nations" (James 1:1). The Jewish people contained elements of all twelve tribes, and they were addressed and recognized as representing all twelve tribes (see #26 and #27).

Having said this, it is certainly possible that the promises to Ephraim or Israel in the prophetic books *prefigure* the promises to the Gentile branch of the Body—Paul quotes words applied to Israel, once alienated from God, and then applies them to the Gentiles in Romans 9, and Peter might do this as well in 1 Peter 2—but it is completely wrong to think the prophets were actually *calling* the Gentiles Ephraim or Israel.

For the sake of brevity, and because this is such a fringe teaching, this short, representative sampling will have to suffice. The position paper, referenced above, is a good place to start (giving a number of key references to proponents of the Two House teaching). Two final comments are in order.

First, as has been emphasized a number of times in this book, in Jesus the Messiah, Jew and Gentile are one, with equal standing and equal status in Him. One is not better than the other, and the only thing that ultimately matters is being rightly connected with Him—the Branch, the Bread of Life, the Redeemer, the Savior, the Head of the Body, the King (see #53). Rather than accepting their exalted status in the Lord as spiritual children of Abraham, these Two House teachers have felt the need to become physical children of Abraham. In so doing, not only do they believe something that is false, but they minimize the reality of their place in God, seeking a lower place rather than the higher place to which He has called them.

Second, there is one good thing that has been accomplished by the Two House theory, and that is to draw attention to passages such as Ezekiel 37:15–25, where God speaks of the reunification of Judah with Ephraim. The Two House proponents do get these texts wrong, but the question must be asked: Were verses such as these fulfilled in the return of the Jews from Babylonian exile, since among them were Israelite exiles as well, or do they point to a yet future restoration, one that could be ongoing this very day, in which scattered remnants of the so-called Ten Lost Tribes—from India and Africa—are returning to the Land?

Questions such as this are worth asking. Adherents to the Two House theory, however, would do best to abandon their error and focus on the Source of their life in God. (For the question of Torah observance, see #48.)

55
What is the difference between a Messianic Jew and a Hebrew Christian?

Jewish followers of Jesus are referred to in a number of ways: Messianic Jews, Hebrew Christians, Jewish Christians or simply Jewish believers. In fact, over the years, when sharing my faith with a stranger, I have often been asked if I am a "Jew for Jesus," as if this was a generic term rather than the name of an organization. (I simply say that, yes, I am a Jew for Jesus, but not part of that particular organization.)

The designation "Jewish believers" is informal and not used to designate any specific group, while "Jewish Christians" is accurate if rightly understood, but it sounds like an oxymoron to most people, and it does not carry a more narrow connotation. The designations "Hebrew Christian" and "Messianic Jew," however, have a more particular history and are often used in a nuanced way.

Beginning in the mid-1800s in England, as thousands of Jews were coming to faith in Jesus but virtually all of them were quickly assimilated into church culture, some of the Jewish believers began to organize themselves into a fellowship called the Hebrew Christian Alliance. This development encouraged many Jewish believers in the churches to be more open about their Jewish background—at that time, this was not as much of a "badge of honor" as it is today—and Hebrew Christian congregations began to be planted.[36]

Why were these believers called Hebrew Christians rather than Jewish Christians? The word *Jewish* can refer to one's ethnicity as well as to one's religious practices, and despite the Jewish origins of the Christian faith, for many centuries, to be "Jewish" has been understood to mean "not Christian." The word *Hebrew*, however, carries a primarily ethnic connotation—in fact, it is strongly biblical—and hence modifies the word *Christian*: We are men and women of Hebrew descent who believe that Jesus is the Messiah!

In the 1970s, however, a proposal was put forth by the Hebrew Christian Alliance of America to change its name to the Messianic Jewish Alliance of America, a primary reason being that, to most Jews, the word *Christian* meant "not Jewish." (It should also be noted that most Jews do not refer to themselves as Hebrews.) To emphasize, then, that these believers were both Jewish and devoted to Yeshua, the term *Messianic Jew* was adopted, and it has proven an effective way to communicate our faith. (In Israel, however, if you tell Hebrew speakers that you are a Messianic Jew—*yehudi meshichi*—very few of them will be familiar with the term. On the other hand, it is important that they understand that you are not a Christian—*notzri*—since that has a very specific meaning in Israel, in particular, Catholic or Greek Orthodox, due to their noticeable presence in Jerusalem—and certainly *not* Jewish.)

Initially, *Messianic Jew* was used primarily by members of Messianic Jewish congregations, and it is still used in this narrower sense today, sometimes referring only to Jewish believers who continue to live a "Jewish lifestyle" and are not church members. In that sense of the word, the vast majority of Jewish believers worldwide are not Messianic Jews. On the other hand, the term has really taken hold in the last two decades, to the point that Jewish believers of all stripes and practices are commonly referred to as Messianic Jews.

In contrast, the term *Hebrew Christian* has been displaced in some circles by *Messianic Jew* to the point that: (1) most members of Messianic congregations do not self-identify as Hebrew Christians; (2) the term *Hebrew Christian* is more frequently used by organizations that are part of evangelical Christian denominations; and (3) in the general Jewish society, concepts like "Jews for Jesus" or "Messianic Jews" are probably better known than "Hebrew Christian."

In an ironic, final twist, the great majority of those attending Messianic Jewish congregations (specifically, in America) are Gentiles, not Jews, and some of them designate themselves as Messianic Gentiles. I expect that we will see more creative terminology in the days to come.

56
Are Messianic Jewish leaders really rabbis?

The answer to this question depends on whom you ask and on how you define "rabbi." According to virtually all Jewish leaders who do not believe in Jesus as Messiah, it is downright deceptive for Messianic Jewish leaders to call themselves rabbis, since the title "rabbi" refers to a leader in the religion called Judaism, not Christianity. And in the eyes of most Jews who do not believe in Jesus, "Messianic Judaism" is a misnomer, since it is not really

Judaism at all but rather just another form of Christianity. In addition to this, some Messianic Jewish "rabbis" are not even Jewish, while many others do not have a strong background in Hebrew and/or Jewish studies. All the more reason, then, it would seem that the term *rabbi* is not fitting for a Messianic Jewish leader.[37]

But it is not that simple. Messianic Jews would argue that Yeshua did not come into the world to establish a new Gentile religion called Christianity but rather to fulfill what was written in Moses and the Prophets. What could be more Jewish than that? Jesus Himself was called "Rabbi" (see #36), and He spoke to His followers about their leadership role in Israel's future restoration: "I tell you the truth, at the renewal of all things, when the Son of Man sits on his glorious throne, you who have followed me will also sit on twelve thrones, judging the twelve tribes of Israel" (Matthew 19:28).

Paul taught the Gentile believers in Ephesus that they had become part of the greater commonwealth of Israel (see Ephesians 2:11–22) while explaining to the Gentile believers in Rome that they had been grafted into Israel's spiritual tree (see Romans 11:13–21). Of course, this does not mean that Gentiles who put their faith in Jesus become Jews (see #53), but it certainly follows that Jews who put their faith in the Messiah of Israel *remain* Jews. (See Romans 11:24, where Paul writes, "After all, if you were cut out of an olive tree that is wild by nature, and contrary to nature were grafted into a cultivated olive tree, how much more readily will these, the natural branches, be grafted into their own olive tree!" It is natural for a Jew to return to the God of Israel and put his faith in the Messiah of Israel!)

In the days of the apostles, the question was this: Can you remain a Gentile and become a follower of Yeshua, or do you have to become Jewish in order to follow Him? (See Acts 15 for the full discussion.) Over the centuries, that perspective changed radically, to the point that it was often assumed that for a Jew to follow Jesus, he or she had to become Gentile. In fact, many Messianic Jews can tell you about their own experience as new believers when they were given pork to eat to "prove" the genuineness of their faith. I kid you not. (For the *horrific* baptismal confessions that Jewish converts to Catholicism were required to recite in the Middle Ages, see *Our Hands Are Stained with Blood*, 95–97.)

So, Messianic Jews would state that they are simply recovering their biblical Jewish roots and reclaiming the authentic Jewishness of faith in Yeshua. They would also emphasize that the term *Christian*, which occurs only three times in the New Testament (see Acts 11:26; 26:28; 1 Peter 4:16), does not refer to the follower of a non-Jewish religion but rather to someone who was associated with this Jesus who was called Christ. (In other words, a "Christian" was a "Christ-one," or, as rendered in the *Jewish New Testament*, a "Messianic." Most scholars agree that the term was originally coined in an insulting way, as seen in the larger context of 1 Peter 4:16.)

It should also be pointed out that a substantial and influential segment of right-wing Orthodox Jews does not believe that non-Orthodox rabbis (referring to Reform and Conservative rabbis) should be recognized as legitimate Jewish rabbis. This was made clear in a major Orthodox Jewish statement issued in March 1997, parts of which declared:

The Union of Orthodox Rabbis of the United States and Canada (Agudath Harabonim) hereby declares: Reform and Conservative are not Judaism at all. Their adherents are Jews, according to the Jewish Law, but their religion is not Judaism.

The Agudath Harabonim has always been on guard against any attempt to alter, misrepresent, or distort the Halacha (Jewish Law) as transmitted in the written and oral law, given by G-d through Moses on Sinai. It has, therefore, rejected recognition of Reform and Conservative movements as Judaism, or their clergy as Rabbis. It has publicly rebuffed the claim of "three wings of

Judaism." There is only one Judaism: Torah Judaism. The Reform and Conservative are not Judaism at all, but another religion.[38]

To this day, religious authority in the State of Israel is under the control of the Orthodox Rabbinate, to the point that even *weddings* performed by non-Orthodox rabbis are not recognized by the Orthodox leaders.[39] And they have no intention of letting this change: "[It] is imperative," they stated, "to support Israel's government in their refusal to change the status quo regarding the exclusive Orthodox Rabbinic authority. Even non-orthodox political leaders recognize that unless Jewish religious family law remains under the authority of the sole Rabbinate, the Jewish nation would be hopelessly divided."[40]

So, in the eyes of many traditional Jews, not even Reform and Conservative rabbis are really rabbis, let alone Messianic Jewish rabbis. Yet this lack of recognition from a significant sector of Judaism does not stop Reform and Conservative Jews from training and ordaining their rabbis. Why then should lack of recognition from the larger Jewish community stop Messianic Jews from training and ordaining their rabbis? (In all this, I am not offering my personal opinion on whether Messianic Jewish leaders should or should not be called rabbis; I am simply discussing the relevant issues involved.) I'm also reminded of the comment made to me years ago by a Messianic Jewish leader who did *not* call himself rabbi. He was speaking of an elderly Jewish woman who had just come to faith in Yeshua and was now attending his Messianic congregation. "To her," he explained, "I'm 'rabbi'—and I'm not about to tell her otherwise."

What about the question of the lack of training of many Messianic Jewish rabbis? In the interest of the integrity of the Messianic Jewish movement, it definitely makes sense that those who want to be called rabbis would get some kind of proper training— this is becoming an increasingly common pattern in the movement—always bearing in mind that our ultimate qualifications are primarily spiritual and practical in nature. As for Gentile leaders being called "Messianic Jewish rabbis," I will leave that for others in the Messianic movement to decide.

What about Yeshua's words in Matthew 23? There He told His followers,

> But you are not to be called "Rabbi," for you have only one Master and you are all brothers. And do not call anyone on earth "father," for you have one Father, and he is in heaven. Nor are you to be called "teacher," for you have one Teacher, the [Messiah]. The greatest among you will be your servant. For whoever exalts himself will be humbled, and whoever humbles himself will be exalted.
>
> Matthew 23:8–12

This raises a very good question, and putting all the previous discussion aside, is it right to call *anyone* rabbi? I remember hearing this passage from Matthew cited in the Italian Pentecostal congregation where I became a believer, and it was based on this passage that our church taught that Catholic priests should never be addressed as "Father" ("And do not call anyone on earth 'father,' for you have one Father"; I should point out that most of the members of that church came out of a Catholic background).

I have no argument with those who are consistent in applying this passage, accepting no titles of any kind for their roles as spiritual leaders—not rabbi, not father, not teacher, not pastor, etc. On the other hand, a good case can be made for a different interpretation of the Lord's words—otherwise, it could be argued that a father should tell his own children not to call him Dad, while Paul could be questioned for telling the Corinthians that they did "not have many fathers" aside from him (1 Corinthians 4:15).

Consider these comments from Messianic Jewish Bible scholar David Stern:

The Hebrew Christian scholar Arnold G. Fruchtenbaum holds that this passage prohibits Messianic Jewish congregations from calling their leaders "rabbis." . . .

My view is that a literalistic approach here is inappropriate, since Yeshua also warns against being called "father" or "leader," terms everyone uses. The context leads me to believe that Yeshua here is prohibiting believers from accepting unearned honors, rather than outlawing three titles. A leader is to be humble, a servant (20:25–28); if he is given any title at all, he is not to become puffed up. Others in the community are to guard against making invidious distinctions between "clergy" and "laity" by bestowing titles.[41]

Stern, however, has some misgiving about the use of the term *rabbi* in some Messianic Jewish circles:

My own objection to the use of the title "rabbi" today is not theological but ideological and practical. What should a "Messianic rabbi" be? A pastor under another name? I think the term "rabbi" sets up Jewish expectations which ought to be fulfilled. A Messianic Jewish congregational leader who accepts the title "rabbi" without having training adequate to qualify him as a rabbi in a non-Messianic Jewish setting is accepting honor which he has not earned and to which he is not entitled; and this *does* violate Yeshua's injunction.

Should a Messianic rabbi have *s'mikhah* (ordination . . .)? If so, should it be Messianic or non-Messianic? If Messianic, who is qualified to grant it? Messianic Judaism at present [writing in 1992] has very few ordained rabbis and no accrediting agency. At present, in order not to embarrass the Messianic Jewish movement, I urge leaders without rabbinic training to resist letting themselves be called "rabbis."[42]

Having said all this, I would point out that in Israel, the leaders of Messianic congregations do *not* call themselves rabbis for a number of reasons, including: (1) as Jews living in the Land, they have no need to "prove" their Jewishness; and (2) the title "rabbi" is associated with Orthodox Judaism, and it is Orthodox Jewish rabbis who most strongly oppose Jewish faith in Yeshua. Outside of the land of Israel, leaders of Hebrew Christian congregations tend not to use the title "rabbi" (see #55 for the semantic difference between "Hebrew Christian" and "Messianic Jew"), while a significant minority of Messianic Jewish leaders choose to use other titles, such as "congregational leader" or "Messianic pastor." Those Messianic Jewish leaders who do choose to be called "rabbis" should have a solid answer to Matthew 23:8–12 and should be able to defend themselves ably against the charge of deception.

57

Is it good for Christians to attend Jewish synagogues?

I'll answer this as succinctly as possible, since this is much more a question of personal preference than it is a question of right or wrong according to the Scriptures. Here are some constructive thoughts:

1. *Christians should not attend Jewish synagogues for the purpose of clandestine evangelism.* This is not ethical, and it only will increase negative thinking of "Christianity" as a deceitful faith, feeding into the worst, false stereotypes. How would you feel if someone from a cult began to attend your congregation, posing as a believer, so as to secretly share his or her faith with others? Given the very ugly history of "Christian" anti-Semitism, practices like this should be firmly rejected.

2. *Christians can certainly inform the local rabbi that they are interested in learning more about Jewish practice and Jewish teaching, but that they are only there to listen and learn rather*

than to proselytize. If the rabbi welcomes them, wonderful. They might enjoy the learning experience and, perhaps, some meaningful dialogue and interaction can come out of this in the long run.

3. *Christians should remember that there is a vast difference between Orthodox and Reform synagogue services.* They might be surprised to see the extremely liberal, humanistic attitudes in a Reform synagogue (called a temple), while if they attended an ultra-Orthodox synagogue, they would feel quite left out, since the entire service would be in Hebrew and there would not even be a sermon.

4. *Christians should not attend synagogues thinking that they will find deeper spiritual truths.* They might be enlightened and even edified, but to the extent that the Jewish people have missed the Messiah, they have missed the heart and soul of divine revelation, and outside of Yeshua, there is no ultimate spiritual truth.

5. *Christians should avoid the "wannabe" syndrome that is all too common among Gentile Christians,* a theme addressed several times already in this book (see especially #54). By this I refer to the practice of Gentile Christians who think that by adding Jewish customs or Jewish dress or Jewish prayers to their lives, they will somehow attain a more legitimate or spiritually higher standing in the Lord. Not at all! (The librarian at a Jewish seminary once commented to me about the "wannabes" who sometimes go in there, meaning Gentile Christians who wished they were Jews; see also #53.) To repeat once more: Everything we need for life and godliness is found in Jesus, and that does not mean that Christian women need to become men (since He was male) or that Gentile Christians need to become Jewish (since He was a Jew). Rather, our spiritual life flows from Him, and His own emphasis was not on being Jewish but on

relating intimately to the Father. And, if I may be allowed a moment of complete candor, there is absolutely no good reason for Gentile (or Jewish) believers in Jesus to wear what appear to be ancient biblical outfits (I've seen this!) or to dress up like ultra-Orthodox Jews (I've seen this, too!). It certainly does not impress the Jewish community—to the contrary, it actually makes our whole faith seem weird, almost like someone showing up for work in a spacesuit—and it completely misses the consistent New Testament emphasis that outward religious things are of no intrinsic spiritual value (see also #50 and #51). This fascination with outward adornments is part of a soulish spirituality that does not flow down from the Head, and they are more unhelpful than helpful.[43]

6. *Christian leaders should be encouraged to reach out to the Jewish community leaders to undo misunderstandings about the Christian faith and to show solidarity with their Jewish neighbors.* In some cases, they will be surprised to see that they are more pro-Israel than some of those in the synagogue! I know of many cases where this has been done, and the fruit has been very good in terms of understanding and breaking down walls. If that is all that comes out of the endeavor, it is still worthwhile. If it leads to further proclamation of the Gospel, all the better.

58
Should Christians unconditionally support the nation of Israel?

I believe that Christians should stand in strong, unshakable support of the nation of Israel, but we cannot *unconditionally* support Israel, since the nation has many flaws and blemishes, and "unconditional support" could imply sanctioning wrong national decisions and refusing to stand against wrong national policies. For example, should we "unconditionally" support the Israeli government in its funding of abortions for women in the military? Should we "unconditionally" support the government when it does not allow Jewish believers in Jesus to immigrate to the Land with total freedom? Should we "unconditionally" support every single decision that is made with regard to the Palestinian crisis?[44] (For the myth of a historic Palestinian people, see #34.)

But to major on these issues is to the miss the point, since there are a number of important reasons that believers today should stand with Israel. Here are a few, which I will present in their simplest form, bearing in mind they all deserve to be developed in depth.

(1) *The restoration of the Jewish people to the Land is an act of historic, prophetic significance. Standing with Israel today means standing with the purposes of God.*

To be sure, there has been a spate of recent books and articles, written and published by respected Christian authors and ministries, dismissing the idea that the modern nation of Israel should be seen as a fulfillment of biblical prophecy.[45] With due respect to the scriptural and historical arguments raised, some of which appear to be influenced by pro-Palestinian sentiments, I must say that the evidence points overwhelmingly to the God-ordained, God-orchestrated regathering of the Jewish people back to their homeland.

On a purely rational level, the ongoing preservation of the Jewish people is a distinct miracle, unprecedented in world history, since no people, scattered from their land for many centuries, has preserved its national identity, let alone returned to its ancient land, let alone resurrected its ancient spoken language as a living, national tongue. And yet all this occurred after Hitler's demonic extermination of two-thirds of Europe's Jews. While the crematoria were still smoldering, Israel was reborn. This was a historic act of God.

More importantly, the Scriptures point to this regathering as an act of God. End time prophecies presuppose the existence of the nation of Israel as a Jewish nation (see Zechariah 12–14), and yet Isaiah 11:11 indicates that there will only be *two times* when God brings His people back to the Land en masse. The first took place after the Babylonian exile (this happened in stages, over a number of years); the second has been taking place for the last century (also in stages, over a number of years). According to Isaiah 11:10, this second return to the Land will take place at a time of great spiritual ingathering: "In that day the Root of Jesse will stand as a banner for the peoples; the nations will rally to him, and his place of rest will be glorious." Is it not significant that the twentieth century saw more people come to the Lord than all previous centuries put together? This was also the time of the beginning of the great *national* regathering, one in which God has been bringing His Jewish people back to the Land—the vast majority of them still not in faith, but more and more of whom are coming to faith once in the Land (cf. Ezekiel 36:22–32, just as happened after the Babylonian exile).

Some of Yeshua's words point in this direction as well, since the Olivet Discourse (see Matthew 24; Mark 13; Luke 21) cannot be understood entirely in terms of the Roman destruction of Jerusalem in A.D. 70—despite preterist arguments to the contrary—and the context of this very discourse speaks of Jewish believers living in a Jewish nation, one that even enforces Sabbath laws.[46] Given the ever-increasing Orthodox Jewish population in Israel today, such a scenario becomes more and more realistic.

There are many other scriptural arguments that can be marshaled to support this position—these few words barely represent the tip of the iceberg—and there are answers for every objection. Interested readers can dig into the books cited in this endnote.[47]

(2) *God promised to preserve His ancient people—as a distinct people—regardless of their sin, and the modern State of Israel is part of that preservation. Listen to the words of the Lord:*

> This is what the Lord says,
>> he who appoints the sun
>>> to shine by day,
>> who decrees the moon and stars
>>> to shine by night,
>> who stirs up the sea
>>> so that its waves roar—
>> the LORD Almighty is his name:
> "Only if these decrees vanish from my sight,"
>> declares the LORD,
> "will the descendants of Israel ever cease
>> to be a nation before me."
> This is what the LORD says:
> "Only if the heavens above can be measured
>> and the foundations of the earth below be searched out
> will I reject all the descendants of Israel
>> because of all they have done,"
>> declares the LORD.

Jeremiah 31:35–37

In light of the first point made, namely, that God Himself is behind Israel's regathering, then those who try to destroy Israel are in opposition to the very purposes of God. In truth, if not for God's merciful and supernatural preservation, we Jews would have been wiped out long ago. Surely Christians today should recognize this and work with the Lord's promises, not against them.

(3) *There is a satanic attempt to destroy Israel (see #30). Believers should therefore recognize that standing with Israel means standing*

against Israel's spiritual enemies—meaning the spiritual forces that provoke and inspire such destructive and venomous hatred against the people of Israel. Every day, every Israeli has to reckon with the fact that many of the neighboring countries share these sentiments spoken by radical Islamic leaders in the 1990s: "Blood must flow. There must be widows, there must be orphans. Hands and limbs must be cut and the limbs and blood must be spread everywhere in order that Allah's religion stand on its feet."[48] That means Jewish blood and Jewish limbs!

Calls for the extermination of Israel are an ongoing reality today, despite the endless negotiations and peace talks. This is ultimately a spiritual battle, and standing with Israel means standing on the right side of this battle.

To be sure, as Christians, we should treat every person with compassion, even if they find themselves on the wrong side of the battle. But the stark realities cannot be overemphasized: In much of the Muslim world, quite notably among the Palestinians, little children are taught to hate Jews (and Americans) from birth, and the hatred is deep-seated and religiously rooted. The unique perspective of Walid Shoebat, a former terrorist who is now a great supporter of Israel due to his dramatic conversion to Christianity, should be heard by all Christians who feel that they should side with the Palestinian side of the crisis. I highly recommend his books *Why I Left Jihad: The Root of Terrorism and the Return of Radical Islam* (2005) and *Why We Want to Kill You: The Jihadist Mindset and How to Defeat It* (2007), for the perspective of an insider. (I do not necessarily endorse all his eschatological interpretations.)

(4) *Jesus will return to a Jewish Jerusalem.* The Lord stated this plainly in Matthew 23:37–39:

> O Jerusalem, Jerusalem, you who kill the prophets and stone those sent to you, how often I have longed to gather your children together, as a hen gathers her chicks under her wings, but you were

not willing. Look, your house is left to you desolate. For I tell you, you will not see me again until you say, "Blessed is he who comes in the name of the Lord."

The Jewish Messiah will not return until His Jewish people, centered in Jerusalem, welcome Him back as King.[49] Why else is there so much controversy over this city? Why else is Jerusalem the only national capital not recognized by the other nations? Why else is there such a determined effort to divide the city and take it out of Jewish hands? And why else did God say through the prophet Isaiah, in chapter 62:6–7, "I have posted watchmen on your walls, O Jerusalem; they will never be silent day or night. You who call on the LORD, give yourselves no rest, and give him no rest till he establishes Jerusalem and makes her the praise of the earth"? (Note carefully that there is no exegetical support for changing "Jerusalem" here to "the church.")

Why Jerusalem? It is because this is the city to which the Messiah will return, and the ultimate battle is the battle for a Jewish Jerusalem.

Now, if you were the devil and you knew this, wouldn't you try to stop the Jewish people from reconstituting a homeland in Israel? And if you couldn't stop this, wouldn't you try to keep Jerusalem out of Jewish control? And if you couldn't stop this, wouldn't you try to keep the Jewish people from recognizing Jesus as Messiah? The answer, of course, is yes to each of these questions—an emphatic yes—and historical events, both recent and distant, give ample evidence to these very activities. Christians, therefore, should stand *with* Israel and *with* a Jewish Jerusalem, praying fervently for God to open His people's eyes to acknowledge Yeshua as Messiah and King.

(5) *In Genesis 12:3, God promised Abram, "I will bless those who bless you, and whoever curses you [literally, reviles you or treats you with contempt] I will curse; and all peoples on earth will be blessed through you."* Over the course of the centuries, it is clear that this promise was

specifically given to Abraham's chosen seed, coming through Isaac and then through Jacob/Israel. Where does the Word specifically state that this promise is no longer in effect? On what scriptural basis can we say that God no longer holds to this principle?

Some have argued that the demise of "Great Britain"—in terms of its world influence—was set in motion when it began to turn against Israel in the early twentieth century. Others argue that one main reason that God has not more severely judged America has been because of our historic commitment to Israel, while our times of vacillating have been accompanied by divine judgments.

For a number of years now, I have heard some teachers propound this argument about God chastening America when we failed to stand with Israel, and I myself was struck by some of these very "coincidences" as they unfolded. And it definitely caught my attention that the Monica Lewinsky affair came to light on the day that President Clinton was scheduled to have a photo op with Yasser Arafat. I thought to myself, *How ironic!*

Recently, more and more Christians have been wondering about these things, and in 2005, many could not help but see some connection between major events in Israel—very historic events— and major events in America. Shortly after we put heavy pressure on Israel to uproot by force Jewish settlers from their homes in Gaza—leaving thousands homeless—we were struck by Hurricane Katrina, leaving thousands of Americans homeless. One Christian news outlet ran the headline, "Did God send Katrina as judgment for Gaza? Eerie parallels between forced evacuations spark speculation."[50] Before scoffing at such connections, you might want to prayerfully consider the issue, also taking a look at some books that make this argument in detail.[51]

In Jeremiah 30:11, God promised the Jewish people, " 'I am with you and will save you,' declares the LORD. 'Though I completely destroy all the nations among which I scatter you, I will not completely destroy you. I will discipline you but only with justice; I will not let you go entirely unpunished.'" Yes, the Jewish people have experienced God's discipline through the ages, but He has supernaturally preserved us. What has happened to the nations who sought to destroy us? Where is Assyria or Babylon? Why was Germany subsequently divided into East and West after the Holocaust, causing much national suffering and pain?

On the flip side, I know many pastors and leaders who are quite sure that God has blessed them because they pray for Israel and bless Israel. I concur with them, understanding, of course, that there are no magical formulas and that blessing Israel is not some kind of spiritual talisman. Nonetheless, when done with right motivations, with a sincere heart and out of love for God and His ancient people—who remain loved by God, even in their disobedience (see Romans 11:29)—I affirm that those who bless Israel will themselves be blessed.

(6) *There really is a world conspiracy against Israel, and as Christians who stand for truth and light, we must stand with Israel.* I once asked a pro-life activist who had issues with modern Israel if he trusted the media's reporting of the abortion debate. "Absolutely not!" was his reply, and for good reason. The "mainstream" news media is decidedly against the pro-life movement, and its reporting on abortion cannot be taken at face value as truthful and accurate. In the same way, especially overseas, reporting about Israel and the Middle East is extraordinarily slanted. Sometimes, while watching world news coverage when ministering outside of the United States, my jaw has dropped because of the overt, undisguised anti-Israel bias. It really is shocking!

In truth, Israel is a tiny island surrounded by committed, often mortal enemies—just look at this map, where Israel is the tiny black strip and all the gray represents Muslim nations—and the only reason for its military buildup is survival.[52]

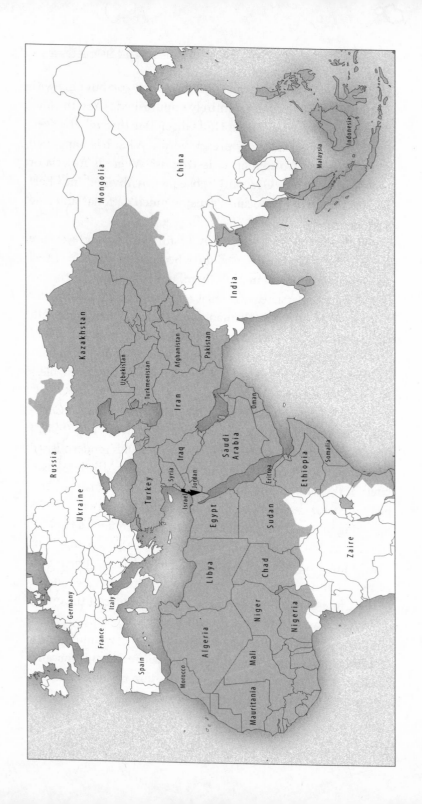

Ironically, as one Middle Eastern scholar said in the 1990s, "When Israel uses tear gas against its enemies, there's a world uproar. When Saddam Hussein uses nerve gas against his own people, no one says a word." Sadly, this continues to be the pattern today, a pattern duly noted by organizations such as CAMERA, the Committee for Accuracy in Middle East Reporting in America. A quick visit to Camera.org will prove painfully enlightening.[53]

Israel went to war in Lebanon in 2006 after its people were bombarded by a constant stream of rockets launched by radical Muslims bent on their destruction, and in the midst of war, there were literally hundreds of rockets exploding in Israel daily. More than one million people—representing one-fifth of Israel's Jewish population—were displaced. (That would be the equivalent of roughly *sixty million Americans* having to be temporarily relocated.) Yet the world wanted Israel to be restrained, and many condemned their military actions. Can you imagine how America would have responded if terrorists in Mexico were launching bombs into Texas every day, killing many and causing rampant destruction?

In 2006, former president Jimmy Carter published a highly controversial book equating Israeli policy toward the Palestinians with South African apartheid.[54] As a result of this highly skewed volume, more than ten members of the advisory board of the Carter Center in Atlanta resigned, stating in part:

> Israelis, through deed and public comment, have consistently spoken of a desire to live in peace and make territorial compromise to achieve this status. The Palestinian side has consistently resorted to acts of terror as a national expression and elected parties endorsing the use of terror, the rejection of territorial compromise and of Israel's right to exist. Palestinian leaders have had chances since 1947 to have their own state, including during your own presidency when they snubbed your efforts.[55]

Without a doubt, Israelis have been guilty of criminal acts in some of their dealings with the Palestinians and the surrounding countries. Yet these acts take place contrary to national policy—something that some anti-Israel, Christian authors fail to note—and you can ask anyone in Israel who has served in the military or who has a family member serving in the military, and they will tell you the extraordinary measures they take to prevent the loss of innocent Arab lives, often at the price of their own safety. Many times during the war with Hezbollah, I received prayer requests from friends living in Israel whose family members were on the front lines, and they would frequently state that the operations were made so much more difficult because of Israeli policies to avoid civilian casualties at all costs.

Put another way, when Israeli troops kill nonaggressors, the nation calls for an accounting and the military launches an investigation. When a terrorist suicide bomber blows up Israeli children on a school bus, his people rejoice and praise him as a martyr.

The bottom line is that, broadly speaking, the same ideology that fueled the 9/11 attacks is the same ideology that is bent on destroying Israel, and as a matter of justice, Christians should stand with the Jewish state while reaching out with compassion to all parties in the Middle East, calling for justice and truth, and recognizing that, ultimately, the only hope of the region—and the world—is the return of the Prince of Peace.

59
What did Paul mean when he said that "all Israel will be saved"?

When Paul wrote that all Israel would be saved (see Romans 11:26), he was speaking of the end time turning of the Jewish people to Jesus the Messiah. This echoes the word of the Lord through Jeremiah: "'At that time,' declares the LORD, 'I will be

the God of all the clans of Israel, and they will be my people'"
(Jeremiah 31:1). Although some interpreters have disputed this
meaning, claiming that Paul meant something different when he
spoke of "Israel," the context is clearly against these views.

Let us first look at the larger context of Romans as a whole. At
the time that Paul wrote Romans, he had not yet ministered to
the believers in Rome, and he wanted to be sure that they understood the foundation of the Gospel message. That's why Romans
is often considered to be the most important doctrinal letter in
the New Testament.

So, after his introductory comments, which include the statement that the Gospel is "the power of God for the salvation of
everyone who believes: first for the Jew, then for the Gentile"
(Romans 1:16), Paul demonstrates that all people, Gentile and
Jew alike, are under sin (1:18–3:31). Then, in chapters 4–5, he lays
out the principle of justification by faith before describing life in
the Spirit and the believer's victory over sin in chapters 6–8, after
which he takes three more chapters, chapters 9–11, to address the
question of Israel. The rest of the letter, chapters 12–16, deals with
the practical application of the Gospel.

Dwight Pryor, a fine teacher of the Jewish background to the New
Testament, once told me that a pastor friend of his commented to
him, "I just finished teaching Romans to my church, but whenever
I do this, I always skip chapters 9–11, because they're not relevant
anymore." What a massive spiritual blind spot! To the contrary, as
my FIRE colleague Bob Gladstone often tells our ministry school
students, "According to Paul, if you don't understand Israel, you don't
understand Paul's Gospel." I'm confident that Paul would agree.

Why was Israel's destiny of such importance to Paul? Why did
their state of spiritual alienation (nationally speaking) cause him
such grief that he would have been accursed from the Messiah if
it would have brought them salvation (see Romans 9:1–3)? It is
because Israel was the chosen nation, the covenant people, and

through them God's salvation was to come to the whole world. Yet when the Messiah of Israel came, the people of Israel rejected Him (again, on a national, not personal level). How could this be?

How could it be that "the Gentiles, who did not pursue righteousness, have obtained it, a righteousness that is by faith; but Israel, who pursued a law of righteousness, has not attained it" (9:30–31)? Have the promises failed (see 9:6)? Has God rejected His people (see 11:1)? "Did they stumble so as to fall beyond recovery?" (11:11). I will let Paul answer for himself: "Not at all!" (11:11).

In the unfathomable wisdom of God, Israel's rejection resulted in the salvation of the Gentiles, and in the end, their turning back will bring glorious spiritual restoration:

> Again I ask: Did they stumble so as to fall beyond recovery? Not at all! Rather, because of their transgression, salvation has come to the Gentiles to make Israel envious. But if their transgression means riches for the world, and their loss means riches for the Gentiles, how much greater riches will their fullness bring!
>
> I am talking to you Gentiles. Inasmuch as I am the apostle to the Gentiles, I make much of my ministry in the hope that I may somehow arouse my own people to envy and save some of them. For if their rejection is the reconciliation of the world, what will their acceptance be but life from the dead? If the part of the dough offered as firstfruits is holy, then the whole batch is holy; if the root is holy, so are the branches.
>
> 11:11–16

"But," you say, "I've heard that when Paul spoke of Israel in Romans, he was actually speaking of spiritual Israel, the Church, rather than the Jewish people."

That is a common misconception, but it is not supported by the text at all. In fact, the verses just cited should make that clear, since *Paul did not tell the Gentile believers that they were Israel.* Instead, he spoke to the Gentiles about Israel, addressing them as Gentiles rather than as spiritual Israelites. (Stop for a moment and read the verses again. They really are quite clear. For Paul's use of the term *Jew*, see #53.)

But there's more. Paul began this section in Romans making reference to "the people of Israel" (9:4), meaning the nation as a whole, the nation for whom his heart was broken. Then he spoke of Israel and Abraham's offspring in a special, spiritual sense (see 9:6–9). After that, for the rest of these critically important chapters (i.e., Romans 9–11), *every time he spoke of Israel, he spoke of the nation as a whole*. Take a moment and look up the references: 9:27, 31; 10:16, 19–21; 11:1–2, 7, 11. It really is quite clear. Every time Paul wrote the word *Israel*, he meant the natural children, the people as a whole.[56]

Then we come to the climax of his discussion in 11:25–29. Let us read verse 25 carefully: "I do not want you to be ignorant of this mystery, brothers, so that you may not be conceited: Israel has experienced a hardening in part until the full number [literally, "fullness"] of the Gentiles has come in."

Tragically, over the centuries, the Church *has* been ignorant of this mystery, thinking that it had replaced Israel and that God was finished with Israel. This ignorance led to the erroneous teaching called supersessionism, or replacement theology, the doctrine that the Church replaced Israel, a doctrine that opened the door to the horrors of "Christian" anti-Semitism in history.[57]

Now, let us look again at the end of verse 25: "Israel has experienced a hardening in part until the full number of the Gentiles has come in." "Israel" does not mean the Gentiles! Notice also that it is this statement that leads into verse 26. The *Israel* that has been hardened in part is the *Israel* that will be saved.

And so [meaning, "on the heels of the fullness of the Gentiles coming in"] all Israel will be saved, as it is written:
"The deliverer will come from Zion;
    he will turn godlessness away from Jacob.

> And this is my covenant with them
>> when I take away their sins."
> As far as the gospel is concerned, they are enemies on your account;
> but as far as election is concerned, they are loved on account of
> the patriarchs, for God's gifts and his call are irrevocable.

Romans 11:26–29, quoting Isaiah 59:20–21

The meaning is quite clear: The Israel that had been rejected is the Israel that will be accepted. The chosen people, who had become enemies of the Gospel, remain the objects of God's covenantal love, and in the end, there will be a national conversion, a national awakening, and "all Israel shall be saved." Praise God!

This is not referring to the Church as a whole (as recognized by virtually all the top contemporary commentators on the book of Romans),[58] nor is it referring to the sum total of Jewish believers through the centuries (really, this is a fringe interpretation not supported in the least by the context, which includes a significant quotation from Isaiah 59).[59] To the contrary, there will be a national turning at the end of this age. Underscoring this is the fact that, outside of Romans 9–11, Paul never speaks of "Israel," although he makes frequent reference to "the Jews." These are national promises!

Does Romans 11:26 mean that every single Jew living anywhere in the world will be saved at the end of the age? That is possible, but that is probably overstating Paul's point. Does it mean that all Jews from all generations will ultimately be saved? Certainly not. Those who have been lost are lost, and Paul's broken heart was occasioned by the genuinely lost state of so many of his people.

Does the verse mean that we don't have to worry about witnessing to the Jewish people, since in the end, they will all be saved? God forbid! First, we are responsible to share the Gospel with our own generation without hedging our witness because of some kind of misguided eschatological expectation; second, there is the excellent possibility that the Jewish person whom God has placed in your life will not be alive when Jesus returns (you and I might not be either!); third, nothing happens automatically in God's Kingdom, and if Jewish people are to be saved, the loving, prayerful witness of the Church will play a major role in this; fourth, who knows what size "all Israel" will be at the end of the age? Perhaps it will be reduced through assimilation and hardship before the Lord's return, underscoring the importance of reaching out to Jewish people with the Good News of the Messiah as the opportunities arise.

However, to return to the glorious news, just as it is said today in broad, sweeping terms, "Jews don't believe in Jesus," on that day, it will be said, "Jews believe in Jesus!" The event will be so glorious that the godly Puritan author Samuel Rutherford wished that he could put off heaven to witness that day.

As the old poem declared:

> Clothed with her fairest hope, the Church
> Will triumph with her Lord,
> And earth her jubilee will keep
> When Israel is restored.

60

Did God make a special way for Jews to be saved without believing in Jesus?

I wish that I could say, "Yes! God has made a special way for Jews to be saved without believing in Jesus." After all, my wife and I are Jewish. Our families are Jewish. Many of our friends growing up were Jewish. To this day, I am in close, ongoing contact with religious Jews, and we have had many in-depth discussions about the things of God. They would tell me plainly that they love God deeply but they do not believe that Jesus is the Messiah. Isn't there a way for them to be saved without faith in Yeshua?

Certainly, each individual, Jew and Gentile, will have to stand before God on his or her own, and we cannot claim to know the fate of every human being. But of this we can be sure: God has not made a special covenant with the Jewish people that allows them to be saved without Yeshua. The testimony of the Scriptures is clear.

Why, then, do some Christians teach that Jews can be saved without believing in Jesus? For some, it is primarily a sentimental issue. That is to say—in overly simplistic terms—they go to Israel, they see Jews praying at the Wailing Wall, they recognize that the Jews are the chosen people, they read about the Church's past persecution of the Jews—in the name of Jesus no less—and they simply cannot imagine them being lost. After all, at certain times in history, it appears that the Jews have been far more righteous than the Christians! Isn't it arrogant, then, to think that believers in Jesus are saved while these righteous Jews are lost? The unspeakable tragedy of the Holocaust has also made it difficult for many Christians to believe that Jews who do not believe in Yeshua will not be saved.

Others, however, base their views on a number of scriptural arguments, most of which boil down to the claim that God gave Israel the Mosaic covenant, and Jews who adhere to that covenant remain in right standing with the Lord. This is allegedly reinforced by Paul, who taught that "it is those who obey the law who will be declared righteous" and that there will be "glory, honor and peace for everyone who does good: first for the Jew, then for the Gentile" (Romans 2:13, 10), implying that Torah-keeping Jews will be accepted by the Lord as righteous.

These arguments, however, do not stand up to close scrutiny, and the overall message of the New Testament stands against this line of reasoning. Jesus told His fellow Jews that if they knew the Father, they would know Him also, and those who rejected Him rejected the Father as well (see Luke 10:16; John 5:36–47; cf. also 9:39–41). In keeping with this, John wrote that "he who has the Son has life; he who does not have the Son of God does not have life," and that "no one who denies the Son has the Father; whoever acknowledges the Son has the Father also" (1 John 5:12; 2:23).

Repeatedly in the book of Acts, the Jewish apostles shared the Good News with their people, and repeatedly their message was rejected by many of their people. Did the apostles say, "Well, that's not that big of a problem. You still have your own way to God"? No, Peter plainly stated to the Sanhedrin, the Jewish governing body, "Salvation is found in no one else, for there is no other name under heaven given to men by which we must be saved" (Acts 4:12—yes, this verse was originally spoken by a Jewish man to a Jewish audience, not by a narrow-minded, fundamentalist preacher on TV). Paul, too, made himself clear when his people rejected the message of the Messiah: "We had to speak the word of God to you first. Since you reject it and do not consider yourselves worthy of eternal life, we now turn to the Gentiles" (Acts 13:46; this is basically how Acts ends; see Acts 28:16–31). That's why Paul had "great sorrow and unceasing anguish" (Romans 9:2) in his heart: so many of his people were not saved, including those whom he said were "zealous for God, but their zeal is not based on knowledge" (10:2). In fact, it was for those very people that he prayed (see 10:1), "Since they did not know the righteousness that comes from God and sought to establish their own, they did not submit to God's righteousness" (10:3).

So, according to Paul, despite the religious zeal of the Jewish people, they failed to understand the gift of God's righteousness and therefore his "heart's desire and prayer to God for [them was] that they may be saved" (10:1). Let me repeat: Even Jewish people who are zealous for God (see 10:2) and are pursuing a law of righteousness (see 9:31; 10:3) are in need of salvation through Yeshua.

As for the notion that Jewish people can be saved by observing the Mosaic covenant, Paul writes:

> Now we know that whatever the law says, it says to those who are under the law, so that every mouth may be silenced and the whole world held accountable to God. Therefore no one will be declared

273

righteous in his sight by observing the law; rather, through the law we become conscious of sin.

Romans 3:19–20

I do not set aside the grace of God, for if righteousness could be gained through the law, Christ died for nothing!

Galatians 2:21

All who rely on observing the law are under a curse, for it is written: "Cursed is everyone who does not continue to do everything written in the Book of the Law." Clearly no one is justified before God by the law, because, "The righteous will live by faith."

Galatians 3:10–11

That is why, to the end of his life, Paul reached out to his people: He longed to see them saved. And that is why he was willing to suffer so much persecution from his own people, coming back again and again to share the Good News (see Acts 21–22; 2 Corinthians 11:24).

It is also important to remember that, in Jesus, God made a new covenant with the house of Israel and the house of Judah (see Jeremiah 31:31–34; Luke 22:19–20; Hebrews 8:7–12), and, "By calling this covenant 'new,' he has made the first one obsolete; and what is obsolete and aging will soon disappear" (Hebrews 8:13). So, Israel's way to God is through the New Covenant rather than the Mosaic covenant, a point made emphatically clear with the destruction of the Temple in A.D. 70, a destruction that has lasted to this day.

Jesus made it clear that He was the fulfillment of the Torah and Prophets (see Matthew 5:17–19), while the disciples recognized Him to be the One of whom Moses and the prophets spoke (see John 1:45; Acts 3:24–26). After His resurrection, the Lord said to His disciples, "This is what I told you while I was still with you: Everything must be fulfilled that is written about me in the Law of Moses, the Prophets and the Psalms" (Luke 24:44), commissioning them to preach "repentance and forgiveness of sins . . . in his name to all nations, beginning at Jerusalem" (verse 47).

All this means that Jesus is either the Messiah of the Jewish people or the Messiah of no people; He is either the Savior of everyone, Jew and Gentile alike, or the Savior of no one.

I personally agonize over these issues, wishing at times that somehow, almost everybody could just make it in, especially my own Jewish people. But I know that all of us fall infinitely short of God's standards and that, without His mercy displayed in the cross, there is no hope for any of us, Jew and Gentile alike. And it is significant that religious Jews who come into a life-transforming faith in Yeshua do not simply say, "I had the same relationship with God before I believed, but now I just understand things a little better." To the contrary, their normal response is, "Now I've found the truth! Now I really know God! Now my sins are forgiven!" That's what happens when we enter into the New Covenant through Messiah's blood.

How, then, should we view Jewish people who died without ever hearing the Gospel, especially those who were only exposed to a hypocritical, anti-Semitic "church"? We must leave their fate as individuals to God—just as we must do for all who died without hearing the Gospel—but we should not hold to the hope that somehow, they were still under the old covenant and were thereby good enough to become accepted by God. That is simply not true, as well-intended as it may be.

And this brings us to a practical ending to this book. Israel's salvation matters dearly to the Lord, and to the extent that Christians share His heart for Israel and pray and intercede, to the extent that Christians better understand the Jewish roots of their faith and become more considerate in their witness, to that extent they can help bring the Good News to the lost sheep of the house of Israel, and to that extent they can help hasten the day in which "all Israel will be saved."

May that day come quickly—even in our lifetimes!

Notes

Part 1: Judaism and Jewish Practice

1. G. Wigoder and R. J. Werblosky, eds., *The Oxford Dictionary of the Jewish Religion* (New York: Oxford University Press, 1997), 577.

2. Ibid.

3. As cited by Rabbi Joseph Telushkin, *Jewish Literacy: The Most Important Things to Know about the Jewish Religion, Its People, and Its History* (New York: William Morrow, 1991), 392.

4. Interestingly, in 1897, Reform leaders initially condemned the Zionist movement for these very reasons, but their position was eventually reversed.

5. Wigoder and Werblosky, *Oxford Dictionary of the Jewish Religion*, 577.

6. There remains debate as to whether the shrimp meal was intentional, but most historians agree that it would have been difficult for such a gross oversight to have occurred without some foreknowledge on the part of the seminary. This event also helped lead to the formation of Conservative Judaism's Jewish Theological Seminary.

7. Herbert Freeden, *The Jewish Press in the Third Reich* (Providence: Berg, 1993), 119.

8. Wigoder and Werblosky, *Oxford Dictionary of the Jewish Religion*, 172.

9. Rabbi Loel M. Weiss, "A Concurring Opinion to Rabbi Leonard Levy's Tshuvah; 'Same-Sex Attraction And Halakhah,'" 3. (This paper was submitted as a concurrence to "Same-Sex Attraction and Halakhah" by Rabbi Leonard Levy on 8 December 2006. Concurring and dissenting opinions are not official positions of the Committee on Jewish Law and Standards.)

10. Wigoder and Werblosky, *Oxford Dictionary of the Jewish Religion*, 173.

11. Telushkin, *Jewish Literacy*, 397.

12. See Isaiah 66:2.

13. Rabbi Jeffrey Wolfson Goldwasser, responding to the question, "Do Reform rabbis believe in God?" See http://judaism.about.com/od/beliefsandlaw1/f/belief_gd.htm. The fact that such a question can be asked is certainly telling. The American-Israeli journalist, Zev Chafets, writing with typical verve, describes his experience as a Reform Jew in Michigan in the mid-1960s: "Around this time a local Reform rabbi named Sherwin Wine announced that he didn't believe in God and that he was starting a congregation for Jewish atheists. This seemed perfectly natural to me. Most of the Jews I knew in Pontiac were Reform Jews. Their denomination (and mine) in those days was almost entirely about civil rights. We didn't speak to one another about God. Our prayers, such as they were, consisted primarily of reflections on an abstract being who resembled Franklin D. Roosevelt. The Bible was second-rate Shakespeare. To the extent we read it at all, we concentrated on those prophets whose teachings were in line with Pete Seeger. The Holocaust was never discussed. Israel was a foreign country." *A Match Made in Heaven: American Jews, Christian Zionists, and One Man's Exploration of the Weird and Wonderful Judeo-Evangelical Alliance* (New York: HarperCollins, 2007), 6.

14. Weiss, "A Concurring Opinion," 3.

15. For a useful summary, see Ian Silver, "Homosexuality and Judaism," http://www.betham.org/kulanu/iansilver.html.

16. Rabbi Steven Leder, cited by Silver, above.

17. See http://newsbusters.org/node/2905; see also http://rac.org/Articles/index.cfm?id=783&pge_prg_id=7037.

18. For this claim, see Ammiel Hirsch's contributions in *idem* and Yaakov Yosef Reinman, *One People, Two Worlds: A Reform Rabbi and an Orthodox Rabbi Explore the Issues That Divide Them* (New York: Schocken, 2002).

19. http://www.artscroll.com/Talmud1.htm. To put this Orthodox revival into perspective, see *Daring to Dream: Profiles in the Growth of the American Torah Community* (New York: Agudath Israel of America, 2003).

20. For a good introduction to Jewish humor (and culture), see Rabbi Joseph Telushkin, *Jewish Humor: What the Best Jewish Jokes Say About the Jews* (New York: William Morrow, 1992); more broadly, see Leo Rosten, *The Joys of Yiddish* (New York: McGraw Hill, 1968).

21. H. Wayne House, *Charts of World Religions* (Grand Rapids: Zondervan, 2006), Chart 26.

22. http://www.jbuff.com/c012501.htm. For some of the Baal Shem Tov's ten principles, see http://www.baalshemtov.com/ten-principals.htm; http://www.baalshemtov.com/sayings.htm.

23. For a sampling of tales of the most famous Hasidic rebbes, beginning with the Baal Shem Tov, see Martin Buber, *Tales of the Hasidim*, new ed. (New York: Schocken, 1991); Elie Wiesel, *Souls on Fire: Portraits and Legends of Hasidic Masters* (Northvale, NJ: Jason Aronson, 1993).

24. For an attack on Lubavitch because of its distinctive Messianic beliefs—some of which, arguably, resemble the Gospel, specifically, the view that the rebbe's death served as an atonement for the generation (a not uncommon, traditional Jewish belief; see Michael L. Brown, *Answering Jewish Objections to Jesus, vol. 2: Theological Objections* [Grand Rapids: Baker, 2000], section 3.15), that he would rise from the dead, that he would return and that he represents the very embodiment of God Himself—see David Berger, *The Rebbe, the Messiah, and the Scandal of Orthodox Indifference* (Oxford: The Littman Library of Jewish Civilization, 2001); for a good overview of the work of Lubavitch, see Sue Fishkoff, *The Rebbe's Army: Inside the World of Chabad-Lubavitch* (New York: Schocken, 2003).

25. http://www.kjvoice.com/aboutkjDet.asp?ARTID=13; for some criticisms of the community—which are many—see the relevant entries in http://en.wikipedia.org/wiki/Kiryas_Joel,_New_York.

26. For a compilation of some of Rav Nachman's sayings (but not his famous, longer parables), see Moshe Mykoff, ed., *The Empty Chair: Finding Hope & Joy—Timeless Wisdom from a Hasidic Master, Rebbe Nachmann of Breslov* (Woodstock, VT: New Lights, 1998). For Internet links, see http://www.breslov.com/.

27. These 39 subdivisions are discussed in massive detail in the Talmudic tractate called *Shabbat*.

28. For an extensive critique of the concept of a binding, oral law going back to Moses, see Michael L. Brown, *Answering Jewish Objections to Jesus, vol. 5: Traditional Jewish Objections* (forthcoming).

29. Foreword to H. Chaim Schimmel, *The Oral Law: A Study of the Rabbinic Contribution to Torah She-be-al-Peh*, 2nd ed. (Jerusalem/New York: Feldheim, 1996).

30. *Nomos* occurs 194 times in the New Testament, with meanings including "custom," "rule," "principle," "norm," "law," "sacred ordinance" and "body of sacred writings."

31. Published in 1975 by Tyndale House.

32. For caveats to this, see Michael L. Brown, *Answering Jewish Objections to Jesus, vol. 2*, 60–69.

33. See Michael L. Brown, *Answering Jewish Objections to Jesus, vol. 4: New Testament Objections* (Grand Rapids: Baker, 2006), 62–66.

34. For further thoughts on this, see Michael L. Brown, "Messianic Judaism and Jewish Jesus Research," *Mishkan* 33 (2000): 38–51.

35. Published in 2006 by HarperSanFrancisco.

36. Associated Press, "Comedian Jackie Mason drops lawsuit against Jews for Jesus missionary group," *International Herald Tribune*, 4 December 2006, quoted in Lee Strobel, *The Case for the Real Jesus* (Grand Rapids: Zondervan, 2007).

37. *Hilchot Melachim* (Laws of Kings), 11:4.

38. See the relevant articles in Leo Landmann, ed., *Messianism in the Talmudic Era* (New York: Ktav, 1979).

39. I address these themes in *Answering Jewish Objections to Jesus, vol. 2: Theological Objections*, especially section 3.23.

40. B. Sanhedrin 98a, as rendered in Hayim Nahman Bialik and Yehoshua Hana Ravnitzky, *The Book of Legends: Sefer Ha-Aggadah*, trans. William G. Braude (New York: Schocken, 1992), section 18.

41. To explain one further detail, the vowel *ə* in *yəhowah* is the grammatical equivalent to the vowel *ǎ* in *ǎdonai*, which is why the wrong pronunciation came out *yəhowah* rather than *yahowah*.

42. The adjective *kosher* is derived from the Hebrew *kasher*, again meaning "suitable" or "fit for use." For the root *k-sh-r* in the Tanakh, see Esther 8:5, where it means "it is right" or "acceptable," and, in a causative verbal form, in Ecclesiastes 10:10; 11:6, where it means "to succeed."

43. J. E. Hartley, *Leviticus*, Word Biblical Commentary (Dallas: Word, 2002), 163.

44. For a refutation of the Talmudic interpretation of Deuteronomy 12:21, see Brown, *Answering Jewish Objections to Jesus, vol. 5*, section 6.1.

45. For more discussion about the dietary laws, see Brown, *Answering Jewish Objections to Jesus, vol. 4*, section 5.34. For examples of the tragic medieval baptismal confessions, see Michael L. Brown, *Our Hands Are Stained with Blood* (Shippensburg, PA: Destiny Image, 1992), 95–97.

46. Nahum Sarna, *Exodus*, JPS Torah Commentary (Philadelphia/New York: Jewish Publication Society, 1991), 138.

47. Jeffrey H. Tigay, *Deuteronomy*, JPS Torah Commentary (Philadelphia/New York: Jewish Publication Society, 1996), 140.

48. Sarna, *Exodus*, 138.

49. http://www.jewfaq.org/kashrut.htm.

50. *The Torah: A Modern Commentary* (New York: Union of American Hebrew Congregations, 1985), 122. The preceding paragraphs drew on material that will be part of volume 5 of my series on *Answering Jewish Objections to Jesus: Traditional Jewish Objections*.

51. J. I. Durham, *Exodus*, Word Biblical Commentary (Dallas: Word, 2002), 475.

52. Walter C. Kaiser Jr., "Exodus," *Expositor's Bible Commentary*, ed. Frank E. Gaebelein (Grand Rapids: Zondervan Publishing House, 1990), 488.

53. Sarna, *Exodus*, 194.

54. Wigoder and Werblosky, *Oxford Dictionary of the Jewish Religion*, 400.

55. http://www.askmoses.com/article.html?h=407&o=315.

56. http://judaism.about.com/library/3_askrabbi_o/bl_simmons_shabbat-candles.htm.

57. Yehoshua Y. Neuwirth, *Shemirath Shabbath: A Guide for the Practical Observance of Shabbath*, trans. W. Grangewood, 3rd ed. (Jerusalem/New York: Philip Feldheim, 1995), 1:103.

58. http://www.kosherlamp.com/.

59. http://www.kosherlamp.com/rabbinic.html.

60. *Shemirath Shabbath*, 13:41b, 1:103.

61. http://michaelkress.com/_wsn/page13.html.

62. Ibid.

63. Ibid.

64. http://www.askmoses.com/article.html?h=208&o=262.

65. Another issue is that of moving an object from a private domain to a public domain, something also prohibited on the Sabbath based on an expansive interpretation of Jeremiah 17:19–27, and thus a car could not be driven for that reason as well. For Yeshua's intentional challenging of this concept, see John 5.

66. Wigoder and Werblosky, *Oxford Dictionary of the Jewish Religion*, 179.

67. Telushkin, *Jewish Literacy*, 664.

68. Wigoder and Werblosky, *Oxford Dictionary of the Jewish Religion*, 180. Note that while Isaiah 3:17 is subject to different interpretations, it is clear that in most cultures baldness and loss of hair is especially undesirable for women.

69. John H. Walton, Victor H. Matthews, and Mark W. Chavalas, *The IVP Bible Background Commentary: Old Testament* (Downers Grove, IL: InterVarsity Press, 2000), 589.

70. Craig S. Keener, *The IVP Bible Background Commentary: New Testament* (Downers Grove, IL: InterVarsity Press, 1993), 476.

71. David H. Stern, *Jewish New Testament Commentary* (Clarksville, MD: Jewish New Testament Publications, 1992), 474, with further reference to his *Messianic Jewish Manifesto* (Clarksville, MD: Messianic Jewish Resources International, 1988), 170–71.

72. Ibid., 180.

73. Ibid.

74. Yet another answer was passed on to me by a former Hasid whose great-grandfather claimed to know the exact origins of the tradition, namely, that a problem arose when the Jewish women went into town "to party" while their husbands were working. To stop this behavior, the most respected rabbi of the generation ordered that the women shave their heads, and if they refused to comply they would not be buried in a Jewish cemetery, which to them would have been unthinkable. Another scholarly rabbi, however, disputed the correctness of this tradition based on sources that he studied.

75. For additional Talmudic discussion concerning questions about shaving with a razor or with scissors, see b. Makkot 20b–21a.

76. Jacob Milgrom, *Numbers*, JPS Torah Commentary (Philadelphia/New York: Jewish Publication Society, 1990), 160.

77. Although some scholars have pointed to some folk beliefs that there was special healing power in the fringes of a Jewish holy man's garments, the

evidence for this is scant at best, and there is no support at all for the notion that this was a well-known fact in Yeshua's day, based on Malachi 4:2, which states, "But for you who revere my name, the sun of righteousness will rise with healing in its wings." This view is to be rejected for several reasons: (1) There is no evidence whatsoever for any such ancient interpretation of Malachi 4:2. (2) The verse in question has to do with solar imagery, not clothes, as noted in the *IVP Bible Background Commentary: Old Testament,* addressing Malachi 4:2: "It is not unusual in the Old Testament for Yahweh's work to be depicted using this metaphor of solar terminology. 'Healing in its wings' is a symbolic use of the wings of a bird with the rays of the sun. The wings denote protective care (hence the healing). An ancient Near Eastern motif in astral religions has the sun depicted as a winged disk. This is especially pervasive in the Persian period." (3) Although the Hebrew word *kanaph,* or "wing," can be used for the end of a garment (see 1 Samuel 15:27), it is never used specifically to refer to the ritual fringe. (4) There is scant ancient evidence for the idea that the fringes of a Jewish holy man were thought of as having special healing power. (5) In Matthew's gospel—the most "Jewish" of the gospels in terms of its intended audience—the woman with the issue of blood simply says, "If I only touch his cloak, I will be healed" (9:21) rather than, "If I only touch His (holy, healing) fringes."

78. D. A. Carson, "Matthew," *Expositor's Bible Commentary,* 474.

79. For the minor (albeit significant) variations between the Dead Sea phylacteries and the rabbinic phylacteries, see Brown, *Answering Jewish Objections to Jesus, vol. 5,* 6.3.

80. Nathan T. Lopes Cardozo, *The Written Torah and Oral Torah: A Comprehensive Introduction* (Northvale, NJ: Aronson, 1997), 84–85.

81. I am aware, of course, that there are critical biblical scholars who claim that Deuteronomy was not written until after the time of this inscription, and so the question of the application of Deuteronomy 6:9; 11:20 would be moot. I am assuming, however, the Mosaic authorship of the Pentateuch.

82. The actual meaning of *Shaddai* is a matter of scholarly dispute. It has been associated with Akkadian *sadu,* "steppe" or "mountain," similar to concepts like "God is my Rock" (see Deuteronomy 32:4), and thus related to meanings such as "powerful" or "strong." The ancient rabbis sometimes took *Shaddai* to mean "more than enough," based on the Hebrew *she* (pronounced *sheh*), "that is," and *day* (pronounced like English "die"), "enough," but this is a popular etymology, not to be taken as a serious philological observation. *Shaddai* is used in a wordplay in Joel 1:15, literally, "it will come as a *shod* (pronounced like English "showed")—destruction—from *Shaddai,*" but it is fairly certain that *Shaddai* itself is not derived from the verb meaning "destroy." There is a popular Christian view that *Shaddai* means "the many-breasted one," hence the Provider, related to the Hebrew word for "breasts," *shadayim.* This, however, is

the least likely view of all, since such imagery is associated with a female deity, as seen in some ancient iconography, not with a male deity.

83. http://www.jewfaq.org/signs.htm.

84. Shaye D. Cohen, "Was Timothy Jewish (Acts 16:1–3)? Patristic Exegesis, Rabbinic Law, and Matrilineal Descent," *Journal of Biblical Literature* 105 (1986), 251–68.

85. Cited by Lisa Katz, "Who Is a Jew?" http://judaism.about.com/od/whoisajew/a/whoisjewdescent.htm. Katz plainly states: "Matrilineal descent, the passing down of a child's Jewish identity via the mother, is not a biblical principle. In biblical times, many Jewish men married non-Jews, and their children's status was determined by the father's religion."

86. This is the footnote to the Soncino Talmud, *ad loc.*

87. Other Talmudic references to the 613 commandments include: b. Shabbat 87a; b. Yevamot 47b; 62a; b. Nedarim 25a; b. Shevuot 29a.

88. To b. Sanhedrin 56a.

89. For one such example, see J. David Davis, *Finding The God of Noah: The Spiritual Journey of a Baptist Minister from Christianity to the Laws of Noah* (Hoboken, NJ: KTAV, 1996). To me, these accounts are terribly painful, and I cannot fathom how anyone who had a vibrant relationship with the Lord Jesus would ever abandon Him for this (or anything else).

90. See http://www.vendyljones.org.il/; http://en.wikipedia.org/wiki/Indiana_Jones.

91. Other books are cited on http://www.faqs.org/faqs/judaism/reading-lists/general/section-8.html.

Part 2: The Jewish People and Jewish History

1. For refutation of Koestler's theory, which is not taken seriously by the vast majority of scholars, see Brown, *Our Hands Are Stained with Blood*, 66–68.

2. See http://www.radioislam.org/koestler/.

3. For a balanced discussion about the alleged African origins of the Israelites, see Glen Usry and Craig S. Keener, *Black Man's Religion: Can Christianity Be Afrocentric?* (Downers Grove, IL: InterVarsity Press, 1996), and remember that Moses' wife was an Ethiopian.

4. See Nicholas Wade, "Geneticists Report Finding Central Asian Link to Levites," 3 September 2003, *NY Times*, http://www.nytimes.com/2003/09/27/science/27GENE.html?ex=1169614800&en=0e6d3bb8fbd1c3ff&ei=5070. Wade writes, "If the patrilineal descent of the two priestly castes had indeed been followed as tradition describes, then all Cohanim should be descended from Aaron, the brother of Moses, and all Levites from Levi, the third son of the patriarch Jacob. Dr. Hammer and Dr. Skorecki found that more than half the Cohanim, in both the Ashkenazi and Sephardi communities, did indeed carry the same genetic signature on their Y chromosome. Their ancestor lived some

3,000 years ago, based on genetic calculations, and may indeed have been Aaron, Dr. Skorecki said. But the picture among the Levites was less clear, suggesting that they had a mixed ancestry."

5. See http://www.davidicdynasty.org/dna.php. Note that the DNA testing is still in its infancy with regard to alleged Davidic descendants.

6. Telushkin, *Jewish Literacy*, 88–89.

7. http://www.britishisrael.co.uk/; according to the website, this group considered itself Christian as well.

8. C. H. Gordon, "The Ten Lost Tribes," in Shalom Goldman, ed., *The Hebrew Bible and America: The First Two Centuries* (Hanover, NH/London: University Press of New England, 1993), 61–69. Note that Gordon, who was known for his wide-ranging erudition, was also known for some highly speculative theories as well. For a refutation of the association between the Ten Lost Tribes and the American Indians, see Richard H. Popkin, "The Rise and Fall of the Jewish Indian Theory," in *The Hebrew Bible and America*, 70–90.

9. Published in 2004 by Signature Books.

10. For Southerton's response to some of his Mormon critics, see http://www.irr.org/MIT/southerton-response.html.

11. http://wnd.com/news/article.asp?ARTICLE_ID=53068.

12. http://www.shavei.org/article.php?id=47.

13. Ibid.

14. http://wnd.com/news/article.asp?ARTICLE_ID=53068; for relevant DNA studies, see http://www.khazaria.com/genetics/abstracts-nonjews.html.

15. DNA studies have also confirmed the Jewish ancestry of many Spanish-speaking people who claimed that they are the descendants of Spanish-speaking Jews who were forced to convert to Catholicism in past centuries, often secretly retaining their Jewish identity. See http://www.khazaria.com/genetics/abstracts-nonjews.html, under "Latinos with traditions of Spanish Jewish ancestry."

16. For photos of recent high priests, see http://www.the-samaritans.com/gallery/gallerymain.htm.

17. http://www.the-samaritans.com/info.htm, italics in original. Today's Samaritans speak modern Hebrew or Arabic, and the English website has clearly been produced by those whose first language is not English. In navigating through the site, one can quickly feel the historic rejection these ancient people have suffered.

18. Ibid.

19. According to Peidong Shen, Tal Lavi, and others, "Reconstruction of Patrilineages and Matrilineages of Samaritans and Other Israeli Populations from Y-Chromosome and Mitochondrial DNA Sequence Variation," *Human Mutation* 24 (2004), "Based on the close relationship of the Samaritan haplogroup J six-microsatellite haplotypes with the Cohen modal haplotype, we speculate that the Samaritan M304 Y-chromosome lineages present a subgroup

of the original Jewish Cohanim priesthood that did not go into exile when the Assyrians conquered the northern kingdom of Israel in 721 B.C., but married Assyrian and female exiles relocated from other conquered lands, which was a typical Assyrian policy to obliterate national identities. This is in line with biblical texts that emphasize a common heritage of Jews and Samaritans, but also record the negative attitude of Jews towards the Samaritans because of their association with people that were not Jewish. Such a scenario could explain why Samaritan Y-chromosome lineages cluster tightly with Jewish Y-lineages (Fig. 2A), while their mitochondrial lineages are closest to Iraqi Jewish and Palestinian mtDNA sequences (Fig. 2B)." Cited on http://www.khazaria.com/ genetics/abstracts-nonjews.html.

20. Merrill C. Tenney, "John," *Expositor's Bible Commentary*, 55.

21. http://www.karaite-korner.org/history.shtml; emphasis in the original.

22. Ibid.

23. For the online edition, see http://www.jewishencyclopedia.com/view .jsp?artid=1460&letter=A (the "Anan ben David" entry).

24. See, conveniently, http://www.karaite-korner.org/salmon_ben_yeruham .shtml#canto1, citing from Salmon's *Book of the Wars of the Lord*, as translated by Leon Nemoy.

25. According to the *Jewish Encyclopedia*, the Karaites "were a Jewish sect, professing, in its religious observances and opinions, to follow the Bible to the exclusion of rabbinical traditions and laws. But Karaism in fact adopted a large part of rabbinical Judaism, either outright or with more or less modification, while at the same time it borrowed from earlier or later Jewish sects—Sadducees, Essenes, 'Isawites, Yudghanites, etc.—as well as from the Mohammedans. The founder of the sect being Anan, his followers were at first called Ananites, but as the doctrines of the sect were more fully developed, and it gradually emancipated itself from Ananism, they took the name of 'Karaites.'" See *Jewish Encyclopedia*, "Karaites, Karaism," http://www.jewishencyclopedia.com/view.jsp?artid=108 &letter=K&search=karaites.

26. http://en.wikipedia.org/wiki/Karaite_Judaism. As far as I can tell, this statement is accurate.

27. Edward H. Flannery, *The Anguish of the Jews: Twenty-three Centuries of Anti-Semitism* (New York/Mahwah: Paulist Press, 1985), 284, cited in *Our Hands Are Stained with Blood*, 221, n. 7. Note also that some scholars, especially Jewish thinkers, prefer to use the spelling *antisemitism*, since, technically speaking, there is no such thing as racial "Semitism" ("Semitism" is a linguistic term, not a racial term, referring to a Semitic style of expression), and the term Semite includes the Arabs as well.

28. This is documented throughout my book *Our Hands Are Stained with Blood*. Amazingly, a popular (and quite sensationalist) Christian ministry is now pushing the notorious and completely fictitious *Protocols of the Elders of Zion*;

see http://www.texemarrs.com/, where another libelous book, *The Synagogue of Satan: The Secret History of Jewish World Domination*, has been prominently offered (as of February–March 2007). With reference to the *Protocols*, the website states, "The most banned book in all the world! It is a crime in many nations to even possess this incredible book. Coming out of Russia in the early 20th Century, it was said to be the Zionist Jews' Secret Plan for global domination. Henry Ford, industrialist and inventor of the auto assembly line, believed it to be legitimate. So, too, did famous aviator Charles Lindbergh and many others. Read and study it for yourself; but hurry: at any moment, this book may be declared illegal by opponents of Free Speech! 'This ingenious, yet monstrous plot surely was hatched from the pit of hell.'—Texe Marrs." See http://www.texemarrs. com/Merchant2/merchant.mvc?Screen=PROD&Store_Code=catalog&Product _Code=bboa_learned_elders_of_zion. It is truly remarkable to read such quotes from a professing evangelical, Christian author, especially in the 21st century, but this simply underscores the point we have been making.

29. http://www.rael.org/rael_content/rael_summary.php.

30. http://rael.org/.

31. I am not sure if Rael's current message has been modified, given the fact that his materials are now available in Hebrew. The anti-Israel message can be found at http://www.rael.org/int/english/raelspeaks/raelspeaks/april56.html, entitled, "If only there was a Palestinian Gandhi," and dated 2 April 2002.

32. Irving Greenberg, "Cloud of Smoke, Pillar of Fire: Judaism, Christianity and Modernity after the Holocaust," in E. Fleischer, ed., *Auschwitz: Beginning of a New Era?* (New York: Knopf, 1977), 25.

33. Article Seventeen of the Hamas Covenant, 18 August 1988, http://www .yale.edu/lawweb/avalon/mideast/hamas.htm.

34. The statement was made in 1927, but I do not have the original source.

35. Brown, *Our Hands Are Stained with Blood*, 221, n. 5.

36. Ibid., 163–164.

37. In His humanity, Yeshua remains the Lion of the Tribe of Judah and the Root and Offspring of Jesse; see Revelation 5:5; 22:16.

38. For a convenient introduction to the Amidah online, see http://www.he brew4christians.com/Prayers/Daily_Prayers/Shemoneh_Esrei/shemoneh_esrei .html.

39. http://www.nkusa.org/; this official website features articles explaining all of their positions.

40. For video footage of this, which is almost surreal to watch, see http:// www.youtube.com/watch?v=2GsdC_ZboeE.

41. See http://www.templemountfaithful.org/.

42. Taken verbatim, in abbreviated form, from http://www.templemount faithful.org/obj.htm. See the same for their short-term objectives.

43. See their "Challenge to the Believers from the Nations," http://www .templemountfaithful.org/challeng.htm.

44. See Mitchell G. Bard, *Complete Idiot's Guide to Middle East Conflict* (New York: Alpha, 2005). As reviewers have pointed out, the book's title belies its depth and balance.

45. This position has been argued strongly by Joan Peters in her controversial but copiously documented book *From Time Immemorial: The Origins of the Arab-Jewish Conflict over Palestine* (New York: Harper & Row, 1984); a convenient summary of the controversy surrounding the book can be found at http://en.wikipedia.org/wiki/From_Time_Immemorial. For a good example of a strongly opposing view, see Rashid Khalidi, *Palestinian Identity* (New York: Columbia University Press, 1998). While Peters is a journalist rather than a trained academic—hence some of the searing academic criticisms of her work—it appears clear that her overall arguments carry some real merit, as other scholars such as Professor Daniel Pipes have pointed out. For a recent, popular presentation by a leading attorney, see Alan Dershowitz, *The Case for Peace: How the Israeli-Arab Conflict Can Be Solved* (Hoboken, NJ: John Wiley, 2005).

46. The third edition was published in 2006 by the American-Israeli Cooperative Enterprise (AICE).

47. Mitchell G. Bard, http://www.jewishvirtuallibrary.org/jsource/myths/ mf1.html.

48. This was spoken in 1946 when Professor Hitti testified before the Anglo-American Committee.

49. See www.shoebat.com. Shoebat had a life-changing encounter with Jesus and now works tirelessly on behalf of the Jewish people worldwide. His 2005 book, *Why I Left Jihad: The Root of Terrorism and the Return of Radical Islam* (n.p.: Top Executive Media, 2005), gives important insights from someone who was on the inside.

50. *Myths and Facts*, http://www.jewishvirtuallibrary.org/jsource/myths/ mf1.html#b.

51. Yehoshua Porath, *Palestinian Arab National Movement: From Riots to Rebellion: 1929–1939*, vol. 2, (London: Frank Cass and Co., Ltd., 1977), 81–82.

52. Samuel Katz, *Battleground: Fact and Fantasy in Palestine* (New York: Bantam Books, 1977), 55. Katz's book, although dated, remains essential reading on the subject at hand.

53. For documentation of this and much more, see Arieh L. Avneri, *The Claim of Dispossession: Jewish Land Settlement and the Arabs, 1878–1948*, trans. Kfar-Blum Translation Group (New Brunswick, NJ: Transaction Books, 1984).

54. Brown, *Our Hands Are Stained with Blood*, 70.

55. From *Innocents Abroad*, 1867; although some have challenged this description, other sources point to its accuracy; see http://www.palestinefacts.org/ pf_early_palestine_zionists_impact.php.

56. For further pertinent data, see Avneri's *The Claim of Dispossession*.

57. Propagandists put this number at one million; the UN, at the time, put it at 427,000; see Bard, *Myths and Facts*.

58. Brown, *Our Hands Are Stained with Blood*, 72.

59. http://www.forzion.com/full-article.php?news=3497.

60. Accounts such as that of Elias Chacour, with David Hazzard, *Blood Brothers* (Grand Rapids: Chosen, 1984), have greatly influenced the thinking of some Christian leaders who have sided with the Palestinians on humanitarian grounds, often vilifying the Israelis in the process. It is not surprising, then, that some recent books advocating replacement theology—namely, that the Church has replaced Israel and that national Israel has no special place in God's redemptive plan—have also been influenced by perceived humanitarian issues. See Stephen R. Sizer, *Christian Zionism: Road-Map to Armageddon?* (Downers Grove, IL: InterVarsity Press, 2005). Sadly, both the theology and the assessment of human suffering in works such as this are quite skewed; for more on this, see #58.

61. http://www.palestinefacts.org/pf_early_palestine_name_origin.php.

62. Ibid.; see also http://christianactionforisrael.org/isreport/july01/history_palestine.html.

63. Walter W. Wessel, "Mark," *Expositor's Bible Commentary*, 751.

64. Keener, *IVP Bible Background Commentary: New Testament*, 248.

Part 3: Rabbi Yeshua and the Jewish Background to the New Testament

1. For the position that, generally speaking, Jesus adhered to the Pharisaic oral traditions, see David Bivin, *New Light on the Difficult Words of Jesus: Insights from His Jewish Context* (Holland, MI: En-Gedi Resource Center, 2005).

2. This view was communicated to me privately by the Messianic Jewish scholar Dr. Dan Gruber.

3. Nehemia Gordon, *The Hebrew Yeshua vs. the Greek Jesus: New Light on the Seat of Moses from Shen-Tov's Hebrew Matthew* (Chicago: Hilkiah Press, 2005), 48.

4. Ibid., for discussion of the Shem-Tov manuscript. In addition to the treatment in Gordon, see especially the studies of G. Howard, W. Horbury, W. L. Petersen, and R. F. Shedinger cited in Gordon, *The Hebrew Yeshua vs. the Greek Jesus*, 103–7.

5. For a more full discussion, see volume 5 of my series *Answering Jewish Objections to Jesus: Traditional Jewish Objections* (forthcoming), section 6.15.

6. The King James actually reflects the fact that *yehōshu'a* could sometimes be called *yeshu'a*, referring to both Joshua and Jesus by the same name in Hebrews; see Hebrews 4:8, where "Jesus" refers to Joshua. (The Greek name *Iesus* is used in the Greek for both Jesus and Joshua in Hebrews, but most modern translations distinguish between the two simply as an aid to the reader.)

7. For a more detailed explanation, with easy-to-follow charts, see http://www.aramaicnt.org/NEW/index.php?p=23.

8. Here is a typical, error-filled statement: "Although some would argue 'YA-HUshua' -vs- 'Yâhuwshú`a' -vs- Yahshua' -vs- 'Yeshua' -vs- 'Jesus' till the Messiah returned, my studies and belief, as well as the works of experts in the Hebrew language, show me that Yahushua [YAH-hoo-shu-ah] is probably the most accurate pronunciation of the Messiah's name. It makes perfect sense as this pronunciation is the exact name of the Messianic 'Branch' prophesied in Zechariah 6:11–12 as well as Moshe's (Moses') successor (known in English as Joshua) who led the Israelites over the Jordan, therefore, with abundant and scholarly evidence [sic], I personally use Yahushua." See http://www.wwyd.org/. The alleged experts in Hebrew are found at the www.eliyah.com website, specifically the http://www.eliyah.com/yahushua.html. Anyone with a scholarly knowledge of Hebrew will recognize at once that there is no Hebrew expertise on this website at all.

9. http://www.sacrednamemovement.com/JesusZeus2.htm.

10. Ibid.

11. http://www.wwyd.org/. This is the aptly named "What Would Yahushua Do?" website. It begins with the comment, "As my brother in Messiah, Michael Rood would say, 'First off, he would answer to HIS REAL NAME!'"

12. http://www.sacrednamemovement.com/JesusZeus2.htm.

13. As stated by former Hasidic Jew Menachem Korn, jesusoverisrael.blogspot.com/2006/11/daniel-code-christian-zionism.html. On other subjects, Korn has some very unusual views—to say the least—especially regarding modern Israel.

14. Simply stated, this is the etymological history of the name Jesus: Hebrew/Aramaic *yeshu'a* became Greek *Iēsous*, then Latin *Iesus*, passing into German and then, ultimately, into English, as Jesus.

15. For this and other views, see http://www.truthnet.org/islam/Islam-Bible/5MuslimJesus/index.htm.

16. The expected Aramaic form would have been *koumi*, which is reflected in some Greek manuscripts, as opposed to *koum*. Aramaic scholars, however, recognize that this could reflect a dialectical variant in colloquial Galilean Aramaic.

17. The Aramaic is actually *shabaqtani*, but Greek did not have the "sh" sound, so, e.g., Hebrew *Shaul* would become Saul in Greek. For a recent, nonscholarly (and, candidly, quite unsuccessful) attempt to minimize the presence of Aramaic here, see Douglas Hamp, *Discovering the Language of Jesus* (Santa Anna, CA: Calvary Chapel Publishing, 2005).

18. A typical case in point would be Hamp.

19. Notice also Acts 2:7, recording the surprised reaction of the Jews who heard the 120 speaking in new languages at Shavu'ot/Pentecost, "Utterly amazed, they

asked: 'Are not all these men who are speaking Galileans?'"—which would refer either to their accent or to their expected native language, namely, Aramaic.

20. Richard Bauckham, *Jesus and the Eyewitnesses: The Gospels as Eyewitness Testimony* (Grand Rapids: Eerdmans, 2006), 205–206, citing M. Bockmuehl, "Simon Peter and Bethsaida," in B. Chilton and C. Evans, eds., *The Missions of James, Peter, and Paul*, NovTSup 115 (Leiden: Brill, 2004): 82. See also J. N. Sevenster, *Do You Know Greek? How Much Greek Could the First Jewish Christians Have Known?* trans. J. de Bruin (Leiden: E. J. Brill, 1968).

21. Bauckham, 206, n. 9.

22. For further discussion of the degree of Peter's knowledge of Greek, see Bauckham, 205–10.

23. Keener, *The IVP Bible Background Commentary: New Testament*, 338.

24. Bivin, *New Light on the Difficult Words of Jesus*, xxv (this section was written by the editors, Lois Tverberg and Bruce Okkema, not David Bivin, although he would surely concur with these words).

25. For details on this, see Michael L. Brown, "Recovering the Inspired Text? An Assessment of the Work of the Jerusalem School in the Light of *Understanding the Difficult Words of Jesus*," *Mishkan* 17/18, 30, with n. 108. The article can be accessed online at http://caspari.com/mishkan/zips/mishkan17-18.pdf. For other issues of *Mishkan* online, see http://caspari.com/mishkan/.

26. James Trimm, http://www.isr-messianic.org/.

27. Ibid.

28. David Bivin and Roy B. Blizzard Jr., *Understanding the Difficult Words of Jesus* (Arcadia, CA: Makor Foundation, 1983), 21.

29. Ibid., 105, my emphasis.

30. Ibid., 105, 37; for further discussion of such statements, see Brown, "Recovering the Inspired Text?"

31. For typical conspiratorial rhetoric, see http://www.remnantofyhwh.com/Hebrew%20Origin%20NT.htm.

32. The problems involved in such an undertaking can be well illustrated by means of the children's game called "telephone"—but played with the following rules: The first player speaks several sentences in German into the ear of the player to his right; that player then translates the words into Arabic and passes them on secretly to the next player, who puts the Arabic sentences into a non-chronological, topical order and passes them on. The next player, who knows Arabic very well, improves the grammar of the previous player, shortens the sentences, attempts to put them back in their original order and then whispers them into your ear. Now it's your turn: Translate these Arabic sentences back into the original German, word for word. You will need more than good luck to succeed in this endeavor! And playing this game with written sources would not make the task any easier, since the difficulties are created by the distance from the original source—be it oral or written.

33. From the ninth century to 1976, there have been as many as 68 different Hebrew reconstructions of the Lord 's Prayer. There have also been many Aramaic reconstructions.

34. Brown, "Recovering the Inspired Text?" 41.

35. For convenient reference to some of the evidence, see http://www.biblical hebrew.com/nt/hebrewgospel.htm.

36. Most recently, see Gordon, *Hebrew Yeshua.*

37. I take for granted that most readers will understand that Paul's letters were written in Greek to Greek-speaking congregations, while Mark and Luke in particular also had Gentile audiences in mind, and so for them, it would also be quite natural to write in Greek.

38. According to www.peshitta.org, it means "straight."

39. A very rough comparison in terms of the closeness of these languages would be this: Hebrew is to Aramaic as Italian is to Spanish; Aramaic is to Syriac as Spanish is to Portuguese.

40. http://www.peshitta.org/, following the link "Peshitta"; I have removed the various fonts and emphasis in the original.

41. Modern Aramaic today is spoken in only a few parts of the world, primarily in the Middle East.

42. George M. Lamsa, *Holy Bible: From the Ancient Eastern Text* (San Francisco: HarperSanFrancisco, 1985); among his other writings, see *Idioms in the Bible Explained and a Key to the Original Gospels* (San Francisco: HarperSanFrancisco, 1985).

43. http://www.aramaicnt.org/NEW/index.php?; links are provided on the website in support of these claims.

44. For details, see Brown, "Recovering the Inspired Text?"

45. See Andrew Gabriel Roth, *RUACH QADIM: Aramaic Origins of the New Testament* (Malta: Tushiyah Press, 2005); idem, *Ruach Quadim: The Path to Life* (Malta: Tushiyah Press, 2006).

46. Ibid., n. 33.

47. Keener, *IVP Bible Background Commentary: New Testament,* 283. He also notes, "Because the water of verse 38 flows to and not from the believer (v. 39), 7:37–38 may be punctuated to read: 'If anyone thirsts, let this one come to me; and let whoever believes in me drink. As the Scripture says . . .' (The original manuscripts had no punctuation.) Verse 38 may thus declare that Jesus fulfills the Scriptures read at the feast, as the foundation stone of a new temple, the source of the water of life (see 19:34; Revelation 22:1)."

48. Michael L. Brown, *Revolution in the Church: Challenging the Religious System with a Call for Radical Change* (Grand Rapids: Chosen, 2002), 174.

49. Even the Spanish "Santiago" is actually a corruption from Jacob, being a contraction of San Diego (Saint Diego = Jacob).

50. Brown, *Revolution in the Church,* 175–76.

51. Donald A. Hagner, *Matthew 1–13*, Word Biblical Commentary (Dallas: Word, 2002), 158.

52. Some would argue that it is wrong to speak of "Jewish roots," since "Jewish" speaks of the Jewish religion, which developed in its own way after the time of Jesus, and it would therefore be better to speak of "biblical roots." The problems with this are: (1) the church has effectively made Jesus and the apostles into Gentiles; (2) Jesus Himself said that "salvation is from the Jews" (John 4:22) while Paul spoke clearly of Israel's place in world redemption (see Romans 11:11–15, 25–27); (3) Jesus was part of the Jewish religion of His day (see #36 and #46); (4) if we speak of "biblical roots," most of us assume that we are being faithful to the Bible already, so this may not adequately challenge us to reexamine the Scriptures; and (5) speaking of "recovering our Jewish roots" calls for a tangible connection with Jews today, also revealing any latent anti-Semitism that may exist in the lives of some believers.

53. Most recently, David Klinghoffer, following Hyam Maccobby.

54. The paragraphs that follow are adapted from Brown, *Answering Jewish Objections to Jesus, vol. 4*, 192–94, with permission. See there for further discussion of Paul's Jewish background.

55. Joseph Klausner, *From Jesus to Paul* (New York: Macmillan, 1945), 453–54.

56. Ibid., 452.

57. Ibid., 453–54, with examples on 454–58.

58. Ibid., 458; also for an explanation of why he quoted the Septuagint. In addition, Klausner notes, "But sometimes he quotes precisely according to the Hebrew text," with reference to the Finnish scholar Antti F. Puuko.

59. David Daube, *The New Testament and Rabbinic Judaism* (Peabody, Mass.: Hendrickson Publishers, 1994), 336ff. See further Michael L. Brown, *Answering Jewish Objections to Jesus, vol. 1: General and Historical Objections* (Grand Rapids: Baker, 2000), 1.5.

60. Alan F. Segal, *Paul the Convert: The Apostolate and Apostasy of Saul the Pharisee* (New Haven: Yale University Press, 1990), xi–xii.

61. Daniel Boyarin, *A Radical Jew: Paul and the Politics of Identity* (Berkeley: University of California Press, 1994), 2.

62. Cited by Harvey Falk, *Jesus the Pharisee* (Eugene, OR: Wipf & Stock, 2003), 18.

63. Peter J. Tomson, *Paul and the Jewish Law* (Minneapolis: Fortress Press, 1991), 52–53.

64. John Dominic Crossan and Jonathan L. Reed, *In Search of Paul: How Jesus's Apostle Opposed Rome's Empire with God's Kingdom. A New Vision of Paul's Words & World* (San Francisco: HarperSanFrancisco, 2004), 4.

65. W. R. Stegner, "Paul the Jew," in Gerald F. Hawthorne and Ralph P. Martin, eds., *Dictionary of Paul and His Letters* (Downers Grove, IL: InterVarsity, 1993), 506, 500.

66. Jaroslav Pelikan, *Jesus through the Centuries* (New Haven, CT: Yale University Press, 1999), 18, my emphasis.

67. See also Risto Santala, *Paul the Man and the Teacher: In Light of the Jewish Sources* (Jerusalem: Keren Ahvah Meshihit, 1995); the entire book can be accessed online at http://www.kolumbus.fi/hjussila/rsla/Paul/paul01.html. The early church leaders Eusebius and Jerome testified to Paul's fluency in Hebrew.

68. For further discussion, see Brown, *Answering Jewish Objections to Jesus, vol. 4*, section 5.26.

69. Flannery, *The Anguish of the Jews*, 1. This quote is so poignant that I have cited it numerous times in my books, lectures and debates, and it always resonates with the Jewish audiences that hear it.

70. For a vivid example of the sensitivities involved, see the debate between Rabbi Shmuley Boteach and myself, "Who Really Killed Jesus?" available on DVD or video; http://www.icnministries.org/resources/video.htm.

71. For a detailed discussion of 1 Thessalonians 2:13–16, see Brown, *Answering Jewish Objections to Jesus, vol. 1*, 164–67.

72. See again Brown, *Our Hands Are Stained with Blood.*

Part 4: Contemporary Christians, the Law of Moses and the State of Israel

1. John Nolland, *The Gospel of Matthew: A Commentary on the Greek Text*, New International Greek Testament Commentary (Grand Rapids: Eerdmans, 2005), 217–18.

2. For an interesting treatment of this passage in the context of answering Muslims, see http://answering-islam.org/Authors/Arlandson/fulfilled.htm.

3. Michael L. Brown, *Answering Jewish Objections to Jesus, vol. 4: New Testament Objections* (Grand Rapids: Baker, 2006), 209–10.

4. Ibid., 174–75.

5. "For the goal at which the *Torah* aims is the Messiah, who offers righteousness to everyone who trusts" (Romans 10:4, *Jewish New Testament*; note that this verse was cited, above, as one of Paul's *negative* statements about the law).

6. For a very useful summary, see Stephen Westerholm, *Perspectives Old and New on Paul: The "Lutheran" Paul and His Critics* (Grand Rapids: Eerdmans, 2004).

7. For a more detailed treatment of Paul and the Law, see Brown, *Answering Jewish Objections to Jesus, vol. 4*, section 5.29.

8. See ibid., 282, for further details.

9. I am, of course, oversimplifying this, but the overall point stands; for another view, see Peter Tomson, *Paul and the Jewish Law: Halakha in the Letters of the Apostle to the Gentiles* (Assen/ Minneapolis: Van Gorcum/Fortress, 1990).

10. I address this subject in the first lecture of my DVD series *Homosexuality, the Church, and Society*. The first lecture is titled, "The Bible and Homosexual Practice: Separating Fact from Fiction." See http://www.icnministries.org/re sources/resources.htm.

11. The most comprehensive argument for this is Dr. Mark Kinzer's *Postmissionary Messianic Judaism: Redefining Christian Engagement with the Jewish People* (Grand Rapids: Brazos, 2005). Kinzer brings excellent scholarship to the table and raises many important issues. He should not, however, be followed: (1) in a number of his scriptural interpretations, especially those that make it mandatory for Jewish believers to observe the Torah; (2) in his opening the door to the possibility of Jews being saved without explicit faith in Yeshua; (3) in his call for Jewish believers to submit to rabbinic traditions; and (4) in his calling to lessen the bold, forthright, "missionary" proclamation of our faith to other Jews. I hope to address these issues at greater length in an article to be published in an honorary volume for Moishe Rosen. See also my paper, "Is a Postmissionary, Truly Messianic Judaism Possible?" delivered April 18, 2007, at the annual North American gathering of the Lausanne Consultation on Jewish Evangelism, where I take strong issue with some of Kinzer's main conclusions. The paper is available online at http://www.icnministries.org/resources/resources.htm.

12. For further, practical insights, see Jews for Jesus, *The Messianic Movement: A Field Guide for Evangelical Christians* (San Francisco: Purple Pomegranate Publications, 2005), 97–105; see also 131–47.

13. http://www.messianicliturgy.com/spiritual_biography_of_jeremiah_ .htm. Jeremiah's special contribution to the Messianic movement has been the development of Messianic Jewish liturgy, since synagogue worship is completely liturgical and it is important for many Messianic Jewish congregations to have some form of liturgy.

14. For a still-useful study of ancient proselytes to Judaism, see Alfred Edersheim, *The Life and Times of Jesus the Messiah* (electronic edition; Albany, OR: AGES Software, 1999), Appendix 12, "The Baptism of Proselytes," 2:640–43.

15. See the discussion in the recent major Romans commentaries, including those of James D. G. Dunn, Douglas J. Moo, and Thomas R. Schreiner. For a different but highly questionable approach, see Mark D. Nanos, *The Mystery of Romans: The Jewish Context of Paul's Letter* (Minneapolis: Augsburg Fortress, 1996).

16. Samuele Bacchiocchi, *From Sabbath to Sunday: A Historical Investigation of the Rise of Sunday Observance in Early Christianity* (Rome: Pontifical Gregorian University, 1977); D. A. Carson, ed., *From Sabbath to Lord's Day: A Biblical, Historical and Theological Investigation* (Grand Rapids: Zondervan, 1982).

17. http://www.worldslastchance.com/full_article.php#topic15.

18. As to the fact that December 25 was originally a pagan holiday, a common, traditional Christian understanding is that the Catholic Church moved

the celebration of Jesus' birth to this day so that pagan converts to Christianity would have something spiritual to celebrate in place of their historic, idolatrous celebration. So then, there is no attempt to deny the (originally) pagan signifi-cance of December 25, but the argument is that the date has been redeemed for holy purposes. I have no interest in either defending or attacking this position; I am simply explaining how some Christians defend their reason for celebrating Jesus' birth on December 25.

19. Michael J. Rood, *The Pagan-Christian Connection Exposed* (Gainesville, FL: Bridge-Logos, 2004), 87. This pales, however, in comparison to his attacks on Easter: "Easter is the rehearsal of child sacrifice and fertility rites of pagan sun god worshipers" (64); "I will not subject myself to their perverted, disgusting forms of satanic worship. . . . I have died to their world, and I will not return to the vomit of Tammuz worship" (91–92).

20. While it is possible to interpret 1 Corinthians 5:7–8 as a command to celebrate the Passover, it is best to understand Paul's language there as meta-phorical.

21. For various interpretations, see the Galatians commentaries of Ronald Y. K. Fung, F. F. Bruce, and Richard N. Longenecker. For a different approach, see Mark D. Nanos, *The Irony of Galatians: Paul's Letter in First-Century Context* (Minneapolis: Augsburg Fortress, 2001). Contrast Vincent M. Smiles, *The Gospel and the Law in Galatia: Paul's Response to Jewish-Christian Separatism and the Threat of Galatian Apostasy* (Collegeville, MN: Liturgical Press, 1998).

22. Although Matthew Henry in his commentaries oversimplifies things by speaking of the difference between Judaism and Christianity, his overall observa-tion is absolutely correct: "He would do this *after Easter, meta to pascha—after the passover,* certainly so it ought to be read, for it is the same word that is always so rendered; and to insinuate the introducing of a gospel-feast, instead of the passover, when we have nothing in the New Testament of such a thing, is to mingle Judaism with our Christianity" (see Acts 12:4).

23. See Kinzer, *Post-Missionary Messianic Judaism*, 200.

24. Ibid., 199.

25. Ibid., 201.

26. Ibid., citing *Nicene and Post-Nicene Fathers of the Christian Church,* second series, vol. 14, *The Seven Ecumenical Councils,* eds., Philip Schaff and Henry Wave (Grand Rapids: Eerdmans, 1983), 54.

27. In D. R. W. Wood, and I. H. Marshall, eds., *New Bible Dictionary* (Downers Grove, IL: InterVarsity Press, 1996), "Easter."

28. Rood, *The Pagan-Christian Connection Exposed,* 64.

29. The New Living Translation completely misses the mark here, rendering, "May God's peace and mercy be upon all who live by this principle. They are the new people of God." The footnote, however, contains the correct translation: "*this principle, and upon the Israel of God.*"

30. Some have pointed to Revelation 2:9 and 3:9, which speak of "those who say they are Jews and are not, but are a synagogue of Satan," to argue that Jews who deny Jesus—or, more specifically, who oppose the Gospel—are not really Jews. There are several responses to this charge: (1) Even if this was the correct interpretation of these verses, it would be in keeping with prophetic usage in which God indicted Israel for not really living as Israel (see Hosea 1). (2) In keeping with this, throughout the Old Testament, God still addressed His people as Israel (or, the people Judah, etc.), even while saying that they were not really His people. (3) Some interpreters, especially Messianic Jews, take the verses at face value: These were people who claimed to be Jews but were not—in other words, they were Gentiles! In any case, regardless of which interpretation is followed, these two verses can hardly negate the overwhelmingly clear, cumulative evidence of the New Testament.

31. Kay Silberling, Ph.D., "The Ephraimite Error," 1; http://mdl.heartofisrael.org/EphraimiteError.pdf

32. Ibid., 1.

33. For further references to the primary writings of the Two House camp, with clear refutation of this erroneous teaching, see *The Messianic Movement: A Field Guide for Evangelical Christians*, 121–129. See also Tim Hegg, "The Two-House Theory: Three Fatal Flaws," http://www.torahresource.com/English%20Articles/Two%20House%20Fatal%20Errors.pdf.

34. Silberling, 2, points out that in the New Testament, the equivalent Greek term for Hebrew *goy*, namely *ethnos*, "refers to the Jewish people in Luke 7:5; 23:2; John 11:48–52; 18:35; Acts 10:22; 24:2,10,17; 26:4; 28:19; 1 Corinthians 10:18; Philippians 3:5."

35. Ibid., 3.

36. For a convenient overview, see David Sedaqa, "The Rebirth of Messianic Judaism," http://www.imja.com/rebirth.html. See also, *The Messianic Movement: A Field Guide for Evangelical Christians*, 1–85.

37. Even for those who are sympathetic to Messianic Judaism, there can be some ambiguity with the statement that someone is an "ordained rabbi." By what Jewish authority has this person been ordained? On the other hand, there is a similar ambiguity when someone states that he or she is an ordained minister. Ordained by what Christian authority? In the case of the title of "ordained rabbi," however, believers might mistake this title with that of someone who was an ordained rabbi *before* coming to faith in Yeshua, which is an entirely different matter in terms of being able to say to the larger Jewish community, "Here's the testimony of a rabbi who is a believer!"

38. http://www.orthodoxrabbis.org/halachic_ruling.htm.

39. This means that all marriages performed within the Land are performed by Orthodox rabbis, while marriages performed outside the Land—be they

civil or religious—receive full status within Israel but are "registered" rather than recognized.

40. http://www.orthodoxrabbis.org/halachic_ruling.htm.

41. Stern, *Jewish New Testament Commentary*, 68.

42. Ibid., 68–69.

43. For this concept of "soulish spirituality," expressed in Greek with the word *psuchikos*, literally, "soulish," see 1 Corinthians 2:14 (NASB); see also James 3:15; Jude 19.

44. A good example of a respected, contemporary Christian voice speaking against Israel specifically *because* of its handling of the Palestinian crisis would be David Hazzard.

45. For some recent books, see Sizer, *Christian Zionism*; Colin Chapman, *Whose Promised Land?* (Grand Rapids: Baker, 2002); idem, *Whose Holy City?: Jerusalem and the Future of Peace in the Middle East* (Grand Rapids: Baker, 2005); for two articles in major cult-watch publications, see Alan Morrison (a Jewish believer), "The Two Jerusalems: A Biblical Look at the Modern State of Israel, Judaism and the Church" in the *Spiritual Counterfeits Project* (2004) and Stephen Sizer, "Modern Israel in Bible Prophecy: Promised Return or Impending Exile?" in the *Christian Research Journal* (2006). For a clear and healthy antidote to these recent books and articles, see Sandra Teplinsky, *Why Care about Israel?: How the Jewish Nation Is Key to Unleashing God's Blessings in the 21st Century* (Grand Rapids: Chosen, 2004). See also #32 above.

46. Preterists believe that Matthew 24 and related passages found their complete fulfillment in the destruction of Jerusalem by the Romans in A.D. 70, seeing no future application to any of the verses, including those that speak of the glorious return of Jesus.

47. A good starting point is Dan Juster and Keith Intrater, *Israel, the Church, and the Last Days*, repr. (Shippensburg, PA: Destiny Image, 2005); see also Teplinsky, *Why Care about Israel*; Brown, *Our Hands Are Stained with Blood* (with documentation and a bibliographical supplement). For a dispensational approach, see Arnold G. Fruchtenbaum, *The Footsteps of the Messiah: A Study of the Sequence of Prophetic Events* (rev. ed.; San Antonio: Ariel Ministries, 2003).

48. Islamic radical Fayiz Azzam, addressing a gathering in Atlanta, 1990, documented in the film *Jihad in America*.

49. See Brown, *Our Hands Are Stained with Blood*, 165–`73.

50. http://www.wnd.com/news/article.asp?ARTICLE_ID=46178; the article was by Aaron Klein and was posted 7 September 2005, offering detailed parallels between the two tragic events.

51. William R. Koenig, *Eye to Eye: Facing the Consequences of Dividing Israel* (n.p.: About Him, 2006); John P. McTiernan, *As America Has Done to Israel* (Longwood, Fla.: Xulon Press, 2006).

52. See http://www.masada2000.org/geography.html.

53. See further Brown, *Our Hands Are Stained with Blood*, 43–57, with reference to other important works.

54. Jimmy Carter, *Palestine: Peace Not Apartheid* (New York: Simon & Schuster, 2006).

55. http://www.cnn.com/2007/US/01/11/carter.resignations/index.html. Mr. Carter did, in fact, apologize for one statement that was especially poorly worded, implying that terrorists should continue to kill Israelis until a peaceful settlement was negotiated. See http://www.allheadlinenews.com/articles/7006261535.

56. As noted above, #53, in Romans, Paul speaks of "Israel" only in Romans 9–11, making reference to "Jews" in the other chapters, but not here. This underscores the fact that he is referring to God's purposes for the nation as a whole in these chapters.

57. Once again, I refer the reader to my 1992 study, *Our Hands Are Stained with Blood*, which has been translated into more languages than anything I have written, reflecting Christian interest in the subject; among many other important studies, see Dan Cohn-Sherbok, *The Crucified Jew: Twenty Centuries of Christian Anti-Semitism* (Grand Rapids: Eerdmans, 1997).

58. See the works cited above in part 4, n. 15.

59. I only cite this because it gained some circulation in the article by Alan Morrison in the *Spiritual Counterfeits Project* magazine, cited above in part 4, n. 45.

Index

Abraham, 71, 112, 113, 243, 262
Ajami, Fouad, 144
Amidah, 137
Anan ben David, 125
Ananites, 125
antirabbinic movement, 125–26
anti-Semitism, 128–35, 143, 254, 285n27. *See also* Holocaust, the; Protocols of the Elders of Zion
explanations of, 132–34
irrationality of, 131–32
length of throughout history, 129–30
and the Raelians, 130–31
role of Satan in, 134–35
as a spiritual phenomenon, 135
viciousness of, 131
widespread nature of, 130–31
Apocrypha, 46
Aramaic, 168–70, 175–80, 291nn38–39, 291n41
Assyrians, 116, 121–22
Avneri, Arieh, 145

Babylon, 142
Bard, Mitchell, 139, 145
Bauckham, Richard, 167
Beth Simchat Torah, 22
Black, Matthew, 179

Book of the Commandments (Maimonides), 102
Boyarin, Daniel, 193
Bruce, F. F., 234

Cairo Genizah, 44
Canaanites, 143–49
candles, lighting of on the Sabbath, 72–79, 103
and the Kosher-Lamp, 77–78, 81
among Messianic Jews, 75
among traditional Jews, 75–76
Cardozo, Nathan, 94
Carson, D. A., 158
Carter, Jimmy, 265, 298n55
Chafets, Zev, 278n13
Christianity, 130, 248–49, 254. *See also* Christians; Judaism, differences of from Christianity
Jewish roots of, 187–91, 292n52
Christianity Is Jewish (Schaefer), 49
Christians, 250
and adherence to dietary laws, 226–28
arguments for the support of the nation of Israel by, 256–63, 265–66

and God's promise to Abram, 261–62
and God's promise of Israel's preservation, 259
how standing with Israel means standing with God's purposes, 257–59
and the promise of Jesus' return to a Jewish Jerusalem, 260–61
and the reality of a satanic attempt to destroy Israel, 259–60
and the world conspiracy against Israel, 263, 265–66
and attendance at Jewish synagogues, 254–56
Gentile Christians as spiritual Jews, 235–40, 295n29, 296n30
Hebrew Christians and Messianic Jews, 246–48
and keeping of the Law (Torah), 215–21
and observance of biblical Jewish holidays, 228–30
and observance of the Sabbath on Saturday, 221–26
lack of biblical command for seventh-day Sabbath, 224–25

Index

and praying with phylacteries (*tefillin*), 92–95, 128
and the wearing of long black coats, 97–98
and the wearing of white fringe outside the shirt, 88–92, 281–82n77
Jewish New Testament Commentary (Stern), 185, 186, 187
Jewish Theological Seminary, 22
Jewish women
and the wearing of wigs, 84–86, 281n74
Jews. *See also* Israel; Jesus; Jewish beliefs; Jewish men; Jewish women; Judaism; Karaites
Ashkenazi Jews, 113
Black Hebrews, 114
DNA studies concerning, 114–15, 117–18, 284n15, 284–85n19
Ethiopian Jews, 114, 118
Hellenized Jews, 167–68
Indian Jews (Bnei Menashe), 119–20
Khazar Jews, 113
Messianic Jews, 101, 226, 241, 247–48, 296n30
difference between Messianic Jews and Hebrew Christians, 246–48
Messianic Jews as rabbis, 248–54, 296n37
Neturei Karta Jews, 137–38
origin of the term "Jew," 112–15
Hebrew word for (*y'hudah*), 115
and salvation for without belief in Jesus, 271–75
Slavic Jews, 26
Jill-Levine, Amy, 56
John, 272
Jones, Vendyl, 109
Judaism
acronyms used in, 39
beliefs of concerning a literal Messiah, 57–60

and the "Messiah son of David," 57–58
and the "Messiah son of Joseph," 58
dietary laws of, 65, 66
and separate dishes for meat and dairy products, 67–71
differences of from Christianity, 49–54
concerning the afterlife, 51–52
concerning atonement, 51
concerning God, 50
concerning the Messiah, 50
concerning mission, 52–53
concerning salvation, 51
concerning sin, 50–51
and the deeds of Judaism versus the creeds of Christianity, 52
and the Jewish/Christian calendar, 53
holy (foundational) books of, 45–49
jokes concerning, 24–25
teaching centers of, 24
use of acronyms in, 39
use of the name "Jehovah," 60–64
Judaism, Conservative, 13, 16–17, 60, 251
number of adherents to in the United States, 23
views of concerning homosexuality, 22
Judaism, Hasidic, 25–30, 85–86
Breslov sect of, 29–30
etymology of the term "Hasidic," 30
Lubavitch sect of, 28, 88, 279n24
mission work of, 109–10
and the mystical importance of the rebbe, 27–28
Satmar sect of, 28–29, 88, 138
Judaism, Orthodox, 13, 15–16, 17–18, 83
differing beliefs of Orthodox and Reform Judaism, 18–20

Modern Orthodox, 18
number of adherents to in the United States, 23
"revival" of, 23–24
and the *baal teshuvah*, 24
safeguards of against assimilation, 80–81
ultra-Orthodox (*Haredi*), 18, 24, 55, 74, 81, 83, 98, 256
participation of in the Holocaust denial conference, 137–38
views of concerning homosexuality, 21–22
views of concerning non-Orthodox rabbis, 250–51
Judaism, Reform, 13–15, 16, 82, 136, 251, 278n13
differing beliefs of Orthodox and Reform Judaism, 18–20
number of adherents to in the United States, 23
position of concerning Zionism, 277n4
views of concerning homosexuality, 22–23

Kabbalah, 47
Karaites, 123–28, 285n25
decline in the number of, 127
origins of, 124
as a percentage of the world's Jewish population, 127
and the Torah, 124–25
Katz, Lisa, 283n85
Keener, Craig, 84, 152, 167–68, 185
Ketuvim (Writings), 35–36
Khazars, 113
Kimchi, David, 39
Kinzer, Mark, 232–34, 294n11
kippah. *See* yarmulke
Kiryas Joel community, 29
Klausner, Joseph, 192
Koestler, Arthur, 113
Koran, the, 174
Korn, Menachem, 289n13
kosher
etymology of the term "kosher," 64, 280n42

Michael L. Brown (Ph.D., New York University) is the founder and president of FIRE School of Ministry in Concord, North Carolina. He has written numerous books and articles ranging from scholarly studies in the Hebrew Bible and Semitic languages to calls for church renewal and spiritual revolution, and he is widely considered to be the foremost Messianic Jewish apologist today. He has preached around the world and has served as visiting professor at Trinity Evangelical Divinity School and Fuller Theological Seminary School of World Mission.